Carlton J. Ketchum

June 2, 1932

Cleveland

SIR BILLY HOWE

* * *

BOOKS BY BELLAMY PARTRIDGE

Novels

SUBE CANE
COUSINS
A PRETTY PICKLE

Biography

AMUNDSEN: THE SPLENDID NORSEMAN

GENERAL SIR WILLIAM HOWE
After the portrait by Corbett, 1777

SIR BILLY HOWE

BY

BELLAMY PARTRIDGE

LONGMANS, GREEN AND CO.
LONDON · NEW YORK · TORONTO
1932

LONGMANS, GREEN AND CO.
55 FIFTH AVENUE, NEW YORK
221 EAST 20TH STREET, CHICAGO
88 TREMONT STREET, BOSTON
128 UNIVERSITY AVENUE, TORONTO

LONGMANS, GREEN AND CO. Ltd.
39 PATERNOSTER ROW, E C 4, LONDON
6 OLD COURT HOUSE STREET, CALCUTTA
53 NICOL ROAD, BOMBAY
36A MOUNT ROAD, MADRAS

PARTRIDGE

SIR BILLY HOWE

FOR

M. P. M.

Poor Tammy Gage within a cage
Was kept at Boston-ha', man;
Till Willie Howe took o'er the knowe
For Philadelphiá, man;
Wi' sword an' gun he thought a sin
Guid Christian bluid to draw, man;
But at New York wi' knife an' fork
Sir-Loin he hackèd sma', man.

Robert Burns.

Awake, awake, Sir Billy,
There's forage in the plain.
Ah ! leave your little filly,
And open the campaign.

Contemporary rhymster.

FOREWORD

A BIOGRAPHY of Sir William Howe presents to the biographer almost as many difficulties as delights. There is a great fascination about writing the life of a man who has never before been under the biographical ether. Then there is a certain satisfaction in having as a subject a man who was somebody and who did things, and still who did not take himself and his affairs so seriously as to dampen the joy of living. And there is an added attraction in writing a life that is touched with mystery. Indeed, Howe's entire American career is a series of mysteries. Why should a Whig general take a Tory command? Why did Howe spare Washington at Brooklyn, White Plains, and Brandywine? Did he, as charged, calculate the exact time necessary for Washington to escape at Princeton? Why did he abandon Burgoyne and an almost certain military victory for the will-o'-the-wisp of a marine expedition against Philadelphia?

It may seem strange that the general who was Washington's opponent in all but two of the major engagements in which the American commander took part, should have been overlooked by the biographers during all this time. But Sir William was not overlooked. He has from time to time aroused the interest of more than one ambitious writer, who, after a survey of the available material, has turned sadly away to write another book about Washington or Franklin, or perhaps about himself. For, so far as anyone knows, there are no "Howe Papers."

Historians and biographers are not the only ones who have searched in vain for any considerable collection of documents that may have been left by Sir William or his brother, Admiral Lord Howe. Collectors have been thorough in their quest of the dusty muniment rooms of English country houses where it was hoped some trace might be found. Sir John Barrow, while writing his rather stilted life of the Admiral a century ago, came perhaps a little nearer the goal than any of the others when he learned that a chest of papers, after the death of the Admiral, and another upon the death of his sister, came to the youngest daughter, Louisa Catherine Marchioness of Sligo, and that "the present Marquis had them sent to his seat in Westport, Ireland, where, in consequence of a fire they were apparently destroyed."

It was the custom in Sir William's day for field officers to retain permanent possession of their papers when they relinquished a command. General Gage, and General Clinton on quitting the American command retained huge collections of papers gathered in America, and Lord George Germain, on retiring as Secretary of State for the Colonies, took his records with him. Even William Knox, his under-secretary, kept such papers and documents as he could get his hands on when he left the Colonial Office.

Fortunately these great collections were not lost though their whereabouts was unknown to historians for a century and a half. First the *Clinton Papers* turned up, then the *Germain Papers,* later on the *Gage Papers,* and only recently the *Knox Papers.* All these priceless collections have been brought to this country and housed in the splendid William L. Clements Library on the campus of the University of Michigan. Among them are many of the originals of supposedly lost letters and documents written by Sir William and the Admiral to Germain, to Clinton and to others as well, for both Clinton and Germain had all the instincts of the collector of valuable documents: whenever possible they kept the originals and sent copies.

Though the final sorting and arrangement of the papers in these collections has not been completed, enough has been found to lay the ghost that has been stalking the battlefields of Long Island, New Jersey, White Plains, and Brandywine for many a year.

Much of the source material in this volume is new, and some, though not entirely unknown, has not been in print since 1779. The *Narrative* of Sir William before Parliament, reproduced in the appendix, has not been in type since the year of the Enquiry, and many of the rare letters and documents brought together here have been heretofore widely scattered.

The author is indebted to Dr. Randolph G. Adams, Director of the Clements Library for valuable assistance and advice; to Mr. Victor Palsits, Chief of the American History and Manuscript Divisions of the New York Public Library; to Mr. E. H. Anderson, Director of the New York Public Library; to the New York Historical Society, the Pennsylvania Historical Society, the Massachusetts Historical Society, the British Museum, the Library of Congress, and the very patient and efficient staff in the American History Room of the New York Public Library.

B. P.

New York City
December 24, 1931

CONTENTS

LIST OF ILLUSTRATIONS

SIR BILLY HOWE

* * *

SIR BILLY HOWE

CHAPTER I

HE COMES TO BOSTON

WHEN in the spring of 1775 the good ship *Cer-berus* set sail from England she carried in her cabins three young and ambitious generals going out to America to seek the bubble Reputation in the cannon's mouth.   Two of these young fighting-men, Sir William Howe and John Burgoyne, in addition to being soldiers, held part-time jobs as members of Parliament. The third, Major-General Henry Clinton (he had not yet become Sir Henry), did not, it might be said, mix his drinks. He took his military career straight.   He was a soldier, nothing more, and certainly nothing less.   And when, some four years later, General Howe, who had not quite succeeded in quelling the American Revolution though he had given it some pretty bad scares, set sail for London, it was this same Major-General Clinton who took over the job of subduing the colonists.   Clinton had ideas of his own as to how a revolution should be put down, and at once set them in operation. He may not have proved very conclusively that he could win a war, but it took him only two years to show how well he could lose one.

By this time Burgoyne would have met his Saratoga and have made his fame secure as a participant in one of the seven decisive battles of the world, albeit on the red side of the ledger; and Sir William would have goaded a contemporary wit into the saying that any other general than Howe would have beaten Washington and any other general than Washington would have beaten Howe.*

But these things were still far off as the three young generals in their bright red uniforms went clanking down the dock and grouped themselves on the quarter-deck of the *Cerberus*. Their departure was regarded in London with no small satisfaction. It had been felt that Gage, who was already in Boston (and in hot water as well) was not quite equal to the situation with which he was confronted. That these Three Musketeers could not fail to bring Gage out of his difficulties was everywhere the consensus of opinion.

It should be borne in mind, however, that Sir William was the real head of the expedition. He had made an enviable reputation for himself in the field and was much "in fashion" at home. He it was who was coming over to supersede Gage. Burgoyne and Clinton were present largely as scenery. They were at this time little more than guest artists. But it was on the whole an imposing party, and England saw them off with the feeling that all would soon be well in America.

The reception at Boston was in quite another vein when on the 25th day of May 1775 the battered *Cerberus* came nosing into port and dropped her rusty anchors not far from the spot where the 342 chests had been heaved overboard at the somewhat tumultuous Tea Party put on a few months before. America hailed the arrival of the Three Musketeers with an outburst of doggerel, a snatch of which went like this:

---

* This saying was credited to Lafayette, but obviously does not convey his sentiments. Besides, Lafayette was no wit. It was taken from a letter reproduced in the *Gentlemen's Magazine*, 1778.

Behold the *Cerberus* the Atlantic plough,
Her precious cargo, Burgoyne, Clinton, Howe.
Bow, wow, wow !

This may have been a bit disrespectful, but that was the frame of mind of America at the time. America suspected that the shipload of generals was meant to overawe her, and she was in no mood to be overawed. Nor was Sir William himself any too well pleased with his role in the revolutionary drama of which the curtain was about to go up.

Service against the colonies was, quite naturally, a bit distasteful to him. His brother, George Augustus, the third Viscount, who had fallen at Ticonderoga during the war with the French and Indians, had been immensely popular with the people of New England; and in spite of the unpleasantness afterward occasioned by the younger brothers a certain cordiality still exists. This is apparent from the demeanor of New England tourists who seldom fail to pause for a moment of silence before the memorial to the fallen hero long ago placed in Westminster Abbey by the Province of Massachusetts.* What these reverential travelers behold is a figure representing the "genius of the Province of Massachusetts Bay" amid the family arms and military trophies of the Howes, lamenting the fall of a hero. The visitors may shed a tear, or as is more likely they may make a brief entry in a notebook. But at least they furnish proof that New England has not forgotten.

There is a curious legend about the mortal remains of the young viscount. After his fall at Ticonderoga his body was taken in charge by Philip Schuyler, then a major, and removed

---

* The inscription on the monument reads: "The Province of Massachusetts Bay in New England, by an Order of the Great and General Court, bearing date February, 1759, caused this monument to be erected to the memory of George Lord Viscount Howe, Brigadier General of his Majesty's Forces in America, who was slain July 6, 1758, on the march of Ticonderoga, in the thirty-fourth year of his age; in testimony of the sense they had of his services and military virtues, and of the affection their officers and soldiers bore to his command."

to Albany where it was entombed in the family vault of the Schuylers. Here it rested undisturbed for some years before the Schuyler family decided that the presence of a visitor among its dead was no longer desirable. Arrangements were accordingly made to transfer the remains to a leaden coffin in which they were subsequently deposited under the chancel of St. Peter's Church in Albany. When the time came to remove the body from the vault to the leaden coffin, however, it was found that the hair, which had been "cut short as an example to his soldiers," had in the meantime grown out into "long, flowing, and beautiful locks." *

Whether this was considered as an omen by Sir William, we have no way of knowing. One cannot be sure that he had even heard of it at the time of his arrival at Boston. His manner of wearing his hair is none too conspicuous in any of his pictures, which, it will be seen, usually depict him with his hat on.

Sir William was at this time in his 45th year. He was tall, nearly as tall as Washington, and like all the Howes he was dark with a rather thick nose and snapping black eyes. Though he had up to this time been noted as a fearless leader of his men when there was any fighting to do, he was also known as one who liked to have a good time when the fighting was over. He was inclined to be a dandy as to his dress, and still he was a man with a great deal of maleness about him.

There was royal blood in the veins of the adventurous nobleman whose goings and comings had such a way of inspiring budding poets to bantering rhyme. His great great grandfather was John Grubham Howe of the County of Notts, one of two brothers who had been knighted in recompense for their services to Charles II. John Grubham married Annabella, an illegitimate daughter of the Earl of Sunderland, a lady afterward legitimatized by an act of the Par-

* Harper's *Encyclopedia of U. S. History,* Vol. 4.

liament which is understanding about such things. A son born of this union, Scrope Howe, was the grandfather of Sir William. Scrope was made Baron Clenawly and the first viscount of the line. He was succeeded by a son, Emanuel, who married Sophia Charlotte Mary Kielmansegge, usually conceded to have been an illegitimate daughter of George I, and therefore a half-sister of George II. This was very convenient for Sir William and his two brothers, for it made them cousins to Frederick, the Prince of Wales, and second cousins to the King.

As is often the case among the mighty of the earth these various bar sinisters did not prevent the Howes from becoming one of the great Whig families of England. Franklin, who by the way was not above having a bar sinister under his own rooftree, was only too honored to be entertained by the Howes as a house guest. He played chess with Sir William's sister, and with his customary tact, was beaten. The friendship of the Howe family for America was traditional. Perhaps friendly feelings would do more than force.

When the fighting Viscount had fallen at Ticonderoga, the good people of Nottingham, at the urgent request of his mother, had sent young William, then a colonel of thirty, to Parliament. Through thick and thin they kept him there until 1780. When one stops to recall, however, that he was in Canada with Wolfe and later with Murray, that he fought in Cuba, and that he was engaged in America for more than three years and a half with the war against the colonies, it is easy to imagine that his parliamentary duties could not have been very pressing.

It was when Sir William came up for re-election in 1774 that he was quizzed by the tax-payers as to his attitude towards the Americans. He told them that if a war with America should come and he should be offered a command in the British army, he would decline. This satisfied his constituency and he was elected. But when, soon afterwards, the war did break out, the situation presented difficulties that the young gentleman had not foreseen. He was not merely *offered* a command, but was informed by his Majesty that he had been *given* one.

Much embarrassed, he asked if he was to consider his Majesty's message as a request or as an order, and was told that it was an order. Whereupon Sir William bowed and withdrew. He could not decline, but there was nothing to keep him from making a few mental reservations. His constituents at Nottingham were not so easily satisfied, and one of them, a grocer named Kirk, addressed to Sir William Howe, M.P., the following letter:

SIR:

I cannot easily describe the discontent and disappointment which appears among a very great number of your constituents here, on account of your having accepted *a command in the expedition against our American brethren.* From the opinion I had of your integrity in general, I voted for you at the late election, notwithstanding you had in some recent instances, acted contrary to my sentiments. I took the liberty to tell you so, and asked you the following questions, viz.

Whether you thought our whole army would be insufficient to *conquer America?*

If you did not think *the Ministry had pushed this matter too far?*

Whether, if you should be appointed to a command, you would refuse? And whether you would vote for the repeal of the four acts of Parliament, which *you are now going to enforce?*

If I am not mistaken, and I believe that you will allow that I am not, *you answered to every one of these queries in the affirmative.* . . We are however assured that General Howe is preparing to embark *for America to enforce the acts. Judge, if you can, the confusion this occasions among your friends.* The most plausible excuse that is made among us is, that the King sent for you, and what could you do? . . . I believe you have not even an enemy, who would impute *your refusing to go,* to want of courage; nay your courage would be made more *conspicuous by the refusal.*

If you should resolve, *at all events, to go,* I don't wish you may fall as many do; but *I cannot say I wish success to the undertak-*

ing. These, Sir, are the sentiments of many here, as well as of
Your obedient servant
SAMUEL KIRK

Nottingham
Feb. 10, 1775

Though this is not, strictly speaking, putting a curse upon
the General, surely it is not sending him off with any great
amount of cordiality. It was a rather bitter pill for a *bon
voyage,* and Howe resented it; but he was some ten days in
framing an answer:

SIR,
I have read your letter of the 10th, with so much the greater
degree of concern, as I had flattered myself I had *removed all
those prejudices you had entertained against me,* when I had
the pleasure of being with you at the election. The rancour
and malice of those who were not my friends at the election, fill
me with astonishment as the instance you mention of their
wishes for my fall in America.

My going thither was not my seeking. I was ordered, and
could not refuse, without incurring the odious name of backwardness to serve my country in distress. — So contrary are *men's
opinions here,* to some with you, that instead of the grossest
abuse, I have been *most highly complimented upon the occasion,
by those who are even averse to the measures of Administration.*

Every man's private feelings ought to give way to the service
of the Public at all times; but particularly when of that *delicate
nature* in which our affairs stand at present. . .

One word for America: you are deceived if you suppose there
are not *many loyal and peaceable subjects* in that country. I
may safely assert that the insurgents are very few, in comparison
of the whole people.

There are certainly those who do not agree to a taxation from
hence, but who do not wish to sever themselves from the supremacy of this country. This last set of men, I should hope,
by their being relieved from *the grievance,* will most readily
return to all due obedience of the laws.

With respect to *the few,* who, I am told, desire to separate
themselves from the Mother country, I trust, when they find
they are not supported in their frantic ideas by the more moderate, which I have described, they will, from fear of punishment, subside to the laws.

With regard to trade, this country must now fix the foundation

of its stability with America, by procuring a lasting obedience
to our laws, without which it can never arrive at that permanency
so absolutely requisite for the well being of this empire.

I am Sir,
your faithful and
obedient Servant
WILLIAM HOWE

Queen Street
Feb. 21, 1775

This is hardly the letter of a blood-thirsty militarist.   Are
we to believe that Sir William is going to the defense of his
country merely to avoid the "odious name of backwardness,"
and not to make the world safe for anything?   There is, however, a hint of something else here: he has been "complimented upon the occasion, by those who are even averse to
the measures of the Administration."   In other words by the
Whigs.   Why should the Whigs compliment him on being
called to the colors for a war to which they are bitterly opposed?   This is a question that obtrudes itself with arrest-
ing significance as the war gets under way.

Like many of his contemporaries Howe did not realize the
height to which the revolutionary tide in America was rising.
To him it was a little matter of taxation to be straightened
out by some tactful conciliation and perhaps a show of arms.
The insurgents were a handful of madmen with frantic ideas
who would scurry for cover as soon as they saw a few regiments of Redcoats.   How mistaken he was and how the madmen scurried at the sight of the British Redcoats were shown
soon afterwards at Lexington and Concord.

The tradesmen of Nottingham, however, were not the
only ones to look askance at the entry of Sir William into
the fray.   Charles Lee, who afterwards became a general in
the rebel armies, exclaims in a letter to Burgoyne, "Gracious
God! is it possible that Mr. Howe should be prevailed upon
to accept such an office!   The brother of him to whose memory the much-injured people of Boston erected a monument,

employed as one of the instruments of their destruction."
Lee was also horrified to find Burgoyne aligned against the
colonies, and undertook to argue him out of the British
forces by a number of rather long-winded letters. It might
have been better for Gentleman Johnny if Lee's arguments
had prevailed. But, alas, they failed, and into the mess at
Boston went Burgoyne, Clinton and Howe. Bow, wow,
wow !

William Howe was born under the fiery, commanding,
changeable sign of Leo, whose children are said to act from
the heart rather than the head. He came into the world
August 10, 1729, the third son of the second viscount. His
father died in Barbados while there as governor in 1735.*
The title thereupon passed to George Augustus, who, as we
have seen, fell at Ticonderoga and was remembered by the
Province of Massachusetts Bay. Upon the death of Sir
George the title descended to Richard, the Admiral. Lord
Richard died in 1799. It was accordingly not until the year
of George Washington's death that Sir William actually be-
came the fifth viscount of the line.

Young William, as soon as he was old enough, was furnished with a top hat and an abbreviated jacket and sent to
Eton. But he was an indifferent student and was destined
for neither of the great English universities. He was to complete his education, such as it was,† in the army; for at seventeen (this was in 1746) we find him receiving a commission in
the Duke of Cumberland's Light Dragoons. The following
year he went to the continent for some spirited fighting in
which his regiment greatly distinguished itself, especially at
the battle of Lauffield where with the Greys and the Innes-
killings the Light Dragoons participated in a famous charge

---

* Sir John Barrow in his life of the Admiral says that Emmanuel died from
drinking while overheated the cooling milk of the cocoa nut.

† Charles Lee speaks of his education as "corrupt" or "more properly speaking no education," which he excuses as being the fashion of the times. *Lee
Papers,* Vol. II, p. 397.

led by old Ligonier to extricate the infantry from a dangerous salient into which it had thrust itself.

Just what part the tall gangling youth had in these bloody
doings does not appear.   But he evidently liked this taste of
army life, for when the regiment returned to England in 1749
after the Peace of Aix-la-Chapelle and were disbanded, he
went into the 20th Foot where he was posted as a captain in
January of the year 1750.   This was a famous regiment in
which Wolfe was at one time a major.

Six years passed before young Captain Howe was promoted
to major.   He had been a long time making the grade, but
once he had made it he was only two years in securing a
command of his own.   With his new regiment he was sent
to America and plunged into the spirited campaign against
Louisburg.   He had apparently not forgotten the fierce
charges at Lauffield, for soon Wolfe was to write of him,
"Our old comrade Howe is at the head of the best trained
battalion in all America, and his conduct in the last campaign corresponded entirely with the opinion we had formed
of him."   Just what this opinion may have been the reader
is left to conjecture for himself, but in those days the dashing
youth had very much of a reputation as a daredevil.   No
hope was too forlorn for him to undertake, no chance too
long.

He fought brilliantly under Wolfe in the fierce struggle
that led to the capture of Quebec.   Indeed, it was young
Howe who with a small detachment of men scaled the
Heights of Abraham under cover of darkness and made
Wolfe's victory possible.   Wolfe fell, but Howe fought on.
After Quebec he led his old regiment, the 58th, in the bloody
battle of St. Foy, an engagement in which the British lost
thirty out of every hundred men employed.   They finally
managed to withdraw, and took refuge inside the fortifications of Quebec where they were besieged for eighteen days

before the British warships could come up the river and drive off the French. Young Major Howe remained after Murray had succeeded Wolfe. He did not leave Canada until the final blow had been struck at French domination in the new world. When he did return to England he was just in time to command a brigade in the expedition against Belle Isle.

Though the Belle Isle campaign was not without its comic aspects — with the French commander parading in uniform all the females in the garrison to mislead the British as to the number of his available troops — the citadel held out for a full two months after the British had effected a landing. So there must have been some real fighting, although the British after they had taken Belle Isle were at very much of a loss to know what to do with it. Historians have ever since been hard at work to find any advantage that was gained from this rather senseless campaign. So far as the fighting-men were concerned, however, that was neither here nor there. British arms had triumphed, and British officers and men had been given an opportunity to show their valor. Young Sir William returned with a full share of such glory as there was, and was soon afterwards promoted to colonel.

His next active service was against the Spanish in Cuba where he served with distinction in the campaign of 1762. The British had little difficulty in routing the Spanish and capturing Havana, but they were no match for the tropical diseases which laid low more than 5000 of their officers and men. Again young Mr. Howe came back without so much as a scratch or a headache, and after the peace of 1763 was stationed in Ireland with the 46th Regiment. In time of war he had led a charmed life, but peace, he found, was not without its perils; for after a siege of a year the gallant young soldier surrendered to a colleen named Fannie Conolly, a daughter of the Rt. Hon. William Conolly of Castletown in

County Kildare, and on the 4th of June 1765 the wedding bells pealed gaily over the green hills of Erin. And so they were married.

Had the people of Nottingham selected the sailor of the family instead of the soldier to represent them in Parliament they might have had an occasional glimpse of their member. When a sailor goes to places he is very likely to come back again; but with the wars and rumors of war young Colonel Howe seems always to have been at the ends of the earth. Though he did not shine as a statesman he made his way rapidly up the ladder that leads to military fame. In 1772 he was gazetted a major-general. Two years later he was to be found on Salisbury Plain training the "light companies" which were just then coming into vogue. Where the fair Fannie may have been at this time we are not told. But if she was as much in love with her tall and dashing husband as some of the other women he met, it is to be surmised that she was not far in the offing. At the conclusion of the training of these detachments there would be a gala demonstration at which his Majesty the King would come in person to inspect them. After they had been thus inspected they were regarded as fit and were returned to their various regiments.

Meanwhile the revolution in America had been slowly brewing, and when finally the pot did boil over and the tea was actually thrown into Boston Harbor Parliament retorted with the Port Bill. The harbor of Boston was to be closed and General Gage was instructed to sit on the lid until the Americans had recovered their equilibrium. It was a task for which Gage, even after years of almost princely powers as military governor of the colonies, was pre-eminently ill suited. His show of arms had led to an encounter with the Minute Men. Blood had been shed and soon Gage and his Redcoats were cooped up in Boston by a "rabble" of colonists who, though they were unfamiliar with the manual of arms, could pick off a squirrel at a hundred paces.

The situation was not one to contribute materially either to the dignity or to the respect of British arms in America. It must on the contrary have been very mortifying to the Government. Better days were in sight, however, for even before news of the little matter at Lexington and Concord had crossed the sea his Majesty George III had risen to the occasion and presented to General Howe the command in America that first embarrassed, then embroiled, and finally obliterated the career of one of the most promising soldiers of his time.

It was this command that gave Sir William his page in history, a page on which are written many things that are splendid, many that are diverting, and few that are calculated to inspire any great amount of pride in the heart of the average Englishman.

CHAPTER II

HE CLIMBS BUNKER'S HILL

ON THE 17th of June 1775 General Howe was rudely awakened at daybreak by the thunder of heavy guns. Boston was in a turmoil. Terrified people were running to and fro trying to find out what was happening or likely to happen, when it was discovered that the gunfire was coming from a British man-of-war lying in the harbor. Presently word came ashore from the captain that he had discovered with the coming of daylight that the high ground over beyond Charlestown had been seized during the night by the rascally rebels and fortified by a sizable earthwork, and that upon making the discovery he had immediately opened fire upon them.

At first the British could hardly take the situation seriously. That the rabble who called themselves the rebel army should have had the temerity to make an organized move on the town was scarcely credible. But there they were, and one look through the glasses was enough to show that they were still digging in as if they expected to stay there in spite of the cannonading of the *Lively* and some of the other warships which happened to be within range.

There was a brief respite from the firing when the admiral of the fleet, who happened to be sleeping ashore and did not know what it was all about, sent word to the captains to desist. After he had breakfasted and heard the news, how-

ever, he directed them to resume, and from that time until
the rebels had been dislodged from the high ground over beyond Charlestown the warships continued to thunder.

The location of Boston is peculiar. It lies in the midst of
the Bay of Massachusetts like an island. It would have been
an island had it not been for a narrow strip or neck of land
by which it is attached to the mainland on the southwest.
To the north of the city stand the heights of Charlestown, a
like formation connected with the mainland by Charlestown
Neck, while to the south are the heights of Dorchester.
With the enemy in possession of either of these heights the
town of Boston was, in a military sense, untenable. General
Gage was well aware of this fact, and he was intending in his
good time to occupy both positions. Indeed, the plans had
been drawn and were about to be executed by his Majesty's
troops, when the news leaked through the lines to the rebels.
General Ward at once took the position that if these heights
were important to the British they must be of equal importance to the rebels themselves.

The colonial army had had plenty of opportunity to study
the lay of the land. They had held the town in a virtual
state of siege since the middle of April, and should after all
this time have known the strategic value of every acre of
the neighboring topography. There is evidence that General Ward did appreciate the importance of these heights,
though he took no steps to occupy them until the night of the
16th of June when he dispatched Colonel Prescott with a
small force (the number is disputed and is not now important) to take and fortify a portion of the heights of Charlestown known as Bunker's Hill. Prescott exceeded his authority, however, and marched beyond Bunker's Hill to
another height somewhat nearer the tip of the promontory,
called Breed's Hill. Though some thirty-five feet lower than
Bunker's Hill, the top of Breed's Hill was a fairly stiff climb
from the beach. Whether Prescott went on to Breed's Hill

by mistake or thought it a better position in which to make
a stand does not appear.   In either event he led his men to
the top of Breed's Hill under cover of darkness and ordered
them to dig in.

With feverish haste the men began the construction of an
earthwork known as the Redoubt.   To prevent the Redoubt
from being surrounded Prescott threw out a line to the right
towards Charlestown, and to the left towards the Mystick
river which empties into the bay near this point, directing his
men to take such cover as the country would afford.   Part of
the line was able to entrench itself behind the substantial
protection of a stone fence, though the greater part of the
left was not so fortunate.   Here the only cover at hand was a
rail fence which the colonists quickly stuffed with armfuls of
hay.   Scarcely a bullet-proof arrangement, and still it was
something behind which they could hide, and through which
they could poke the barrels of their muskets in order to take
aim.   Indeed, it was from this rail and hay obstruction that
General Howe met the most stubborn resistance when he led
the attack against the hill.

The British did not dally long over their breakfasts on
that historic morning.   Boston had overnight become untenable.   Something must be done about it.   But what?
With four accomplished military men on hand, all of them
major-generals in his Majesty's service, this ought to have
been a comparatively easy question to answer.   The only
difficulty was that the four military men did not see eye to
eye.   Clinton, the practical fighting-man, wanted to seize
Charlestown Neck, the narrow strip of land leading out from
the mainland to the heights, and thus slip the enemy into
the sack where he could be smothered at leisure by gunfire
from the fleet assisted by floating batteries.   But General
Howe scorned the idea of defeating his adversaries by a
trick.   The capture of the heights was not all he had in
mind.   He wanted to show the Americans how hopeless it

was for them to think that they could ever win their freedom from Britain by force of arms. He wanted to humiliate them, to prove to them how inferior they were to the British as fighting-men. He was therefore in favor of taking his men up the steepest part of the hill in a frontal attack.

Obviously the British could not use three major-generals against a mob of ragamuffins, so Clinton and Burgoyne were sent to the sidelines and Howe was given the command. Some time had been required to make the dispositions and arrangements, however, and it was not until after lunch that General Howe and his troops landed on the beach at the foot of Breed's Hill.

As General Howe looked around the situation seemed to take on a different view. The hill was higher than he had supposed, the nature of the terrain more difficult, and the Redoubt much more substantial than had appeared through the glasses. All things considered, a bit of exhortation seemed to be called for, and the General is quoted by Frothingham as having said:*

Gentlemen, —
    I am very happy in having the honor of commanding so fine a body of men: I do not in the least doubt but that you will behave like Englishmen, and as becometh good soldiers.
    If the enemy will not come from their entrenchments, we must drive them out, at all events, otherwise the town of Boston will be set on fire by them.
    I shall not desire one of you to go a step farther than where I go myself at your head.
    Remember, gentlemen, we have no resources if we lose Boston, but to go on board our ships, which will be very disagreeable to us all.

Not a very fiery speech as we read it today, but General Howe thought it would suffice, for after he had closed his remarks he gave the order for the attack to begin. The British went forward in three columns, one at the extreme right

* *Battle of Bunker Hill*, Richard Frothingham.

of the hill led by General Howe in person, a second up the
center of the slope, and a third at the left just outside the
limits of Charlestown.   According to the plan of battle the
three columns were to reach the Redoubt at the same time
and join in a concerted attack from three sides.   Had the
march up the hill been unimpeded the plan would have been
quite perfect.   This, however, was not to be.

General Howe's column as it approached the hay and rail
entanglement found the barrier a murderous nest of gunfire.
The rebels waited until the Redcoats had come near enough
to show the whites of their eyes.   Then they fired, and they
shot to kill.   One blast from the colonists and the regulars
gave way and fell back leaving the turf red with the blood
and the scarlet coats of their fallen comrades.   General
Howe rallied them with spirit.   He reformed the column
and led his men for a second time against the murderous hay.
Again the British were turned back by the deadly fire of the
straight-shooting rebels.

An "Exact Reproduction" of the battle hanging on the
walls of the New York Public Library depicts the regulars as
falling back in perfect formation, their ranks unbroken, their
hats still on, and their guns resting on their shoulders.   It is
a quaint picture, but wide of the truth.   The repulse of the
regulars amounted almost to a rout.   They fell back in the
utmost confusion, and had it not been that the backward
movement was arrested by the waters of the bay the affray at
Breed's Hill might have developed into something not unlike
the disaster before Duquesne where some of the regulars had
retreated for nearly forty miles before they could be stopped.

Here, however, they had no choice but to stop or swim.
They stopped; and once more General Howe rallied them.
His fighting blood was aroused.   He had forgotten all about
humiliating the enemy.   His one thought was to take the
Redoubt.   By this time he was seriously hampered by the
want of field officers on whom the enemy seemed to have

been concentrating their fire. After one of the volleys
Howe was the only man in the front rank still on his feet.
But he did not think of giving up the attempt. On one of
his charges up the hill he had caught a glimpse of an open
angle where the hay and rail obstruction approached the Redoubt. On his third attempt he made for this open angle —
and went over the top.

The other two columns had met with a stubborn resistance. General Piggot who was leading the left was harried
by snipers from the houses in Charlestown, and the center
column was thrown back in such confusion that General
Clinton rushed over from Boston by rowboat to help reform
the units and get them into action for the final attack.

General Burgoyne took no part in the battle. Instead he
posted himself on Copp's Hill in Boston with a good glass
where, with General Gage, he watched the progress of the
battle from beginning to end. His description of the fight
written a few days afterwards to a Noble Lord, though too
lengthy to be quoted in full, is characteristic of Gentleman
Johnny:*

. . . Howe's disposition was exceedingly Soldier like, in my
opinion it was perfect. As his first arm advanced up the hill
they met with a thousand impediments from strong fences and
were much exposed. They were also exceedingly hurt by musketry from Charlestown, though Clinton and I did not perceive
it till Howe sent us word by a boat, and desired us to set fire to
the town, which was immediately done. . . And now ensued
one of the greatest scenes of war that can be conceived; if we
looked to the height, Howe's corps ascending the hill in the face
of entrenchments and in the face of a very disadvantageous
ground, was much engaged; to the left the enemy pouring in
fresh troops by thousands, over the land, and in the arm of the
sea our ships and floating batteries cannonading them; straight
before us a large and noble town in one great blaze; the church
steeples being of timber, were great pyramids of fire above the
rest; behind us the church steeples and heights of our own camp,
covered with spectators of the rest of our army who were (not)

* Letter of June 25, 1775.

engaged; the hills round the country covered with spectators, the enemy all in anxious suspense; the roar of cannon, mortars, and musketry, the crush of churches, ships upon the stocks, and whole streets falling together in ruin to fill the ear; the storm of the redoubts with the objects above described to fill the eye, and the reflection that perhaps a defeat was the final loss to the British Empire in America, to fill the mind, made the whole a picture and a complication of horror and importance beyond anything that ever came to my lot to be witness to. . .

As the oldest settlement on the bay Charlestown had come to be venerated by the colonists as more or less of a shrine, and its ruthless burning aroused the most spirited protest, although the colonists at first supposed the fire to have been of accidental origin. They were even more bitter when they found that the match had been applied by orders of the British high command. Just who issued the actual order for the burning of the town is not clear. Burgoyne's letter seems to intimate that the firing was ordered by himself and Clinton at Howe's request, and Gage's report does not deny this. The letter from General Gage to Lord Dartmouth as reprinted in the *Remembrancer* from the London *Gazette* of July 25th follows: *

My Lord,
I am to acquaint your Lordship of an action that happened on the 17th instant between his Majesty's troops and a large body of rebel forces.

An alarm was given at break of day, on the 17th instant by a firing from the *Lively* ship of war; and advice soon afterward received that the rebels had broke ground, and were raising a battery on the Heights of the peninsula of Charlestown, against the town of Boston. They were plainly seen at work, and in a few hours, a battery of six guns played upon their works. Preparations were instantly made for landing a body of men to drive them off, and ten companies of the grenadiers, ten of light infantry, with the 5th, 38th, 43d, and 52d battalions, with a proportion of field artillery, under the command of Major-General Howe and Brigadier-General Pigot, were embarked with great

* Almon's *Remembrancer*, 1775.

expedition, and landed on the peninsula without opposition, under the protection of some ships of war, armed vessels, and boats, by whose fire the rebels were kept within their works.

The troops formed as soon as landed; the light infantry posted on the right and the grenadiers upon their left. The 5th and the 38th battalions drew up in the rear of those corps, and the 43d and 52d battalions made a third line. The rebels upon the heights were seen to be in great force and strongly posted. A redoubt thrown up on the 16th at night, with other works, full of men, defended with cannon, and a large body posted in the houses of Charlestown, covered their right flank; and their center and left were covered by a breast work, part of it cannon-proof which reached from the left of the redoubt to the Mystick or Medford river. . .

These troops advanced, formed in two lines, and the attack began by a sharp cannonade from our field pieces and howitzers, the lines advancing slowly, and frequently halting to give time for the artillery to fire. The light infantry was directed to force the left point of the breast work, to take the rebel line in flank, and the grenadiers to attack in front, supported by the 5th and 52d battalion. These orders were executed with perseverance, under a heavy fire from a vast number of rebels; and notwithstanding various impediments before the troops could reach the works, and though the left under Brigadier General Pigot who engaged also with the rebels at Charlestown, which at a critical moment was set on fire, the Brigadier pursued his point, and carried the redoubt.

The rebels were then forced from other strongholds, and pursued until they were drove clear of the peninsula, leaving five pieces of cannon behind them.

The loss the rebels sustained must have been considerable from the great numbers they carried off during the time of the action, and buried in a hole since discovered, exclusive of what they suffered by the shipping and boats. . .

This action has shown the superiority of the King's troops, who, under every disadvantage, attacked and defeated above three times their own number, strongly posted and covered by breast works.*

The conduct of Major General Howe was conspicuous on this occasion, and his example spirited the troops, in which Major General Clinton assisted, who followed the reinforcement. And in justice to Brigadier General Pigot, I am to add that the success of the day must in great measure be attributed to his firm-

* A slight exaggeration !

ness and gallantry. . . The valor of the British officers and soldiers in general was at no time more conspicuous than in this action.

I have the honor to be, &c.

THO. GAGE

To this day there is disputing among the statisticians and historians as to the number of troops engaged on both sides. A fair average of the authorities seems to indicate that for every three Americans engaged in holding the fort there were four British attacking it, say 3000 Americans to 4000 British. As to casualties, however, there is less room for dispute if we take the official returns.

Americans		British	
Killed	115	Killed	226
Wounded	350	Wounded	828
Missing	30	Missing	0
	495		1054

It will thus be seen that in proportion to the number engaged the British losses were staggering — one man out of every four was shot down — twenty-seven of them officers. Channing gives the British losses of officers killed in the twenty battles of the war as 198, one-eighth of which were killed in an afternoon's engagement that resulted in the capture of Breed's Hill.

The battle was over by five o'clock, and General Howe, though smeared with the blood of those who had been shot down all around him, was uninjured. General Clinton begged and besought Sir William to organize a vigorous pursuit of the confused and panic-stricken rebels who had thrown down their guns and were running for their lives. A spirited pursuit by the British at this time might have so scattered the American forces that there would have been no army for Washington to receive under the historic if imaginary elm at Cambridge when he arrived some three weeks later. But Howe had done enough for one day. He had charged up that hill under fire three times and was in no mood to chase a terrified rabble around the countryside. Then, too, he felt that the British had given the rebels their lesson and would hear nothing further from them for a long time. He ordered his soldiers to invest the heights and to build with all speed an impregnable fortification there. Then he went down to the shore, clambered into his boat, and was rowed back to Boston.

This was the beginning of the rift between Sir William and Clinton that was to continue so long as they both remained in America. And it may have been the beginning of the rift that developed in Sir William's own two ways of thinking. What must have been his thoughts as his boat moved slowly away from the shore and he had time to stop and think ? Did he by any chance suddenly remember that he had spent the afternoon shedding the blood of the kindly people who had erected a monument to his fallen brother ? Did he think of the grocer of Nottingham and others at home who were against the war ? Did he have any apprehensions that possibly the British had gone a bit too far that day ? He had fought a good fight. He had been where the bullets flew thickest. He had won the day — but how would the news be received at home ? He must have wondered about that.

In any event, he did not follow the advice of Clinton. He did not make his victory decisive. Whether a policy of extermination at this time might or might not have convinced the rebels of the hopelessness of their cause, we have no way of telling; but as we look back we see something prophetic in the inconclusive victory. Other victories would be won — and would not be driven home. Whatever his thoughts may have been as he crossed the bay Sir William did not turn around and resume the battle, but went back to Boston to change his clothes.

Bunker Hill left the Americans in a rather cheerful state of mind. They had, it was true, been dislodged from their position, and though General Ward was fearful that the attempt to take the hill would arouse the British to a general attack, Colonel Prescott was of a very different opinion. He came storming into Cambridge after the battle and demanded three fresh regiments with which, he said, he could easily retake the hill. They were not given to him.

In his Orderly Book under the head of "General Orders" for the 19th of June 1775 General Gage made an entry to the effect that the Commander-in-Chief returned his "most gratefull thanks to Major General Howe for the Extraord'ry Exertion of His Military Ability's on the 17th Inst." He also returned his thanks to the officers and soldiers "who by remarkable Efforts and Courage and Gallantry Overcame every Disadvantage and Drove the Rebells from their Redoubt and Strongholds on the Heights of Charlestown and gained a compleat Victory."

This sounds like war, whereas only two months before a newspaper in Boston * was running in its columns a peaceful announcement to the effect that "a Wet Nurse with a Good Young Breast of Milk, would go into a Gentleman's Family to Suckle a Child," and one Thomas Turner begged leave to acquaint the public he had opened a school to teach the "elegant art of dancing," and that "any Gentleman or Lady not inclining to attend the publick school, shall be waited on with pleasure and attention." Another advertisement appearing in April announced that Cattanach, Hair Dresser to Ladies and Gentlemen, was to be found at Mr. John Field's, "at the Sign of the Buck and Breeches, opposite the Old Brick Meeting House, Boston, where Ladies and Gentlemen may be waited on at the shortest notice." And in the issue for April 17, 1775, the following notice appeared:

* Boston *Gazette.*

RAN AWAY from the Subscriber on the Evening of the 12th instant, a Negro Man, named PRIMUS, about 52 years old. Whoever shall take up said Negro, and secure him in any one of his Majesty's Gaols, shall have ONE DOLLAR Reward, paid by

JOSEPH HOYH

CHAPTER III

HE MEETS A LADY — AND QUITS BOSTON

IN ADDITION to rendering the town of Boston once more tenable the taking of Bunker's Hill relieved General Gage of a rather delicate question: it made a place for General Howe.   Up to this time matters had been under a slight restraint between the two.   That General Howe had been sent to Boston for some very definite purpose of the Ministry was obvious to Gage.   What the purpose might be, was not so clear.   Gage had not been superseded.   He was still in command — and yet, there was General Howe at his elbow.   Just what was to be done with him Gage did not know until the capture of Bunker's Hill provided him with an answer.

He immediately established separate headquarters there and placed General Howe in command; and from this time until Gage's recall in the autumn, general orders were issued from both Charlestown and Boston.   The orders emanating from Charlestown were presumably the orders of General Howe, while those given at Boston were supposedly the orders of General Gage.   Both were entered in the official Orderly Book which, happily, has been preserved for posterity.*

A quaint order from the headquarters in Boston appears under date of June 20th 1775:

* Published as *Gen'l Sir William Howe's Orderly Book at Charlestown.*

Two women from each Corps to be sent to the Gen'l Hospital as soon as possible and four per Company to go to the troops on the Charlestown side, the latter will be ordered to assemble on the Market Place at 2 o'Clock. A list of those Women to be given to a Serjeant who will attend to conduct them to the Ferry, see them in the boats and will be answerable that no more go than the Number Order'd.

Not long afterwards the women again found their way into general orders, this time in an entry issuing from the Charlestown side: *

Some of the Soldiers wives having brought spirituous Liquors from Boston to this Camp, contrary to Orders: the permission for their passing from thence, hither, is stopt, until further Orders.

And it was a woman who got herself into difficulties over the theft of the town bull, and was haled before a general court-martial for trial, and on whom the august General Gage delivered the following sentence: †

Winifred Mc Cowen retainer to the Camp, tryed by the above General Court Martial, for having stolen the Town Bull and Causing him to be killed is found Guilty of the same and Sentenced to be tied to a Cart's tail, and thereto receive 100 lashes on her bare back in different portions in the most public parts of the town and Camp and to be imprisoned three months.

What a spectacle for the streets of Boston to have witnessed in the most public parts ! But the streets of Boston were to witness many strange sights as the siege gradually tightened its grip.

The British had been beleaguered on the land side since their return from their somewhat disastrous spring outing at Lexington and Concord. Of course they were free to come and go by sea, but their supply of fresh fruits and vegetables for themselves and fodder for their beasts did not come from

* *Orderly Book*, July 5, 1775.
† id., Sept. 26, 1775.

this direction. Indeed they had great difficulty in bringing in enough fresh meat by water to supply the needs of the garrison and the city, and were driven to foraging for supplies wherever they could find them. There is a pertinent item in the *Boston Gazette* of August 14th. The *Gazette* had by this time been driven out of the city and was being published at Watertown:

We are informed that last Thursday evening returned to Boston, after about 3 weeks cruize, twelve Transports (having on board about 1000 Ministerial Butchers) * under convoy of three men of war. During their cruize they plundered and pillaged about 130 sheep and 30 head of cattle off Fisher's & Gardner's Islands near New London, tho' tis said, after they were secur'd they tender'd payment. Tis also said they took and carried in with them an outward-bound vessel with about 40 head of cattle, and 30 sheep. With this trophy of victory on their arrival at Boston, the bells, we hear, were set to music, to the no small joy and rejoicing of the Tories there.

In this same issue of the *Gazette* is an item to the effect that the Hon. Continental Congress have established a continental Post-Office and appointed Dr. Benjamin Franklin to be the Postmaster General, at a salary of a thousand dollars a year. And a further item notes that "Tis said Ben Faneuil and a number of other Tories have purchased or chartered a large vessel to transport their families and effects to. . . *Look Sharp, take care.* . . See how the . . . prepare. Bonum securum. She is near ready to sail."

One or two further items from this issue of the *Gazette* may prove illuminating:

Elisha James, Esq; late of Weston, appointed Overseer of Gage's Haymakers upon Bunker's Hill in Charlestown. Drummer Rogers, Esq; late an attorney at Littleton, appointed superintendent of a Grog Shop in Charlestown; the former is waiter to the Horses, and the latter attends to the Camp Women with a Jill of Rum &c. upon occasion.

From these Specimens of Merit finding a reward we may suppose that the *Great Men* among the *Tories* will be provided for.

* British soldiers and sailors.

Taken out of the Subscriber's House near Mr. Wood's Farm the upper end of Charlestown, the Day after the Destruction of that town, a very good Feather Bed, a good Riding Hood, a Broad Cloth Coat, a Brass Kettle, a pair of boots and a number of Books. Whoever has the same in Possession and will bring them to the Printing Office will be well rewarded for their trouble.

BEN. JENNINGS.

And from the issue of September 4th:

We hear that a number of Officers Ladies have lately arrived at Boston, from England, Ireland &c. and on their landing they were to a Woman *Widows*.

General Gage's report of his large success at Bunker Hill was not well received at home. England was aghast at the price that had been paid for the possession of an outlying height that should and very easily could have been occupied at the beginning of the siege and for two months afterward without firing a shot. Orators thundered about the staggering loss of British soldiery and asked each other hortatory questions concerning the probable cost of winning the war at the same rate. The result was that Gage was at once recalled to the very great relief of Sir William who had long distrusted Gage's ability to cope with the situation. Indeed, this lack of confidence in Gage coupled with the traditional family friendship for the people of Boston had greatly influenced Howe in his decision to accept the American command in the first place.

Some uneasiness on the part of the patriots was felt when the news leaked out that Gage had been superseded by General Howe. The old adage about the new broom filled them with forebodings, and they began to wonder where the first blow would fall. But their fears were groundless. The situation in and around Boston remained unchanged. General Howe kept the fortifications on the heights of Charlestown well manned, but he was as negligent as his predecessor about the occupation of the equally important heights at Dorchester. The British had already paid for one such piece of carelessness by the bloody encounter at Bunker Hill, and if the Continentals had seized the heights of Dorchester, Howe would have been faced by another bloody affray. His only alternative would have been to evacuate.

However, the Continental army showed not the slightest inclination to invest this important position. Weeks passed, and months, and still the strategic key to the situation was stubbornly disregarded by both sides. Howe's excuse was that he was planning to evacuate Boston and was waiting only for the arrival of the necessary supplies and transport facilities to enable him to move on New York. This was, of course, true. It was equally true that a small garrison on the heights of Dorchester would have insured the safety of the town until such time as he was ready to move.

The excuse made for Washington was that he was short of powder. This, too, was true. But not a great deal of powder would have been required to hold an earthwork on the heights, and so long as he was able to hold it he would have had the town of Boston at his mercy. The lack of powder did not prevent Washington from planning various attacks on the town itself. He would have launched an offensive over the ice in the winter had he not been dissuaded by a council of his officers; and on another occasion he seriously advocated making an assault on the British garrison by means of rowboats, powder or no powder.

The Battle of Bunker Hill occurred in June, and it was not until the following March that the heights of Dorchester were to feel the thrust of an entrenching tool. Meanwhile as Howe waited and Washington delayed, life in the beleaguered city became more and more difficult. Smallpox broke out, and scurvy took a heavy toll from both soldiers and civilians. Spruce beer, which was supposed to be good for scurvy, was offered for sale at a dollar a barrel, delivered, if the empty casks were returned as the full ones were put in.

And we find in the *Orderly Book* an entry to the effect that
"Sower Crout" is to be given out only to those who are sick
of the scurvy. As the cold weather came on fuel for the ordinary enlisted man was practically non-existent, and depredations of firewood by soldiers were made punishable by
death.* Several wood thieves were hanged and it was not
until the 19th of January 1776 that the fuel crisis was removed by the arrival of a cargo of coal. During this terrible
winter thievery was rife among the soldiers and the record
bristles with courts-martial for larceny, robbery, burglary,
and plain everyday stealing. The execution of a man for
theft was an ordinary occurrence. The reprieve of a convicted man, however, was quite another matter. This required a royal pardon.

Extract of a letter written by General Howe to the Earl of
Dartmouth on January 22nd:

Robberies, and housebreaking in particular, had got to such
a height in this town, that some examples had become necessary
to suppress it. Two soldiers, late of the 59th regiment of foot,
have been tried, convicted, and sentenced to suffer death, for
breaking into and robbing the storehouses of Messrs. Nathaniel
and William Coffin; one of them has suffered: the other, Thomas
Owen, as a young offender, and having circumstances to plead
in his favor, I have thought proper to reprieve, conforming to
the power expressed in my commission as follows: "We are giving you power to reprieve any person under sentence, until our
pleasure be known:" and I humbly entreat your Lordship to
recommend the said Thomas Owen for his Majesty's royal
pardon.

I am, &c.   W. HOWE

Desertions from the British camp must have been frequent,
and the entries in the *Orderly Book* show that deserters were
sometimes recaptured. One of these unfortunates was young
William Beck, a private in Captain McKenzie's Company of
the 43rd Foot. Beck was tried for desertion and found
"Guilty of the Crime laid to his charge and Sentenced to

---

* *Orderly Book*, December 5th.

Suffer Death, by being hanged by the Neck till he is dead, being the most Ignominious manner of inflicting the punishment of Death, due to so infamous a Crime as Desertion to the Rebels of his Country." The Commander-in-Chief approved of the sentence and ordered an immediate execution in such place as the Major-General "shall think fit to order."

The Major-General was not long in making up his mind. He chose a pleasant spot on Bunker's Hill in front of the camp of the culprit's own regiment where the poor fellow would perhaps feel a little more at home when he faced his ordeal.

After Orders ½ past One oClock

The Picquets of every Corps Encamped and Cantooned on this side (The Light Cavalry included) to parade at four this afternoon in Front of the 43rd Regiment to Attend the above mentioned Execution.

So far as the records are concerned the brief history of young William Beck ends here. The erection of a scaffold or the burial of a corpse is not of sufficient importance to warrant an entry in an orderly book. A little quiet gambling on the part of the soldiers is quite another matter, however, and we find an order from General Howe to the effect that since "some Soldiers of the Different Corps have been observed Gaming, the Commiss'd and non Commiss'd Officers are desired to be attentive that for the future nothing of this sort appears among the Men, Such instances of Idleness & Depravity are always (& particularly at this time) to be prevented and suppressed."

It is to be noted that this rather rigid regulation applies only to the Men, not to the Officers. What delight has the kettle taken since the beginning of time in drawing the color-line on the pot! Major-General Howe was perhaps the most persistent gambler in the entire British army, and there are those who believe that it was his love for the gaming

table and the felicitous company of the gentler sex that were
directly responsible for the loss to Great Britain of her American Colonies.

Just when Howe fell in with the notorious Mrs. Loring
would be hard to say. It is probable that he met her soon
after coming to Boston, for he was an attractive male, and his
conspicuous bravery at Bunker Hill must have brought him
very much to the forefront of army social circles in Boston.
Little is known of the lady herself, save that she was a Miss
Lloyd and was married to Joshua Loring at the house of
Colonel Hatch in Dorchester at some time during 1769 when
Loring was High Sheriff, and a member of the Ancient &
Honorable Artillery Company. Howe had been in the
country less than two weeks when General Gage appointed
Loring as "sole vendue-master and auctioneer" of Boston.
Very probably this appointment was made because of Loring's experience as High Sheriff rather than because of any
amiability on General Howe's part towards the husband of
the flashing blonde who was to be his mistress during the
whole of his stay in America, though Howe did take care of
him subsequently by appointing him to a position as Commissary of Prisoners from which Loring was able to extract a
very handsome graft. Nor is a great deal known about
Joshua Loring except that he was the son of a commodore
in the navy, and had a twin brother named Benjamin. The
antecedents of Mrs. Loring appear to be entirely unknown.
She came into prominence when General Howe came over
the horizon, and she dropped out of sight when he went back
to England. While he was here she lived in a blaze of glory.

Judge Jones calls her an "illustrious courtesan" and says
that she lost Sir William "the honor, the laurels, and the
glory of putting an end to one of the most obstinate rebel-
lions that ever existed." The statement has been copied by
historians for a century and a half for want of more definite
information. Belcher, in his *First American Civil War,* adds

that Sir William "liked his glass, his lass, and his game of cards, as did indeed all British warriors at that time, and American too." Belcher also notes that Mrs. Loring was "as fond of cards as Baroness Bernstein, and would gamble away a hundred guineas or so with any pretty fellow in love with sport."

It would thus appear that in spite of the suffering and deprivation that was rampant in the little town of Boston during the winter of 1775–1776 Sir William Howe and his officers passed their time very pleasantly. Washington sent an occasional cannonball over that way, and Howe, if he was not too busy, returned the compliment. This intermittent boom of a cannon helped to keep up the interest in the siege, and nobody was hurt. Washington's army, however, was being demoralized by idleness, and the general himself was longing for action. It was because of this, no doubt, that he made the rash proposals to move his army across the bay and hurl it against the redoubtable fortifications the British had by this time erected.

By spring the Americans had augmented their supply of powder, and had greatly increased the strength of their artillery with guns drawn over the snow from Ticonderoga. Sir William was still in Boston. He was still meaning to evacuate as soon as he could. But he was still hampered by an insufficiency of the sinews of war. The question of abandoning Boston had been under discussion between the strategists in the field and those in the armchairs of the Ministry ever since Howe's arrival there. New York had from the first been practically agreed upon as the seat of their further operations in America, but they had, as is not unusual with army men, continued the discussion long after an agreement had been reached.

Sir William was anxious to be on his way, but he needed men and supplies, as well as the transports in which to move

Etched by H B Hall Morrisania N.Y 1872

GEN. SIR WILLIAM HOWE.

W Howe

them, and he especially needed more of a navy than was
then available if he was to stand any chance of taking and
holding New York. That he would eventually be furnished
with all these things he did not doubt. But he was still
waiting for them to come, when, disagreeably enough, Washington decided that the time was ripe for him to take possession of the heights of Dorchester.

He had been a long time making up his mind, but once it
was made up Washington moved quickly. At sunset on
March 4th, 1776 he ordered a heavy bombardment on the
town, under cover of which his men moved rapidly across the
neck and up into the heights of Dorchester where a working
party of some twelve hundred proceeded to erect a breast-
work afterwards admitted by the British to have been unas-
sailable.* Artillery was hauled into place, five companies of
riflemen were ambushed at the water's edge, and Putnam was
stationed with a fleet of rowboats in the Charles river to move
on Boston in case a sally should be made against Dorchester.
In spite of the bright moonlight the work was finished without discovery by the British or by any of the numerous Loyalists who were furnishing the British with eyes and ears.

Howe was willing enough to go; indeed, there is evidence
that he had already issued orders for the embarkation of his
troops to begin on the following day,† but he did not relish
the idea of being driven out. He thought that evacuation
under fire would lower the prestige of British arms, and was
preparing to launch an attack against the American position,
when a violent hurricane blew up. The storm not only
lashed the British soldiers in the flatboats, but drove some of
the larger vessels aground and completely paralyzed Howe's
offensive.

Had Sir William felt so inclined he could have dealt the

* *History of the American War,* C. Stedman.
† *Artemus Ward,* C. Martyn.

Americans a heavy blow by hastily embarking his troops and setting fire to the town; but once more his kindly feelings for Boston came to the fore. He could not bring himself to burn the place that had honored his dead brother. Then, too, there was the civil population to think of; he could not leave to the fury of the rebels (which was believed at this time to be fanatically murderous) all these people whose only crime was their loyalty to their king. And there were the accumulated stores and munitions to be considered — he would need all that he had, and more. It was a difficult situation; but the shrewd Sir William thought of a way out. He would not treat with the rebels. To do that would have been too great a compromise with his dignity. There was no reason, however, why he should not deal with them indirectly. So he let it be known around Boston that if the provincials would not molest him, he would evacuate without destroying the town. The news was not long in penetrating the rebel lines. Washington took no official action, but he withheld his fire.

Shipping was scarce, and Sir William was two full weeks in loading his boats and embarking his troops and passengers. The evacuation was completed on St. Patrick's Day when the last of the overloaded vessels put out to sea and headed for Halifax.

The first year of the Revolution was coming to a close, and the outlook for Britain was not promising. Little had been achieved by the three major-generals who had ploughed the Atlantic on the *Cerberus* with so much self-confidence. Burgoyne had gone back to England. Clinton was off on the ill-starred expedition against Ft. Moultrie. And Howe was retreating to Halifax to await developments.

Sir William was in no cheerful mood when he took his pen in hand on board the *Chatham* off Nantasket Road to write the Earl of Dartmouth the latest news from America. His letter reads:

March 21, 1776

MY LORD,

It is with great regret that I am obliged to inform your Lordship, that after all my struggles to supply the army with provisions from the southern provinces and the West Indies, from whence none of the vessels have yet returned, and after an anxious expectation of more transports to convey the troops, stores, civil officers, inhabitants and effects, the enemy, by taking possession of, and fortifying the commanding Heights on Dorchester Neck, in order to force the ships by their cannon to quit the harbour, has reduced me to the necessity either of exposing the army to the greatest distresses, by remaining in Boston, or of withdrawing from it under such straightened circumstances. The importance of preserving this force, when it could no longer act to advantage, did not leave any room to doubt of the propriety of its removal; and since my determination taken on the 7th instant, I have exerted every expedient to accomplish the arduous task, which was executed on the 17th following in the forenoon, without the least molestation from the rebels, the transports having been previously watered, and fitted for sea in every respect, excepting the article of provisions, in the view of complying with his Majesty's for a movement from Boston, as soon as I might be enabled to effect it.

In order to explain to your Lordship more clearly the state I was reduced to in the article of provisions, I have enclosed a return, extracted from the Commissary General's reports between the 12th of February and the 4th of March; also the tonnage of transports at the time of embarkation.

The rebels about the latter end of January erected new works and batteries on a point of land opposite to West Boston, at a place known by the name of Phipps's Farm, which laying under cover of their strongest posts, and so situated as to be supported by their whole force from Cambridge, was not to be prevented; soon afterwards the militia of the country was called in, and having intelligence that the enemy intended to possess themselves of Dorchester Neck, I ordered a detachment from Castle William, on the 13th of February, under the command of Lieutenant Leslie, and one composed of Grenadiers and light infantry from Boston, commanded by Major Musgrave, to pass over the ice, with directions to destroy the houses and every kind of cover whatever upon the peninsula, which was executed, and six of the enemy's guard made prisoners.

On the 22nd instant, at night, the rebels began a cannonade upon the town, from Roxbury and Phipps's Farm, and threw some shells from both places, without doing any personal dam-

age, and but little to the buildings; the same was repeated on
the evenings of the 3d and 4th, by which only six men were
wounded; the fire being returned from our batteries, but at
such a distance, as to be very uncertain in the execution.

It was discovered on the 5th in the morning, that the enemy
had thrown up three very extensive works, with strong abbaties
round them, on the commanding hill of Dorchester Neck, which
must have been the employment of at least 12,000 * men, in a
situation so critical. I determined upon an immediate attack,
with all the force I could transport. The ardour of the troops
encouraged me in this hazardous enterprize; regiments were ex-
peditiously embarked on board transports to fall down the harbour, and flat boats were to receive other transports, making in
the whole 2,400 men, to rendezvous at Castle William, from
whence the descent was to be made in the night of the 5th, but
the wind unfortunately becoming contrary, and blowing very
hard, the ships were not able to get to their destination, and this
circumstance also making it impossible to employ the boats, the
attempt became impracticable.

The weather continuing boisterous the next day and night,
gave the enemy time to improve their works, to bring up their
cannon, and to put themselves into such a state of defense, that
I could promise myself little success by attacking them under all
the disadvantages I had to encounter; wherefore I judged it most
advisable to prepare for the evacuation of the town, upon the
assurance of one month's provision from Admiral Shuldham,
who in this emergency, as he had on every other occasion, offered all the assistance he could afford.

A thousand difficulties arose on account of the disproportion
of the transports for the conveyance of the troops, the well affected inhabitants, their most valuable property, and the quantity of military stores to be carried away; however, as the enemy
gave no interruption but during the nights, and that incon-
siderable, I found the whole in readiness to depart on the 14th,
if the wind had favored, and assisted by the abilities and assidu-
ities of Captains Reynar and Montagu, of his Majesty's ships
Chatham and *Fowey,* who superintended the embarcation, and
by the alacrity of the officers under them, this operation was
effected on the 17th, and the rear guard embarked at nine
oClock in the morning, without the least loss, irregularity, or
accident. Such military stores as could not be taken on board

* A compliment to the industry of the provincials who sent over 2000 men in
the early evening, and relieved them with a detachment of 2000 fresh men at
three in the morning ! Sir William could never seem to understand the American enthusiasm for using the shovel. And he was as bad at figures as Gage,
which is saying a great deal.

were destroyed * and the utmost expedition is now using to get ready for sea in the best state our circumstances will allow; the admiral having all the ships of war he can spare from the convoy, for the security and protection of such vessels as may be bound for Boston.

Every provision my situation would afford, has been made for the accommodation of the inhabitants, and the preservation of their effects; all the woollen goods also that I could find room for, belonging to those who chose to stay behind, the want of which is more distressing to the enemy than any other article whatever, has been shipped; inventories of them taken in the best manner possible, and put under the charge of proper persons, in order to be hereafter stored. The demolition of the castle had been effectually executed, and an armed ship is sent out by the admiral, express, to advise the different governors on the continent of this removal. . .

I am justly sensible how much more conducive it would be to his Majesty's service, if the army was in a situation to proceed immediately to New York; but the present condition of the troops, crowded in transports, without regard to conveniences, the inevitable dissortment of stores, and all the incumbrances with which I am clogged, effectively disable me from the exertion of this force in any offensive operations, although I should receive a supply of provisions before my departure from hence, which considerations, I hope, will lead his Majesty to approve of my determination (to proceed to Halifax).

The last entry with a Boston dateline in the *Orderly Book* was made on the 16th of March. The Parole is given as "Sicily" and the Countersign as "Malta." The next entry is dated at Halifax the 30th of March, though the *Chatham* on which the General made the journey was only six days on the way.

* According to Stedman, Howe left behind 250 cannon, 4 mortars, 2500 chaldrons of sea coal, 25,000 bu. wheat, 2300 bu. barley, among other things.

CHAPTER IV

THE FIRST PITCHED BATTLE

IF GENERAL HOWE regretted his inability to proceed directly to New York while writing his long letter from Nantasket Road, he regretted it a great deal more after he had been a short time at Halifax. The little seaport had a kind heart, but it also had a limit to its hospitality. It had taken in the poverty-stricken Loyalists who had come with Sir William, and several hundred others who had made their way up the treacherous coast in tiny vessels that were courting disaster when they ventured upon the open sea, but Halifax simply had no place for an army. So the soldiers, after a winter of the most severe privation in Boston were compelled to spend the joyous spring imprisoned like felons on the overcrowded boats in the harbor while the commander-in-chief awaited the arrival of his food-ships, and the necessary gear and reinforcements to enable him to move against New York.

In spite of Washington's almost fantastic precautions to insure the secrecy of Arnold's expedition up the Kennebec, Sir William had been fully informed about it from the start. He had written the Ministry back in November that the party under the command of "a Colonel Arnold" had penetrated some sixty miles from the mouth of the Kennebec and had sent back about two hundred sick. Howe was slightly in error about this. It was not "a" Colonel Arnold, but "the" Colonel Arnold. In his letter of January 23rd Sir William had written of the failure of the expedition, and in his letter of March 21st he had expressed the intention of sending three regiments to Quebec as soon as the St. Lawrence was open for navigation.

It is in this letter that he warns the Ministry that unless the supply-ships are sent under convoy, or of force to defend themselves their safety will become very precarious as the rebels have "greatly increased their naval strength." He also expresses the fear that vessels then on the way may fall into the hands of the enemy, and suggests that all convoys should for the sake of their security be sent first to Halifax, from whence they may proceed with more certainty to the future destination of the army. He adds the doleful news heard from the master of a vessel just arrived from Antigua that "no less than 37 sail of different kinds" forced off their course were taking refuge there when he left that island.

Still at Halifax on April 25th, Sir William writes with keen regret of the capture by the rebels of a brig loaded with shoes and woolen articles much wanted by his men. He also reports that Washington has quit Boston and gone to New York with part of his army, while those left behind are further fortifying the city, which goes to show that the British sources of information were still in good working order. It is in this letter that Howe advances the belief that the Americans, "flushed with the idea of superiority after the evacuation of Boston, may be readier brought to a decisive action, than which nothing is more to be desired or fought for" by the British as the most effectual means to "terminate this expensive war." And from the "present health and high order" of his army Sir William feels that he has the greatest reason to be sanguine in his hopes of success.

Halifax was a stuffy little town. There was nothing to see there, nothing to do, and even though Sir William was in pleasant company (for he had taken the adorable Mrs. Lor-

ing and her complaisant husband along with him) he finally
became so bored with the place that he could endure it no
longer.   He did not wait for the arrival of the fleet under
his brother, the Admiral, which was on its way with abun-
dant stores and ample reinforcements.   Three months of
inactivity had made him restless, and one day he suddenly
ordered the anchors up and set sail for New York.

What a sight the convoy of 110 sail must have been as
they swept silently down the blue Atlantic, their tall masts
piercing the sky and leaning this way and that before the
pressure of the wind, the snowy canvas gracefully billowed
like the skirts of a goddess walking on the breezy slopes of
Olympus.   But sailing ships are temperamental creatures.
They must be petted and humored if they are to be made to
sail at all, and in spite of the efforts of the skippers to keep
the General's flagship, the *Greyhound,* in sight, one fell away
here and another there until the convoy was much reduced.
This did not worry the General.   He was well aware of the
whims of ships and sailors, and when he had reached the
rendezvous off Sandy Hook he dropped anchor and waited
for the stragglers to catch up.   In due time the lookout reported them all.

As the ships came to anchor, Washington who had taken
personal charge of the defense of New York, became more
and more nervous.   He anticipated an early attack, and issued orders that his men should "lay on their Arms in their
tents and quarters, ready to turn out at a moment's warning,
as there is great likelihood of it."   Still the attack did not
come.   The armada made no move to come inside the bay
until the 2nd of July.   Through a strange coincidence this
happened to be the day when the Declaration of Independence was passed by the Continental Congress, though the news
of the passage of the important act did not reach New York
until the 10th.

Washington had very obligingly omitted Staten Island

from his scheme of defenses, so the British were able to land there without opposition. At last the soldiers who had been cooped up on shipboard since the 17th of March were able to stretch their cramped limbs on the shore. They leaped and wrestled and ran races and rolled on the turf — while Washington was writing nervously to Congress that as only 50 of the 110 ships had come into port he was fearful that the British meant to surround Long Island and seize all the livestock there.

Sir William was not bothering his head about the livestock on Long Island, however. He was doing something much more to his liking; he was receiving large delegations of loyal Tories who had come flocking to Staten Island to welcome the arrival of the British. An impromptu celebration was held at which an immense bonfire was started with a huge wad of continental currency. A party of sixty men came over from New Jersey carrying muskets, and offered their services to the Crown. They brought the heartening news that some five hundred more would follow shortly. The Tories wanted peace, they said. They were waiting anxiously for the arrival of the Admiral with the olive branches he was reported to be bringing, but they were dubious about the prospects; they thought that nothing short of a decisive drubbing would ever put the rebels in their place. Sir William listened with interest, but did not do a great deal of talking. He was as anxious as they for the arrival of his brother.

He had not long to wait; for on the 12th of July the Admiral came sailing into port with the ensign of St. George flying at the masthead of his flagship, his peace proposals in his pocket, and 10,000 fighting Hessians in his transports. He had touched at Halifax on July 1st, and finding his brother gone, had hurried on to New York. The Admiral with his huge fleet of warships and transports was received with a general salute from the vessels already lying at anchor. The noise must have been terrific, and doubtless the thunder of all these guns filled the waiting colonials with ominous forebodings.

Soon after the arrival of the Admiral, General Clinton came sailing in with the 2000 men he had taken South for the unsuccessful attempt against Charleston.

That this growing array of men and ships should have made Washington jumpy is not to be wondered at. He was now able to count more than 400 transports, 10 ships of the line, and 20 frigates, with some 1200 big guns. There were 10,000 seamen, and a land force of over 32,000. The British fighting-men were well armed, well found, well fed, well clothed, and well trained, whereas the motley force at Washington's command, which could not possibly have exceeded 20,000 including the sick and disabled, was in a state of the utmost dilapidation. They were poorly armed and insufficiently trained. Many of them were without uniforms. None of them had enough to eat. They were not even concentrated in a single camp. About half of them were stationed in New York "in case the British should make their initial attack there." The rest were over on Long Island to keep the invaders from seizing the high land that commanded the city. Washington had no ships or floating batteries; nothing but rowboats and flatboats, and a few small ferryboats with which to maintain communications between the two parts of his divided army.

The British were not unaware of the spectacular aspects of all this show of strength. They were not at all averse to overawing the colonists as much as they conveniently could, on the theory that a wholesome respect for an opponent is a valuable aid to an understanding of the opponent's point of view. They made no warlike gestures, however, and proceeded to set in motion the machinery by means of which they hoped to settle the American dispute at a conference table instead of on a battlefield.

While Sir William had been hibernating at Halifax, Lord Howe had been closeted with the Ministry. He was ready and willing to take his fleet to America, but he was even more opposed to the American war than Sir William. He believed that peace with the colonies was still possible if the negotiations were properly handled, and he offered the services of himself and his brother as negotiators on behalf of the Crown.

Germain had somewhat grudgingly consented to the commission, but imposed terms so truculent that Lord Howe promptly declined to accept them. A long correspondence ensued * and though Germain was consistently illiberal about making concessions, the Admiral finally succeeded in obtaining terms on which he believed a conciliation might be based, and started for America in high feather. He arrived, it is true, with the most formidable fleet the colonies had ever seen, but his attitude of mind was not unfriendly. He had supplied himself with letters of introduction to a number of influential persons, and in his cabin on the long journey across he had prepared a message to the people of America by which he hoped to impress them with his wide powers and his pacific intentions.

Though Lord Howe and Sir William were as unlike in taste and temperament and habit as it is possible for two brothers to be, they always were able to work together in the greatest harmony. Sir William was as enthusiastic as the Admiral over the peace proposals and as anxious to secure an immediate presentation to the colonial authorities. The well-intentioned commissioners soon found, however, that there were many difficulties in the way.

The ministerial management of American affairs, bad to begin with, had not improved with age. The Port Bill intended for the chastening of Boston had precipitated a war, and the Prohibitory Act had very successfully paved the way

* Found in the *Germain Papers,* W. L. Clements Library.

for the Declaration of Independence. The desire for independence was not a spontaneous impulse. The idea did not
burgeon upon the colonists like a light in the western sky.
It was, on the contrary, a fire started with a slow match which
sizzled for a long time before it burst into flame. Even the
patriotic Washington had not been a convert to the doctrine
when he went to Boston as commander-in-chief of the colonial forces. He still thought reconciliation not only possible but probable. His rancor was against the Ministry
rather than the Crown. And the famous "Olive Branch"
petition to "the King's Most Excellent Majesty" was not
adopted by the Continental Congress until the 8th of July
1775, some three weeks after the Battle of Bunker Hill.*

The Prohibitory Act repealed the Port Bill, which had
closed only the port of Boston, and declared all colonial har-
bors closed. It forbade fishing on the Grand Banks, and
prohibited trade not only with other countries but among
the colonies themselves. Then with a grand gesture of in-
dignation it declared war against the colonies.

Instead of being awed by this august decree the colonists
hailed it with delight. The declaration of war, they said,
had given them the legal status of an independent nation.
The Prohibitory Act had made them free. Here was a fine
bit of grist for the mill of John Adams who immediately
took his pen in hand and wrote: †

I know not whether you have seen the act of Parliament called
the Restraining Act, or Prohibitory Act, or Piratical Act, or
Plundering Act, or Act of Independency — for by all these titles
is it called. I think the most apposite is the Act of Independency; for King, Lords, and Commons, have united in sundering
this country from that, I think forever. It is a complete dis-
memberment of the British Empire. It throws thirteen Colonies
out of the Royal Protection, levels all distinctions, and makes us
independent in spite of our supplications and entreaties.

It may be fortunate that the Act of Independency should come

* Original in the possession of G. C. W. Fitzwilliam.
† *American Archives*, Ser. IV, Vol. V, p. 472.

from the British Parliament rather than the American Congress; but it is very odd that Americans should hesitate at accepting such a gift from them.

The passage of the act had been preceded by an address from the throne in the course of which the King had declared his purpose to conquer and subdue the colonists, and this, coupled with the royal assent of the act after its passage was enough to satisfy the scruples of timid colonists who had up to this time been restrained from joining the independents by their oath of allegiance to the King. Protection and allegiance were reciprocal, they argued, and where there was no protection there need be no allegiance; surely all thought of protection had been annulled by a declaration of war. Following this reasoning hitherto loyal colonists went flocking over to the independents in such numbers that within six months after the Prohibitory Act had been received in America the public mind was ready for the Declaration.

After its adoption the Declaration of Independence was printed and widely distributed over the country. On receiving a copy Washington ordered the several brigades of his army to be drawn up to hear "the declaration of Congress, shewing the grounds & reasons for this Measure, to be read with an audible voice." What the several brigades thought about it may be surmised from their conduct immediately afterwards, for they stormed the equestrian statue of the King in Bowling Green and tumbled it to the ground. This must have been something of an effort, for the leaden likeness of horse and man weighed close to four thousand pounds; but in their enthusiasm they did not stop at hard work, and had soon beheaded their erstwhile monarch, who had been moulded in the role of Marcus Aurelius. They cut off the nose, hacked the wreath of laurels from the brow, shot a bullet into the head and took it up to Fort Washington with the intention of mounting it on the truck of the flag-staff.

There is a popular fable to the effect that the lead from the ruined statue was afterwards made into bullets and fired at the British as "melted George." But Montresor, in his diary, denies this, and says that he sent a man through the American lines to one Cox who kept a tavern near the fort asking him to steal and bury the statue, "Which was effected, and was dug up on our arrival." He adds that he afterward sent the head by Lady Gage to Lord Townshend "to convince them at home of the Infamous Disposition of the Ungrateful people in this distressed Country." And thus perishes another bit of folklore.

The initial move in the new peace offensive was made soon after the arrival of Lord Howe. A naval officer sent forward under a flag of truce requested a conference with Washington. He was met instead by Joseph Reed who was then Washington's secretary. Upon being informed by the envoy that he had a letter from Lord Howe to "Mister Washington," Reed refused to receive it, saying that there was no such person as "Mister" Washington in the army. The visitor expressed great concern and said that the letter was of a civil rather than a military nature, that Lord Howe regretted he had not come sooner. But Reed was firm, and the envoy went away without having delivered his letter. A little later an aide to Sir William called to inquire whether "General" Washington would receive the Adjutant-General of the British army. He was granted an immediate audience, and on being taken into the presence of Washington proffered a letter addressed to "George Washington, Esq., &c. &c."

Washington declined to receive it, whereupon the caller delivered the purported message verbally. It had to do with the treatment of a prisoner, but the caller tactfully brought up the subject of Lord Howe's desire for a reconciliation and mentioned the appointment of the General and the Admiral as peace commissioners.

"From what has transpired," said Washington, "they have

only the power to grant pardons. Those who have committed no fault, need no pardon. We are only defending what we deem our indisputable rights."

"That is a matter that would open a wide field," the visitor replied.

The Adjutant-General had risen to retire when Washington with true southern hospitality invited him to stay for lunch, but the visitor graciously declined. He had partaken of a late breakfast, he said. Still determined to be the perfect host Washington called in his staff officers and introduced them to the distinguished visitor. Then the Adjutant-General retired.

To us all this bowing and scraping seems rather silly. There is no doubt that the Howes were really interested in stopping the shedding of human blood, and it does seem as if they might as well have stopped it in the name of "General" Washington as "George Washington, Esq., &c. &c." Washington himself might have shown a little less concern for rank and a little more for the lives of his countrymen. But both sides were touchy, and the Howes having tried their olive branch without conspicuous success, now unsheathed the sword and went about the bloody business of hacking a little sense into the stubborn colonials.

As ever, they made their preparations slowly, and in the interim Washington, since he had no fleet of his own, tried to set fire to the wooden craft of the enemy by means of fire-rafts which were floated alongside in the darkness of the night well loaded with inflammables and ignited when they were thought to be so near that the flames from the burning rafts would be communicated to the vessels. The attempt provided some thrills for the crews of the fire-rafts, but did so little damage to the enemy boats that the idea was soon abandoned.

"Black Dick," as Lord Howe was affectionately called by his tars, was a real fighting admiral. He had won his way

to the top by his intrepid seamanship. Like his brother, he
did not know what fear was, and as soon as it had become apparent to him that the colonials would listen to no argument
that did not come out of the barrel of a gun, he began to
manœuvre his men-of-war around the harbor, perhaps to get
the lay of the land and to detect any obstructions to navigation,
natural or artificial; and perhaps not wholly without the intention of showing the colonial troops defending New York
how completely he had them in his power. His vessels ran
up and down North River at will, despite the batteries that
the Americans had built to stop them, and two ships dropped
anchor far up the Hudson and lingered there for days while
the distracted Washington shivered for his lines of communication with the mainland. At length gunboats began
to run the East River and anchor near Hell Gate.

According to the military canons New York was untenable
so long as the enemy was in possession of the heights commanding the city. The General and the Admiral were
orthodox enough to believe this. They had, no doubt, acquired their military education from the very books on
which the defense of New York was based. General Charles
Lee, the designer of these defenses, had received his military
training in England. General Lee may have been unreli-
able and mercurial. He may have been, as many believe, a
paranoiac, or a subject of dementia praecox, but he was, according to the books quite sane and sound on his idea for the
fortification of New York. He was not particularly enthusiastic over an attempt to hold a city surrounded by navigable
waters without the assistance of a defending fleet; but if the
place was to be made even temporarily tenable, the army of occupation, he said, must hold the heights of Brooklyn. It was
at General Lee's own request that Washington had sent him
to see to the defenses of New York while the British were still
in Boston, and with the means at his disposal Lee had not
done badly.

Washington has been harshly criticized for permitting the battle of Long Island to be fought at all. To have divided his army so that the British could consume it piecemeal was to furnish a text on which the military commentators have been thundering for a century and a half. But Washington was in a peculiar situation. We have seen that in order to hold New York, he must retain the heights of Brooklyn. If he abandoned Long Island, he must abandon New York. And to abandon New York without making at least a noble gesture of defense would have been politically suicidal to the cause of American independence — or so it was thought at the time. How it would have been any worse for Washington to have burned New York at the approach of the British and have backed his army off out of reach of the naval guns, than to take the beating that he took on Long Island and the chasing that he took throughout the length of Manhattan and Westchester, is hard for the present day commentators to understand.

Two-thirds of the property in New York belonged to the Tories, and, as General Greene pointed out, there was no great advantage in running any considerable risk for its defense. Greene also pointed out that if the enemy got possession of the city the Americans could never recover it without a superior naval force; that to burn it would be to deprive the enemy of an opportunity to barrack their whole army together, and to rob them of a general market which was sure to prove tempting to colonials who had produce to sell. "All these advantages would result from the destruction of the city," he argued, not without astuteness, "and not one benefit can arise to us of its preservation, that I can conceive of."

Shrewd General Greene. Wise General Greene. He is, as Rupert Hughes puts it, writing history before it happens, but nobody pays any attention to him. Washington spared the match, and left half his army to defend New York while he took the other half over to Long Island for the purpose of administering a sound drubbing to a British army four times the size of the force he is sending against it.

The Americans did not, as at Bunker Hill, await an assault within their entrenchments. They were spoiling for a fight. They went out looking for it — and they had no trouble at all finding it. Their thin line was stretched out along the spine of high land that runs from New York Bay easterly to Jamaica. This high land was not yet built up to sky-scrapers, garden apartments and motion-picture palaces. Some of it was planted to corn, but much of it was wooded. The colonial troops took cover behind the trees. The British troops came forward in skirmish formation and made contact with the enemy. Firing began, but the British were cautious. They seemed to be feeling out the situation. The Americans braced themselves for a charge, and when it failed to materialize they began to wonder if the British were afraid of them. Then suddenly they heard the thunder of artillery in the rear. The British had circled their left wing and were coming up behind them. They were all but surrounded!

Two gunshots in the rear were a signal to the British on their front. They no longer held their fire, but went forward in a resistless charge. There were more of them than Washington had been led to suppose. The woods were full of them. All the Americans who could fall back, did; the rest were killed or captured, or driven into the swamps to drown. It was a debâcle. The enveloping movement of the British was so successful as to put the Americans completely at their mercy. Washington himself did not reach the field of battle until the fighting was almost over. He had remained in New York, fearing that the thrust on Long Island was a feint. He is pictured as wringing his hands in anguish and exclaiming, "Great God! What must my brave boys suffer today!"

The battle had begun at daybreak, but by four in the afternoon it had turned into a chase with groups of British and Hessians running down the Americans like hares. It is said that even the camp women "joined in the holiday and actually captured prisoners." * The day's bag included three generals, Sullivan, Stirling, and Woodhull, three colonels, four lieutenant-colonels, three majors, eighteen captains, forty-three lieutenants and more than 1000 privates. Howe computed the total American loss at 2000. Washington's report was indefinite, which was enough to show that it was heavy. The British loss was trifling.

Washington must have shaken his head sadly as he went over the figures. But he was not yet out of the woods; all the Americans who had not been killed or captured were cooped up in flimsy redoubts on Brooklyn Heights with the flower of the British army in front of them, and the flower of the British navy behind them. That trouble was ahead the Americans did not doubt, but for the moment there was a lull. That lull has been perplexing historians ever since. Sir William's men had chased the remnants of the colonial army into the redoubts, and were rushing up with much spirit to take the stronghold by storm — when Sir William called them off. They pretended not to hear, for they were in no mood to abandon what appeared to be an easy victory, and repeated orders were necessary "to prevail upon them to desist from the attempt," as Sir William expressed it in a letter to Lord George Germain who had by this time supplanted Lord Dartmouth as Secretary of State.†

It has been suggested that a recollection of the deadly fire of the colonials at Bunker Hill may have flashed suddenly into Sir William's mind and broken his nerve; or that he may have decided to hold off the attack until the Admiral, who had been beset by adverse winds and tides, could get his

---

* *George Washington*, Rupert Hughes, II, page 446.
† Letter of September 3, 1776.

ships into position to pour in a stream of death and destruction from the big guns on the warships. It has even been intimated that the weather may have caused Sir William to postpone the stroke that must have turned that which was already a brilliant piece of action into a final and conclusive victory; for a downpour of rain began that night which continued without interruption for the next two or three days. Sir William in his report gave as his reason for holding back his men, that as it was apparent the lines must have been his at a very cheap rate "by regular approaches" he did not care to risk the loss that might have been sustained in the assault.

This, however, was not written until a week after the engagement, and a man may think of many reasons in a week that would not have occurred to him on the spot. Whatever his reasons may have been, he recalled his men, stationed them in a hollow out of the reach of the "musquetry," and ordered them to entrench. But let Sir William tell the story:

On the evening of the 27th, the army encamped in front of of the enemy's works. On the 28th, at night, broke ground 600 yards distant from a redoubt upon their left, and on the 29th, at night the rebels evacuated their entrenchments, near Redhook, with the utmost silence, and quitted Governor's Island the following evening, leaving their cannon and a quantity of stores in their works. At day-break, on the 30th, their flight was discovered, the picquets took possession and those most advanced reached the shore opposite to New York as their rear-guard was going over, and fired some shot among them.

The enemy is still in possession of the town and island of New York, in force, and making demonstration of opposing us in their works on both sides of King's bridge.

Not a word about waiting for the Admiral's ships. Not a word about the rain. Not a word about the cloak of fog in which Providence is claimed to have enveloped Washington and his little band of patriots, making them invisible to the British so that they might escape unharmed across the river. If there was an unusual fog, and if it was sent by Providence for the protection of the colonials, surely the favored few made but a poor return for the miracle by their subsequent behavior in New York, where whole regiments of them turned and ran before the British landing parties had even reached the shore.

Strange as it may seem, the Admiral was never blamed because of his failure to get his gunboats into a position from which they could rake the heights of Brooklyn during this battle. It has always been accepted as a matter of undisputed fact that a contrary wind and a treacherous tide were a sufficient exoneration. One of his smaller gunboats did contrive to get within range of a battery at Red Hook for a short time and with only a few shots completely disabled the stronghold. Had he been able to get his larger boats within range the War of the Revolution might have ended that day with Sir William as a hero to be reckoned with in song and story.

Even as it was, the victory of Sir William was at the time regarded as of the utmost importance. His brief report was received at court with "an extravagance of joy," and the jubilant monarch who took it as an indication that all would soon be well in America determined on the spur of the moment to give Sir William "a red ribband." * Lord Mansfield was given an earldom. Bells were rung at Leeds. Windows were illuminated, cannon were fired, and a huge bonfire built. At Limerick a number of ladies and gentlemen were "elegantly entertained at dinner by the Bishop" in honor of the victory. The criticisms of Sir William's conduct were to come later on when the whole story had been told. He had met the enemy on the open field; he had outwitted and out-generalled them; he had beaten them soundly — and then instead of bagging them he had managed to let them

* The insignia of the Order of the Bath.

get away. That was what annoyed the Tories. They were afraid he would never again get so beautiful a chance to put away a good half of the Continental army.

The colonials derived what comfort they could from the "masterly retreat" of Washington. Indeed, they had so much to say in its favor, and sang so many hosannas to the American commander for his part in it that the history books of a later generation treated Washington as the virtual winner of a day, their narratives amounting, as one recent commentator puts it, to "little less than a falsification of history." This same commentator, who has a rank of brigadier-general in the United States army, further finds that Washington in his campaign on Long Island "disregarded almost every known principle of strategy or ruse of tactics, some of them in a way almost grotesque." To quote him further: *

A British division, under the command of Clinton, made a night move on Brooklyn by the eastermost of the three roads. That road, under any known rules of warfare, even the most elementary, should have been picketed, and watched by a mounted patrol. Twenty-five men would have sufficed; fifty would have been ample. Four hundred men could have picketed the whole of Washington's front, and, holding the enemy in check, have given ample notice of his approach.

To neglect so obvious a precaution was so unpardonable as not to admit of explanations. As a matter of fact, the road in question was left not only uncovered, but was not even observed. (This is denied by Stedman who was at the time an officer in Howe's army. Occasional patrols, he says, were sent to watch this road, but one of these being intercepted by a British advanced guard, enabled the pass to be gained without alarming the Americans.†)

The disaster of August 27 on Long Island just failed to bring irretrievable ruin on the cause of American Independence. Even as it was, gravely compromising Washington, its influence was perceptible on the whole course of military operations during the succeeding three years. To Washington it was a lesson from which he learned much. Thenceforth he adopted Fabian tactics.

* *Studies Military and Diplomatic*, Charles Francis Adams.
† *History of the American War*, C. Stedman.

If the "masterly retreat" was the first evidence of an emulation by Washington of the tactics of General Quintus Fabius Maximus Verrucosis, it was a very promising beginning. It saved a full half of his army from an almost certain destruction. It prevented the movement for the independence of America from coming to an untimely end. And it preserved the noble name of Washington that it might in later years be honored by applying it to cities and states as well as to insurance companies, fish-markets, and coffee.

After the departure of the Americans Sir William moved into the abandoned fortifications and put them in order. He mounted his siege guns and trained them on New York. He encamped his splendid armies on the high ground overlooking the American position. The Howes were well content. They had shown the rascally rebels what to expect if they persisted with this foolishness about independence. Now perhaps the colonists would listen to reason. Lord Howe and Sir William laid aside the sword and dusted off the olive branch. Once more they assumed the role of peace commissioners.

CHAPTER V

A PREMATURE PEACE CONFERENCE

ISTORY does not record what Washington said to General Sullivan when the day after the retreat from Long Island he met the captured general on the streets of New York. Washington must have been surprised. Most certainly he was not pleased when he heard that Sullivan had been released on parole to carry further proposals of peace from Lord Howe to Congress.

Washington was still convinced that the authority of the proponents did not exceed the power of granting pardons, and he realized that nothing is so disruptive of the fighting spirit of a country as the continual discussion of peace.* No doubt he would have been happier, although he was too polite to say so, if Sullivan had been back in the cornfield on Long Island where three tall grenadiers had found him in hiding and had dragged him out with glee to add him to the day's bag of prisoners. That Washington had little faith in the success of Sullivan's errand is apparent from his letter to the Congress written on August 31st. He says:

I have consented to his (Sullivan's) going to Philadelphia, as I do not mean, or conceive it right, to withhold or prevent him from giving such information as he possesses in this instance.

* He had also been cold to the well-meaning advances of Lord Drummond some months previous.

The pronunciamento which Lord Howe had composed in his cabin at sea, though addressed to the royal governors of the colonies, was intended for wide distribution among the people. It was, as a matter of fact, no more than an announcement that the Admiral and his brother had been named as peace commissioners by a gracious monarch and endowed with the power to grant pardons upon submission. Lord Howe had taken the precaution to send a copy of the declaration to Congress at the time when he was posting his letters of introduction to Franklin and other influential citizens.

Congress had taken the declaration calmly, and had ordered it printed in the gazettes, "that the few who still remain suspended by a hope founded either in justice of moderation of their late king, may now, at length be convinced that the valor alone of their country is to save its liberties."

The friendly letter to Franklin had not been read into the record, but it had been shown to every member who was interested in seeing it, and a resolution had finally been passed authorizing Franklin to make a reply if he thought proper. Franklin did think proper, and thereupon sat down and wrote one of the most famous letters of his long and useful career. But it is a lengthy letter and only a few of the highlights can be given:

The official dispatches, to which you refer me, contain nothing more than what we had seen in the act of Parliament, viz., offers of pardon upon submission, which I am sorry to find, as it must give your lordship pain to be sent so far on so hopeless a business.

Directing pardons to be offered the colonies, who are the very parties injured, expresses indeed that opinion of our ignorance, baseness, and insensibility, which your uninformed and proud nation has long been pleased to entertain of us; but it can have no other effect than that of increasing our resentment. It is impossible that we should think of submission to a government that has with the most wanton barbarity and cruelty burnt our defenseless towns in the midst of winter, excited the savages to massacre our farmers, and our slaves to murder their masters, and is even now bringing foreign mercenaries to deluge our settlements with blood. . . But your lordship mentions 'The king's paternal solicitude for promoting the establishment of a lasting *peace* and union with the colonies.' If by peace is here meant a peace to be entered into between Britain and America, as distinct states now at war, and his majesty has given your lordship powers to treat with us of such a peace, I may venture to say, though without authority, that I think a treaty for that purpose not yet quite impracticable, before we enter into foreign alliances. But I am persuaded you have no such powers.

Had he not been so determined upon a conciliation, Lord Howe might have taken this as final. At the moment he apparently did. But the setback given to the Americans by the Battle of Long Island seemed to him to have precipitated the psychological moment to renew his negotiations for peace, and the capture of General Sullivan had, he thought, furnished him with a messenger sent directly by the gods.

General Sullivan, however, was more eloquent than accurate, as events were afterward to prove. He harangued Congress to so good an effect that he was invited to reduce his message to writing, which he did. General Sullivan was much better in the role of avenging angel than that of a dove of peace. He could awe the Indians into a state of pacification by burning their villages, but he could not awe Congress at all, and especially that part of Congress represented by the gentleman from Massachusetts, Mr. Adams. John Adams regarded the whole affair of the commission as "a bubble, an ambuscade, a mere insidious maneuver, calculated only to decoy and deceive," and thought that no notice whatever ought to be taken of it.*

The message of Lord Howe as reduced to writing by the rough and ready general, lacked much of the punch of the spoken version, but Congress, after a debate of some three days, concluded that it must overlook no possible chances to put an end to the war and appointed a committee of three

* *Familiar Letters of John Adams and his Wife.*

to wait upon Lord Howe and to hear from his own lips such proposals of peace as he should think fit to make. The committee consisted of Benjamin Franklin, John Adams, and Edward Rutledge who managed to nose out Colonel R. H. Lee on a second ballot, the two having been tied on the first count.

It was at this time that John Adams wrote to his friend James Warren:

> . . . There has been a Change in our Affairs at New York. What Effects it will produce I cant pretend to foretell, I confess, I do not clearly foresee. Lord Howe is surrounded with disaffected American Machiavellians, Exiles from Boston and elsewhere, who are instigating him to mingle Art with Force. He has sent Sullivan here, upon his Parol, with the most insidious, 'tho ridiculous Message which you can conceive. It has put Us rather in a delicate Situation, and gives Us much Trouble.

Two days later he was writing to his wife:

> . . . I requested to be excused, but was desired to consider of it until tomorrow. My friends here advise me to go. All the stanch and intrepid are very earnest with me to go, and the timid and wavering, if any such there are, agree in the request. So I believe I shall undertake the journey. I doubt whether his lordship will see us, but the same committee will be directed to enquire into the state of the army at New York, so that there will be business enough if his lordship makes none.*
>
> It would fill this letter book to give you all the arguments for and against this measure, if I had the liberty to attempt it. His lordship seems to have been playing off a number of Machiavelian manoeuvres, in order to throw upon us the odium of continuing this war. Those who have been advocates for the appointment of this committee are for opposing manoeuvre to manoeuvre, and are confident that the consequence will be that the odium will fall upon him. However this may be, my lesson is plain, to ask a few questions and take his answers.

Mr. Adams had changed his mind since the day when Lord Howe's declaration was first received. He thought that it

---

* Lord Howe had asked for a conference with some of the members as private gentlemen; Congress was sending them as officials.

had, as he put it, "let the cat out of the bag," believing that his lordship was afraid of being attacked on Staten Island, and was "throwing out his barrels to amuse Leviathan until his reinforcements should arrive." Now it is the odium of continuing the war that his lordship is trying to avoid.

The Committee left Philadelphia with John Adams on horseback, and Franklin and Rutledge traveling in chairs. The second night out they lodged in New Brunswick, where owing to the rush of soldiers to help hold New York, they found the tavern so crowded that Adams and Franklin were forced to occupy the same bed. This led to some argument as to whether they were to sleep with the window open or shut, but Franklin won. They slept with it open although they indulged in a long argument about the cause of the common cold that lasted far into the night. Franklin who had a very complicated theory on the subject talked them both to sleep.* The next morning they pushed on to Amboy where they found a barge from Lord Howe awaiting them.

In the boat was a hostage who informed them that he was subject to their orders to insure their safe return. And even though the Crown had placed a price on John Adams's head and he was to appear to Lord Howe as if a halter were already round his neck,† the hostage was invited into the boat and rowed back to Staten Island with the Committee. When Lord Howe saw the barge coming he walked to the shore to meet his callers, and on perceiving the hostage in the boat, he said, "Gentlemen, you make me a very high compliment, and you may depend upon it I will consider it the most sacred of things."

Dr. Franklin shook hands with his lordship and introduced his fellow committeemen, and the party conversing pleasantly started for the house where his lordship had made ready

---

* *The American Revolution*, Sir George Trevelyan.
† Franklin died from a cold caught by sitting in front of an open window.

to receive them through a lane formed by two lines of Hessians which Lord Howe had ordered drawn up as a guard of honor. The sight of these mercenaries so close at hand was a little annoying to the gentleman from Boston, who describes them as "looking fierce as ten Furies, making all the grimaces, and gestures, and motions of their muskets with bayonets fixed, which, I suppose, military etiquette requires, but which we neither understood nor regarded." Probably all that the poor Germans did was to present arms at the order of the commanding officer as the guests of honor were passing.

The house appointed for the interview was a plain old stone farmhouse with a veranda in front. It had once been the residence of a man of wealth but had of late been occupied by the soldiers and was somewhat dilapidated and run down. His lordship, however, had attempted to make the most of his rather limited opportunities and had decorated one of the largest rooms with moss and branches, until, according to Mr. Adams, "it was not only wholesome, but romantically elegant." And here the amiable host had spread a collation consisting of "good claret, good bread, cold ham, tongues, and mutton." Quite naturally pleasure must come before the business of the day, so the good claret, and the good bread, and the ham, tongues and mutton must needs be well threshed over before the little matter of peace between Britain and America could even be touched upon.

So long as there was any food to discuss the Hessian colonel was very much in evidence, but as the conference prepared to convene, he withdrew leaving Lord Howe and his secretary, Henry Strachey, alone to present the case of Britain. Peace was something in which the Hessians took very little interest. It will be noted that although Sir William Howe had been named by the King as joint commissioner with his brother, he had up to this time taken no active part in the proposals looking to the negotiation of peace. Lord

Howe had made all the advances while Sir William had done nothing except to maintain a discreet and dignified silence. It would seem that the moment for his entry had arrived, though none of the congressional Committee appears to have expected him.   If he had come clanking into the conference room by one door as the Hessian colonel was making his exit by the other the setting for the Peace Proposals of Seventy-six would have been perfect.

But Sir William did not come.   Another of those mysteries that surround so many of the acts of the amiable Howe in America.   He may have been engaged with "his glass, his lass, and his game of cards" over on Long Island.   Again it may have been that he and his brother had decided that the blood of Bunker Hill and Brooklyn was a little too fresh on his hands to look well at the preliminary sessions of a peace conference that showed signs of having a very delicate stomach.   It is not to be doubted that Sir William's interest in making a peace with the colonies was fully as deep and sincere as that of his brother the Admiral, although the Admiral on this occasion made no excuses for the absence of his colleague but plunged into the business at hand.*

Lord Howe: Long ago, gentlemen, I entertained the opinion that the differences between the mother-country and her colonies might be accommodated to the satisfaction of both.   I was known in England to be a well-wisher to America — particularly to the province of Massachusetts Bay, which had endeared itself to me by the very high honor it had bestowed upon my eldest brother. I assure you, gentlemen, that I esteem that honor to my family above all things in this world.   Such is my gratitude and affection to this country on that account, that I feel for America as for a brother, and if America should fall, I should feel and lament it like the loss of a brother.

Dr. Franklin: (With a bow and a smile noted at the time by Mr. Adams) My lord, we will use our utmost endeavors to save your lordship that mortification.

* From the minutes kept by Mr. Strachey at the time, with pencil notes by Lord Howe.

ADMIRAL LORD HOWE

Lord Howe: (Never one to see through Franklin's whimseys) I suppose you will endeavor to give us employment in Europe. (Silence on the part of the Committee who must have had a hard time to keep their faces straight. Franklin offered nothing more on the subject, and his lordship resumed.) My going out as a commissioner from the king was talked of long ago, as Dr. Franklin is aware. Then an idea arose of sending over several commissioners, but to this I objected, for my plan was to go alone, with only a civil commission, and proceed straight to Philadelphia, and meet the Congress face to face. I objected even to my brother's being in the commission, from the delicacy of the employment, and from my desire to take upon myself all the reproach that might be the consequence of it. It was thought best, however, that General Howe, being in command of the army in America, should be joined in the commission, and that I should have the naval command; since, in that case, the two commissioners would control the movements of both forces. I acquiesced in this arrangement. I hoped to reach America before the army had made a movement to begin the campaign, and had no doubt that if the disposition of Congress remained the same as expressed in their last petition to the king, I should be able to bring about an accommodation. That petition, I thought, was a sufficient basis to confer upon; as it contained matter which, with candor and discussion, might be wrought into a permanent system. True, the Address to the People, which accompanied the petition to his majesty, had injured the effect of the petition. Nevertheless, to the moment of my arrival in America, I flattered myself that, taking the petition as a basis, I should be able to do some good. But since I left England, you have yourselves changed your ground by the Declaration of Independency. That act, gentlemen, if it cannot be got over, precludes all treaty-making; for, as you are aware, I have not, nor do I expect ever to have, powers to consider the colonies in the light of independent States. You must be sensible, also, that I cannot confer with Congress. I cannot acknowledge a body which is not acknowledged by the king, whose delegate I am, and, for the same reason, I cannot confer with you gentlemen as a committee of the Congress. If you are unwilling to lay aside that distinction, it will be improper for me to proceed. That, however, I trust, you will regard as an unessential form, which may for a moment lie dormant, and give me leave to consider you merely as gentlemen of great ability and influence in the country, who have met here to converse with me, and try if we can devise the outline of a plan to stay the calamities of war. I beg you to consider the delicacy of my situation, and the reproach I should be liable to if I should be understood by any act of mine, to have treated with the Congress or acknowledged its authority. I hope you will not, by any implication, commit me upon that point. Even in the present meeting I have gone rather beyond my powers. (The Committee may as well have gone home at this point, but Franklin was having a good time, and was apparently interested to see what else his lordship would have to say.)

Dr. Franklin: You may depend upon our taking care of that, my lord.

Lord Howe: I think the idea of a Congress may easily be thrown out at present; because, if matters can be so settled that the king's government is re-established, the Congress would of course cease to exist. (David Lloyd George presented the same argument to Woodrow Wilson concerning the "freedom of the seas" at Versailles 143 years later!) And if you really mean an accommodation of that kind, you must see how unnecessary it is to stand upon a form which you are negotiating to give up. (This, too, might well have brought the conference to an end. One can almost hear John Adams scuffing his feet in preparation for rising to leave. But Franklin is not quite ready to go.)

Dr. Franklin: Your lordship may consider us in any view you think proper. (If Franklin had stopped here his lordship would no doubt have felt quite encouraged, but he did not stop.) We, on our part, are at liberty to consider ourselves in our real character. But there is, really, no necessity on this occasion to distinguish between members of Congress and individuals. The conversation may be held as among friends. (This was a little too much for John Adams who now broke into the colloquy.)

Mr. Adams: Your lordship may consider *me* in what light you please. Indeed, I should be willing to consider myself for a few moments in any character which would be agreeable to your lordship, *except* that of a British subject.

Lord Howe: (Turning amiably to Dr. Franklin and Mr. Rutledge) Mr. Adams is a decided character. (We are inclined at this point to think of John Adams as a cantankerous old man, but he was at the time only 41. Franklin was 70. Rutledge was only 27. That Franklin should have made the journey in a chair is not to be wondered at; but we would have expected to find young Mr. Rutledge traveling on horseback.)

Mr. Rutledge: I think, with Dr. Franklin, that the conversation may be as among friends.

Lord Howe: On my arrival in this country, gentlemen, I thought it expedient to issue a Declaration, which one of you has done me the honor to comment upon. I endeavored to couch it in such terms as would be least exceptionable, and I conclude you must have supposed I did not express in it all I had to offer. I thought, however, that I said enough to bring on a discussion which might lead the way to accommodation. But the Declaration of Independency (Lord Howe insists upon calling it thus) has since rendered me more cautious of opening myself, for it is absolutely impossible for me to treat, or even confer upon that ground, or to admit the idea in the smallest degree. If that is given up, I flatter myself there is still room for me to effect the king's purpose. His majesty's most earnest desire is to make his American subjects happy, to cause a reform in whatever affected the freedom of their legislation, and to concur with his Parliament in the redress of any real grievances. My powers are, speaking generally, to restore peace and grant pardons, to attend to complaints and representations, and to confer upon the means of a reunion upon terms honorable and advantageous to the colonies and to Great Britain. You know, gentlemen, that we expect aid from America; our dispute seems only to be concerning the mode of obtaining it.

Dr. Franklin: Aid we never refused upon requisition.

Lord Howe: (thinking that Franklin is referring to monetary aid) Your money, let me assure you, is the smallest consideration. America can confer upon Great Britain more solid advantages; it is her commerce, her strength, her men, that we chiefly want.

Dr. Franklin: (still insisting upon having his little joke) Ay, my lord, we have in America a pretty considerable manufactory of *men.* (Strachey added in his notes, "alluding, as should seem, to their numerous army." But this was later corrected by Lord Howe who penciled in the margin, "No; their increasing population." But as yet the Committee had said nothing about retreating from the Declaration of Independence. His lordship felt that he must have some definite assurance before going much farther.)

Lord Howe: It is desirable to put a stop to these ruinous extremities, as well for the sake of our country as yours. When an American falls, England feels it. The question is: Is there no way of treating back this step of Independency, and thus opening the door to a full discussion? Now, gentlemen, having opened to you the general purport of my commission, and the king's disposition to a permanent peace, I must stop to hear what you may choose to observe.

Dr. Franklin: (now he is getting down to business. There is to be no more cracking of jokes.) I suppose your lordship has seen the Resolution of the Congress which has sent us hither. It authorizes us to inquire what authority your lordship bears, and what propositions you have to offer for the consideration of the Congress. That Resolution contains the whole of our commission. Nevertheless, this conversation, if productive of no immediate good effect, may be of service at a future time. I will therefore say, that America considered the Prohibitory Act as the answer to her last petition to the king. Forces have been sent out, and towns have been burnt. We cannot now expect happiness under the domination of Great Britain. All former attachments are obliterated. America cannot return to the domination of Great Britain, and I imagine that Great Britain means to rest it upon force. (How right he was!) The other gentlemen will doubtless deliver their sentiments.

Mr. Adams: The resolution of the Congress which declared Independency was not taken up upon its own authority. Congress had been instructed so to do by all the colonies. It is not in our power, therefore, my lord, to treat otherwise than as independent states, and, for my own part, I avow my determination never to depart from the idea of Independency.

Mr. Rutledge: I am one of the oldest members of the Congress, my lord, having been a member from the beginning. I think it is worth the consideration of Great Britain whether she would not derive greater advantages from an alliance with the colonies as independent states than she has hitherto done. . . With regard to the people consenting to come again under the English government, it is impossible. I can answer for South Carolina. The royal government there was very oppressive. The officers of the crown claimed "privilege" and confined people for breaches of "privilege." At last we took the government into our own hands, and the people are now settled and happy under that government. They would not, even if the Congress should desire it, return to the king's government.

Lord Howe: If such are your sentiments, gentlemen, I can only lament that it is not in my power to bring about the accommodation I wish. I have not the authority, nor do I ever expect to have, to treat with the colonies as states independent of the crown of Great Britain. I am sorry, gentlemen, that you have had the trouble of coming so far to so little purpose. If the colonies will not give up the system of independency, it is impossible for me to enter into any negotiation.

Dr. Franklin: It would take as much time for us to refer to and get answers from our constituents, as it would the royal commissioners to get fresh instructions from home, which, I suppose might be about three months.

Lord Howe: It is vain to think of my receiving instructions to treat upon that ground.

Dr. Franklin: (after a pause) Well, my lord, as America is to expect nothing but upon unconditional submission — (Unconditional has been an important word in the history of America !)

Lord Howe: (interrupting him) No, Dr. Franklin. Great Britain does not require unconditional submission. I think that what I have already said proves the contrary, and I desire, gentlemen, that you will not go away with such an idea.

Dr. Franklin: (there must have been another pause here although Mr. Strachey has made no note of it) As your lordship has no proposition to make to us, give me leave to ask whether if *we* should make propositions to Great Britain (not that I know, or am authorized to say we shall), you would receive and transmit them ?

Lord Howe: I do not know that I could avoid receiving any papers that should be put into my hands, though I am doubtful of the propriety of transmitting them home. Still I do not say that I would decline doing so.

Here the conference came to an end. Lord Howe, with the utmost courtesy and geniality accompanied his guests to the shore and saw them aboard their barge. If Sir William had been listening in an adjacent chamber, as he might easily have been, he deemed the moment unpropitious for him to put in an appearance. So the Committee went as it came without seeing him. Nor did it so much as catch a glimpse of Mrs. Loring, though she, too, may have been somewhere around.

Two days later the members made a brief report to Congress, which was, as a matter of routine, ordered published in the newspapers. No other action was taken upon it. And thus ended the peace negotiations of 1776, with Washington still holding to the city of New York, General Howe in possession of the whole of Long Island which had by this time turned strongly Tory, and the British fleet in undisputed control of New York Bay and all the rivers, creeks, and other waters tributary thereto. There was trouble ahead.

CHAPTER VI

SIR WILLIAM IN NEW YORK

ND SIR WILLIAM sat on the heights of Long Island and looked down on the little city nestling on the tip of Manhattan very much as a man looks down at an ant that he is about to step on. Sir William was not particularly anxious to step on New York. He had nothing against the place or the people in it. In his heart he must have despised the Tories whose cause he had espoused, for he was as much a Whig as ever; and as the war went on the Tories came to despise Sir William and to assail his conduct as openly as they dared. Some of them, of course, gave him the benefit of the doubt and thought he was doing the best he could to put down the rebellion, but to others he was nothing less than an arch-traitor.

For his own part Sir William was faced with a disagreeable task, and a task that was none of his own making. He had not wanted to lead the army against the Americans in the first place, and, having had the job thrust upon him he had hoped against hope that with the valiant assistance of his brother, the Admiral, some sort of peace might be patched up. *The Treaty of Staten Island!* That would have looked well on paper over the flourishing signatures of *Howe* and *W. Howe.* His portrait as a statesman with a scroll in his hands would have been not unbecoming to the ancestral halls; and perhaps all the American provinces would erect a

monument to him as one of them had already done to his
older brother. But, alas, this was not to be. The conference at Staten Island had come to naught. The rebel army
was still in New York, and instead of getting out as it had
good reason to do, it was digging in and strengthening its
fortifications as if it intended to put up a fight.

Washington's army had come out of the retreat from
Brooklyn in a state bordering on complete disintegration.
It had been terribly punished, and many familiar faces were
missing from the morning roll-call. "The merry tones on
drums and fifes had ceased," says pastor Shewkirk in his
diary. "It seemed a general damp had spread; and the sight
of the scattered people up and down the streets was indeed
moving. Many looked sickly, emaciated, cast down, &c."
The army had been cowering in open entrenchments through
two days of pouring rain and was wet to the skin. It was
gaunt with hunger. It was defeated and downhearted. If
the Howes had gone into action the moment they discovered
the "masterly withdrawal," if they had occupied Washington's attention with a bombardment while they were pushing
a line of troops across the upper end of Manhattan Island,
the dispirited colonials would have thrown down their arms
and given three rousing cheers for the King.

The Howes must have known this; they were intelligent
men. And when they failed to follow up their military advantage to an almost infallible victory, and instead, sent back
a captured general as a messenger of peace, it was not because
theys were dolts, but because they were more interested in
conciliation than conquest.

Congress had, as usual, taken its time in debating the question of sending a delegation to Staten Island. Three precious days were consumed by the useless oratory of the congressmen before they could decide whether to receive the
proposals officially. The Howes might in the meantime
have erased the city of New York from the map, had they

felt so disposed. Instead they refrained from firing a shot until Congress had been given an opportunity to talk itself out. Further time was given for the slow-moving Committee to get itself to Staten Island for the conference. Exactly two weeks had elapsed after the retreat from Long Island before Franklin, Adams, and Rutledge sat down to Lord Howe's "good claret, good bread, cold ham, tongues, and mutton" with which the Conference of Staten Island was opened, and in which the gentlemen from the Congress appeared to be more genuinely interested than in his Lordship's proposals for peace.

During the greater part of this time Sir William did little to strengthen his military position; but the day before the conference, while Ben Franklin and Rutledge were jogging along in their chairs across the flatlands of New Jersey with John Adams as a mounted escort, he seems to have had a premonition that his brother's overtures were doomed to failure, for he landed troops on Randall's Island at the mouth of the Harlem river. This move greatly disturbed Washington who immediately reported it to Congress with the disheartened comment, "How the Event will be, God only knows."

This was slightly in error, for General Greene not only knew but had already put down in black and white how the event would be. General Lee also knew, as did practically all the rest of Washington's staff. Indeed, at a council of war held while the peace commissioners were sitting at Staten Island, ten of Washington's officers out of the thirteen at the meeting voted to abandon the town.

The Peace Conference was held on the 12th, and although hostilities were not renewed, as Washington had feared, before the members of the Committee were beyond the sound of gunshot, the British resumed the war in earnest on the following day. Troops were put in motion on Long Island, and just after the dinner hour three frigates and a forty-gun ship ran the East River, firing as they went, and anchored in the neighborhood of Hell Gate. One of their shot fell within "six foot of General Washington, as he was on horse-back riding into the Fort." *

In his defense before Parliament delivered some three years later Sir William makes no mention of the Conference of Staten Island in accounting for his military inactivity during the first half of September 1776, when with victory in the hollow of his hand he sat on the heights of Long Island and looked idly down at his helpless foe. "The necessary preparations," he says in the *Narrative,* "and erecting batteries to facilitate the landing upon the Island of New York, and battering the enemy's works at Horen's Hook, occupied us till the fifteenth of September, when the possession of New York was effected." His silence about the conference on this occasion may have been construed as one of the "political considerations" mentioned to the Members in his speech. It is not unlikely that Sir William thought that the detailed story of the unsuccessful attempt to negotiate a peace with a foe that was down and practically out would sound a little too ridiculous to the pompous statesmen who, as a committee of the whole, were hearing his defense of his conduct of the war.

In any event the batteries he mentions were inconsequential if not purely mythical. His troops when they landed at New York were, as we shall see, amply covered by the guns of the fleet.

The discussion on Staten Island had taken place on Thursday. The Commissioners had arrived at Philadelphia on Saturday, but had not yet made to Congress the half-humorous report of their proceedings drawn up by John Adams, when the attack on New York began. The first shot was fired as the congressmen and their wives sat comfortably in their pews at church on Sunday morning.

The opening salvo was a well-timed broadside from five

* Letter of Col. Babcock to Governor Cooke, Sept. 21, 1776.

battleships firing point blank. The Continental troops
crouching in their earthworks along the riverbanks on both
sides of the island were not so much hurt as scared by the
thunder of all these guns.   They were rustics accustomed to
the silence of the woods and the peace of the open spaces.
The belching flames and the terrific concussion of the big
naval guns took the fight out of them.   And when they discovered that there were gunboats in both the East River and
the North River, and that their shallow trenches were subject
to a crossfire between them, they did not even wait for the
British flatboats to land before they turned tail and ran.

This might as easily have happened a few weeks before,
when the entire colonial army was concentrated at New
York.   Now, however, all but five thousand men had been
removed.   Congress had tardily agreed to a modified evacuation of the city, and General Putnam was left with what was
supposed to be a skeleton defense that could be quickly withdrawn in case the British should attack in force.

The Americans had been pretty well scattered over the
lower end of the island when the pandemonium broke loose.
But they did not long remain scattered.   Those on the east
side of the island ran west.   Those on the west side ran east.
As soon as they were well back from the waterfront all of
them turned north and started in a wild stampede for Washington Heights where fortifications had been constructed to
which they might "retire" in case of a retreat.

The main landing of the British had been at Kip's Bay,
a little indenture in the coast of Manhattan where the East
Thirty-fourth Street ferry house now stands.   Here the New
Englanders had been posted to prevent a landing on the
East River side, but if the men from New England fired a
single shot it was not heard in all that thundering of guns
from the warships.   The militia from New Jersey and Pennsylvania assigned to protect the shores of North River from
any landing parties on that side did not tarry after the first

broadside. They climbed hastily out of their trenches and ran.

Washington, who was in Harlem when the firing had begun, rode to the scene of action with all speed. He met his stampeding troops opposite the farm of Robert Murray which lay about where the Grand Central Terminal now stands, and tried to rally them, but they had long since passed the rallying-point. There was no fight left in them; nothing but fear. And when he drew his sword and rode among them striking at officers as well as at men with the broad of his blade in an attempt to bring them to their senses — they simply took to the fields and kept on running.

A little alertness on the part of the British might have bagged Putnam's entire army, for an advance guard of the Hessians rounded up some three hundred of the frightened Continental sheep and made them prisoner without the loss of a man. Not a battalion of the Americans would have escaped if Sir William had shown any industry about pushing his lines across the island. His troops were landed before noon, but it was not until mid-afternoon that the British column really began to move. By this time all the Americans on the island were either safe within the fortifications at Harlem or on their way there panting and winded with running. Indeed, the last belated stragglers were scurrying along the west side of what is now Central Park as the British column was pushing along the east side in quest of them. Only the thick woods prevented the two armies from seeing each other.

Blame for the delay has quite naturally been placed upon Sir William. Stedman, who was present, says in his *History of the American War:* *

As soon as the English had taken possession of New York, General Howe and some other general officers, repaired to the house of a Mrs. Murray, with whom they remained in conversa-

* Vol. I, p. 207.

tion so long, that General Putnam, with three thousand five hundred men, was enabled to make good his retreat to the main body
of the American army.

Trevelyan in his *American Revolution* * treats this visit
to the Murray farm as a legend, one of many to arise out of
this eventful day.   He says:

According to a very popular American anecdote, the British
Commander-in-Chief never got further westward than the
country-seat of a New York merchant, which stood on a pleasant
eminence halfway across the peninsula.† The owner of the
house happened to be a Quaker; and, as such, he was almost as a
matter of 'course rich, and a Tory. His lady, however, — the
mother of Lindley Murray the grammarian, — held Revolutionary principles, and was so handsome and attractive that she
might air them with impunity in any company whatsoever.
She enjoys the credit of 'having kept Howe and his generals
drinking her husband's Madeira, and listening to a merry argument on politics between Governor Tryon and herself, until the
day was so far advanced that no time remained for arranging to
intercept Putnam.

The anecdote, as Trevelyan tells it, was undoubtedly bor-
rowed from the Rev. William Gordon's *History of the Rise,
Progress and Establishment of the Independence* which was
published at New York in three volumes in 1794.   Gordon
saw much of the Revolution himself, fairly persecuting Washington with his letters asking for confirmation of this or information as to that.   In spite of his voluminous notes and
his untiring efforts to verify them much of his work is un-
reliable.   His version of this anecdote, however, bears such
obvious evidences of truth that it may be well to examine it:

When the Americans were withdrawn, and no prospect of action remained, the British generals repaired to the house of Mr.
Robert Murray, a gentleman of the quaker persuasion. The
lady of the house being at home, entertained them most civilly,
with what served for, or was,‡ cakes and wine. They were well

* Vol. II, p. 299.
† Now known as Murray Hill.
‡ A most circumspect statement, to be sure !

pleased with the entertainment and tarried there near two hours or more; gov. Tryon seasoning the repast, at times, by joking Mrs. Murray about her American friends, for she was known to be a steady advocate for the liberties of the country. Meanwhile, the Hessians and the British, except a strong corps which marched down the road to take possession of the city, remained upon their arms inactive.

Parson Gordon is also authority for the statement that Colonel Grayson repeatedly said, "speaking humorously," that by her dispensation of all this hospitality "Mrs. Murray saved the American Army." Thus we have the double authority of the parson and the colonel. But regardless of any authority whatever the story is so true to the Howe tradition that it is hard not to believe it. It is so exactly what he would have done.

Howe must have been aware long before he reached the Murray farm that he was facing more of a Marathon than a battle, and since the enemy were running, why not let them run until they got where they were going, or until they fell winded by the wayside? It was, as all commentators agree, a very hot day, and the cooling shade of the wide verandas at Murray farm must have looked very tempting, especially when Governor Tryon remarked that the people who lived there were friends of his and served unusually good Madeira to their callers. Then, too, Howe was moving into New York for a long stay, and it might be just as well to get acquainted with some of the best families. Sir William himself never in any of his official or unofficial correspondence undertook to explain where or how he spent the two hours that elapsed between the time that he rode his horse off the boat at East Thirty-fourth Street and the moment of his arrival at the present resting-place, let us say, of the lions guarding the entrance to the New York Public Library. Perhaps this is a case where "political reasons" would not have been far from the truth.

Casualties were few, not over two dozen in both armies.

And though the British had taken some prisoners they would, with a little more energy have captured thousands where they succeeded in taking only hundreds. It is not at all unlikely that Sir William's men were completely disorganized by the ease of their victory, which must have assumed a comical aspect with the British soldiers taking an occasional pot-shot at a flying militiaman just to see him go faster. Sir William must have known that he could easily have captured Putnam's men if he had tried. If this is true it follows that if he did not try, it was because he did not want to capture them at this particular time and place. Otherwise we must accept the alternative that he would rather have a glass of wine than take an army.

Historians have quite outdone themselves in their descriptions of the rout of Washington's army from New York. It is indeed a test of the adjectives in a writer's vocabulary. Nothing that he can say in the way of cowardice and confusion are too exaggerated or too grotesque. An adequate description seems to be quite beyond the power of words — and for that reason every writer likes to try his hand at it. As an example of literary restraint, however, nothing can equal the entry made by David How, a New England soldier on the American side, in his diary. It reads:

Our people thought best to leave the lower part of the Town so that the shipping might not play on us. Our army all marched to the upper part of the Town this after Noon.

Whether "our people" marched or went in some other way they were as David How says all in the upper part of the Town by after Noon. Information passed freely back and forth between the two armies, perhaps too freely for convenience at times. Sir William knew all about the entrenchments in the upper part of the town, and when his army had been collected, and lined up and counted off, it started up that way to see what could be done in the way of staging a battle. Not that same day, of course. Tomorrow would do just as well. His troops had been through quite a little excitement, enough for one day in any event. So Sir William went into camp about a mile and a half to the south of Harlem Heights.

Washington had selected a strong position for his army. He had taken the high ground that lies along the Hudson River north of the Hollow Way through which 125th Street now runs. The British camp was at about 100th Street, and though their picket line reached as far north as 105th Street they did not push any farther that day. They were no doubt tired in very much the way that a crowd is tired after attending the circus, with its thrills and its laughter.

At daybreak the next morning Washington sent out patrols to locate the British and see what they were up to. The patrols collided with the British outposts and retired after a sharp exchange of musketry, whereupon the British launched a very considerable attack with the buglers blowing a hunting call, the "View halloo!" which, as Washington very well knew, means that the fox is in sight and is on the run. But the buglers were a little premature in their bantering, for the patrol withdrew just fast enough to draw the British into a spirited engagement to which Washington kept adding reinforcements until he had some eighteen hundred men under fire — and to his utter amazement they were standing up to the British in the open.

For two hours of very hot firing the armies faced each other in a buckwheat field that must have been about where the grounds of Columbia University now lie. Then Washington tried a little outflanking movement that came so near succeeding that the British were forced to withdraw into an orchard, and from the orchard back to their original lines.

The engagement came to an end at about three in the afternoon some two miles to the south of Harlem Heights. Howe thought that things had gone far enough and began to throw in his reinforcements in such numbers that the Americans ceased firing and withdrew to their position on the heights.   The British let them go without any further argument.   Captain Harris of the Fifth British Fusiliers in a letter written at the time says of the engagement:

We were trotted about three miles (without a halt to draw breath) to support a battalion of light infantry which had imprudently advanced so far as to be in great danger of being cut off.   This must have happened but for our haste.   The instant the front of our columns appeared, the enemy began to retire to their works, and our light infantry to camp.

Howe reported the engagement as a success, but some of his officers took quite a different view, and Colonel von Donop did not hesitate to say that but for the timely arrival of reinforcements the Light Infantry would have been captured; but of course the reinforcements he had in mind were his own Jaegers.

If Washington was amazed at the way his men, after the rout and stampede of the day before, had stood up and faced the British troops, he must have been even more amazed as one day succeeded another and General Howe made no further move to attack him.   Indeed more than a month of the best campaigning weather of the year was to pass before Sir William was able to tear himself away from the delights of the city he had been so long in reaching.   In his defense before the House of Commons he argued that the loss of a thousand or fifteen hundred troops would have been an excessive price to pay for Harlem Heights, and there was none to deny. It was the truth.   It was sound reasoning so far as it went, but it did not account for the weeks that his army was encamped there facing the Americans.   He could so easily have worked around them and cut them off from the north; and had he done so, with Lord Howe controlling the river, Harlem Heights would have become *ipso facto* untenable.

Sir William also has an excuse for not doing this: he was

ignorant of the mainland that lay off to the east, and the country was "ill-adapted for reconnoitering parties." He was also short of horses both for cavalry and transport, and little or nothing, he said, could be learned from the inhabitants who were unable to give him "a military description" of the neighborhood in which they lived. On this point Sir William has the corroboration of Lord Cornwallis who testified that a knowledge of America, for military purposes, was extremely difficult to obtain from the inhabitants. Little or no information, he said, could be got by reconnoitering, as the country was everywhere hilly and covered with woods; intersected by ravines, creeks, and marshes; and presenting "at every quarter of a mile a post fitted for ambuscades."

But four weeks to find a short-cut across from the Sound to the Hudson River! A matter of from five to eight miles! Washington would have run a survey across there in two days; and in two weeks he could have made a topographical map of the district, with altitudes and the depth of all watercourses plainly indicated, in addition to the roads and clearings and favorable locations for combat.

Though Sir William's excuse might have explained things to a House of Commons on the other side of the Atlantic a century and a half ago, it looks pretty flimsy to us today, and as far back as 1794 when Stedman was writing his *History of the American War,* he remarked:

It has been mentioned that the American army was posted at Haerlem and King's Bridge: Its position at this little place was for the purpose of securing a retreat to the continent, should the pressure of affairs render such a measure necessary. Instead, therefore, of directing his attention to New York, Sir William Howe ought to have thrown his army round King's Bridge, by which means he would have hemmed in the whole American army; and such a step was not at all impracticable, when we consider the extent of the military and naval resources subservient to his will.

In other words, Sir William should not have bothered with New York at all. His army had no business to be on Riverside Heights. It should have circled New York to begin with and thus have bottled Washington and his army on the island without any lines of communication with the outside world. This no doubt would have been good war, but perhaps it would also have been from Sir William's point of view, poor politics.

CHAPTER VII

THE BURNING OF NEW YORK

WITH GENERAL HOWE'S occupation of New York the Loyalists had come flocking in from all sides. Since the arrival of Washington's army their existence had been somewhat precarious. If they spoke their minds freely they were likely to be treated to a coat of tar and feathers and ridden on a rail. If they refrained from speaking their minds they were put on the suspected list, which meant that they were almost certain to be insulted if they appeared in public, that in any event their property would suffer from mysterious depredations usually committed under cover of darkness, and that their barns and even their houses were fair game for any rebel incendiary who happened to be in a mischievous frame of mind. There was no neutral ground in America during the Revolution. One was by profession a noble patriot, or he was regarded as a cowardly Loyalist and treated accordingly.

New York had been a hotbed of Loyalists when Washington's army had arrived there from Boston, and the rebel population had enjoyed a glorious time evening off the old scores with the aid of the rebel soldiers. Street-fighting, horse-whipping, and riding on a rail became so common as to excite very little comment among any except the Loyalists who were invariably the victims. Washington has been severely criticized for permitting this reign of unbridled ruffianism

in a city that was occupied by his army, but is said to have
taken the position that any leniency would have tended to
weaken the rebel cause.   And the persecution of the Loyalists had gone on so long as there were any within reach to
furnish entertainment for the mob.

As soon as the Loyalists realized that because of their
loyalty to their monarch they were losing all their personal
and property rights they began to be more cautious about expressing their views.   All who were able to leave the city
left without delay, and those who were unable to leave kept
themselves out of sight as much as possible.   But in spite of
all they could do they were insulted and imposed upon as if
they had been felons instead of political opponents.

Alas, it has been ever thus.   The freedom of man has never
been won without the use of oppression as one of its most
powerful weapons.

With the coming of Washington, the apostle of freedom,
the Loyalists had fled.   On his being driven out by the instrument of monarchy, however, they came back — and they
came in droves.   Many of them had taken refuge on Long
Island which had been as strongly Tory as it dared to be
even before the British armies had landed in the vicinity of
New York Bay.   Now by ferry and sloop and even by rowboat they were flocking into New York.   Once again the shoe
was on the other foot, and it was the rebel population who
would have to lie low.

In removing his military stores and supplies from the city
in preparation for the British attack, General Washington
had evacuated many of the civil population.   It would not
have been a superhuman task to transfer all the inhabitants
to the Bronx or to Westchester in the two weeks that elapsed
between the Battle of Brooklyn and the attack on New York,
but this was not attempted, and a goodly number of the
women and children as well as the old men were still in the
city at the time of the bombardment.   Their fright while

the city was under fire has been commented on by contemporary writers, but none of them seems to have been hurt, and doubtless after the city had been invested they returned to their homes and went on with the preparation of the evening meal as if nothing of great importance had happened — and perhaps they were right.

They must have slept in the midst of alarums that night, with red-coated sentries passing and repassing their doors where before the sentries had been buff-coated, or homespun-coated, or perhaps not coated at all. But when on the morrow they had heard the firing far off on the heights of Harlem, it is very probable that they regarded the war as something that had come their way and passed, and was now rumbling in the distance like a thunderstorm that had blown over. It is easy to imagine them as gathered in little knots talking over the late excitement, and telling of narrow escapes. There was plenty to talk about, and more coming, for the great fire known as the "burning of New York" was just ahead.

The fire started at about midnight on the 20th of September and blazed well into the fore-noon of the following day. It was thought to be of incendiary origin although the name of the miscreant who applied the match is not definitely known. If so, an ideal night had been selected. The weather was dry. The wind was from the south, and the fire broke out at White Hall near the southerly tip of the island, and made its way rapidly northward. There were no bells in the city with which to give the alarm. Washington had carried them away for the ostensible purpose of having them recast into cannon. Perhaps he did; though the British and the Loyalists never would believe it.

As if the initial blaze in White Hall had been the signal to a band of incendiaries, fires almost immediately afterwards broke out in a dozen other places at once. Sentries spread the alarm, and the troops were impressed into service as firemen. Even the reserve forces who were encamped outside the town were brought in to join the bucket brigade, and Admiral Howe landed men from the fleet on both sides of the city to help in fighting the flames.

New York, it must be remembered, did not at this time extend above the present location of the City Hall, and was built almost entirely of wood. And although the fire was out within ten hours of the time when it started it had swept away every building lying between Broad Street and the Hudson River from St. Paul's Church to the Battery. Somehow St. Paul's was saved, though Trinity Church was burned to the ground, its wooden steeple 140 feet in height making a torch that could be seen for many miles around before it finally crashed to the ground, a glowing mass of embers.

Hugh Gaine, in the *Mercury* published on September 30th, claimed that 1000 houses had been burned, and one-quarter of the city. These figures have been quoted and re-quoted until they have acquired a sort of prescriptive authenticity in spite of which they are undoubtedly wrong. In the excitement of the moment Gaine's estimate overran itself.* A careful compilation from official figures has since shown that the number of buildings destroyed could not possibly have exceeded 500.

A number of lives were lost in the fire, and at least one or two persons supposed to be incendiaries were shot down by the soldiers. Others were said to have been pitched into the flames or strung up by the heels while their throats were cut, though letters written at the time make no mention of these barbarities. The usually imperturbable Sir William, in his letter to Germain written the second day after the fire, still displays some uneasiness at the thought of having his

---

* That the reputation of Hugh Gaine was not noted for accuracy may be gathered from a questionnaire published in *Brasher's Journal* at about this time:
Q. Who is the soggiest man in the world? A. Lord Howe.
Q. Who is the weakest? A. General Howe.
Q. Who is the greatest liar on earth? A. Hugh Gaine of New York, Printer.

winter quarters burned out from under him, and makes it
plain that there is no doubt in his mind about the incendiary
origin of the blaze.

Headquarters, New York, Sept. 23, 1776

MY LORD:
  Between the 20th and 21st instant, at midnight, a most horrid
attempt was made by a number of wretches to burn the town of
New York, in which they succeeded too well, having set it on
fire in several places, with matches and combustibles that had been
prepared with great ingenuity. Many were detected in the fact
and some killed upon the spot by the enraged troops in garrison;
and had it not been for the exertions of Major General Robertson, the officers under his command in the town, and the brigade
of guards detached from the camp, the whole must infallibly
been consumed, as the night was extremely windy.
  The destruction is computed to be about one quarter of the
town; and we have reason to suspect there are villains lurking
there, ready to finish the work they have begun; one person escaping the pursuit of a centinel the following night having declared, that he would again set fire to the town the first opportunity. The strictest search is being made after these
incendiaries, and the most effective measures taken to guard
against the perpetration of their villainous and wicked designs.
  I have the honor to be, &c.

W. HOWE

Governor Tryon, writing to Germain on the following
day, is a little more outspoken. He does not hesitate to name
names. His letter in part follows:

  . . . It grieves me to inform you that on the 21st about two in
the morning, the western part of the town was set on fire by a
number of incendiaries, and which raged with such violence as
destroyed, it is thought, one-fourth part of the city, before the
flames could be extinguished. Many of the incendiaries are now
in confinement, and two of three were killed as they were detected in their hellish design. Many circumstances lead to the
conjecture that Mr. Washington was privy to this villainous act,
as he sent all the bells of the churches out of town, under pre-
tense of casting them into cannon; whereas it is much more
probable to prevent the alarm being given by ringing of the
bells before the fire should get ahead beyond the reach of en-

gines and buckets; besides, some officers of his army were found concealed in the city, supposed for this devilish purpose.

Hugh Gaine mentions no names in the newspaper account of the fire to which we have previously referred, though he does add some details from which an identification may be guessed. His long account of the conflagration ends with the following rhetorical outburst:

During this complicated scene of Devastation and Distress, at which the most savage Heart might relent, several persons were discovered with large Bundles of Matches dipped in melted Rosin and Brimstone and attempting to set Fire to the Houses. A New England Man, who had a Captain's Commission under the Continental Congress and in their Service, was seized with these dreadful instruments of Ruin — on being searched the Sum of 500 pounds was found on him. . .* Surely there must be some Curse — some secret Thunder in the Stores of Heaven; red with uncommon Wrath to blast the Miscreants who thus wantonly sport with the Lives, Property and Happiness of their Fellow Creatures, and unfeelingly doom them to inevitable Ruin.

This reference to the New England Man is taken by many to mean Nathan Hale. And, indeed, it might easily be true. Nathan Hale was a New England man, and he held a captain's commission in the Continental Army. He was also known to have been in New York at the time the fire broke out — but we shall hear more of this later on.

It is a curious fact that in an exchange of letters between General Howe and Washington the day after the fire no mention of the disaster is made. Howe wrote:

My Aide-de Camp charged with the delivery of this letter will present to you a ball cut and fixed to the end of a nail, taken from a number of the same kind found in the encampments quitted by your troops on the 15th instant. I do not make any comment upon such unwarrantable practices, being well assured the contrivance has not come to your knowledge.

* Then as now a sure evidence of guilt as well as the root of all evil.

To this Washington replied:

Your Aide-de-Camp delivered me the ball you mention, which was the first of the kind I ever saw or heard of. You may depend the contrivance is highly abhorred by me, and every measure shall be taken to prevent so wicked and infamous a practise being adopted in this army.

Not a word about the fire that even then must have been smouldering in its ashes. Washington had in the first place been averse to the destruction of New York, but this was when he still had some hopes of being able to hold the city. When finally convinced that he must evacuate he had brought up the question of burning the city to prevent the British using it for winter quarters, and Congress had put a firm foot down. They said the city must not be burned. So Washington had evacuated without putting the match to it. Five days later the city is in flames, its firing the work of incendiaries, and still Washington can write to Howe without making any mention of the holocaust. He needs must speak of it, however, in a letter written on the following day to Governor Trumbull:

On Friday night about eleven or twelve o'clock, a fire broke out in the city of New York, which, burning rapidly till after sunrise next morning, destroyed a great number of houses. By what means it happened we do not know; but the gentleman who brought the letter from General Howe last night, and who was one of his Aides-de-Camp, informed Colonel Reed that some of our countrymen had been punished with various deaths on account of it, some by hanging, others by burning, &c. alleging they were apprehended when committing the fact.

Signs of neither approval nor disapproval are here, but one wonders whether he would have allowed the subject to pass without further comment if he had believed that his countrymen were guiltless of the charge of incendiarism that had been lodged against them. Would not a word of outraged protest have escaped in spite of his reserve ? Soon after the fire Tench Tilghman wrote to his father from the camp on Harlem Heights that some of the rebels were executed the next day "upon good grounds." In a letter to his wife Colonel Silliman wrote that he believed it was not the regulars, "but some of our own people in the city that set it on fire, for they executed several of our friends there for it the next day."

Curious reasoning, it strikes one, to believe people guilty of a crime simply because they were executed for it.

Washington was openly accused at the time of having sent Nathan Hale into the town as a spy to make the arrangements for its destruction. W. H Shelton, curator of the Jumel Mansion, who has made a careful study of all available documents bearing on the case * is convinced that these accusations are well-founded, though one, upon examining his authorities, finds it not too easy to agree with him. There is no doubt that Washington did send Nathan Hale into the city as a spy, and that Hale was still there when the fire broke out. He was captured at East River near 111th Street while trying to make his way back to Washington's army. There was nothing remarkable about his case at the time. Just another spy. He was caught, admitted his guilt when the evidence was found on him, was condemned to death without so much as a court-martial. Here the matter rested for nearly a quarter of a century when the Nathan Hale tradition sprang suddenly into life.

Nathan Hale was born in Connecticut June 6, 1755 and went to Yale when the now famous institution was a little rustic college with some sixty students. He entered at the age of sixteen and was graduated with the class of 1773. He was of sturdy build, six feet tall, a manly fellow, we are assured, with keen blue eyes and soft brown hair. Large as he was, Hale was no mean gymnast, for we are assured that he would spring with apparent ease out of one hogshead and

* *The Jumel Mansion*, Boston, 1916.

into another, through a whole series of hogsheads, though we are not told just what his purpose was in leaping into and out of such things.

After college he taught school at East Haddam for two years, and then joined the Continental Army at the siege of Boston. When the army moved on to New York after the siege was lifted he was not left behind, though he did not engage in the Battle of Long Island. He seems to have been in the detachment that was left to protect New York in case the British should launch an attack there simultaneously with their attack on Brooklyn. Just what part he took in the retreat from New York is not clear, though we find him on the heights of Harlem after the retreat is over. He is now a captain of the famous Knowlton Rangers. Indeed, it was Knowlton who induced Hale to offer his services as a spy when Washington was asking for a volunteer who was not afraid to make the attempt to slip into the city for some secret business that he had in hand.

He was next heard of at Norwalk where he induced the skipper of a small boat to take him across to Huntington, Long Island, under cover of the night. From Huntington he made his way to Oyster Bay where he went about asking for work as a schoolmaster, and not finding any. He was told, however, that workmen were needed on the boats that were carrying farm produce into New York for the use of the British army. So he went to the docks and was taken on as a deckhand, and thus he made his way into New York, jotting down in Latin as he went along notes concerning the British troops and fortifications on Long Island and other strategic approaches to New York. These notes, we are informed, were concealed beneath the removable inner-soles in his shoes.

Hale spent the night of the fire in New York. He could probably have slipped out under cover of darkness and made his way to Harlem without molestation had he tried that

night. But he apparently did not try. He seems to have
made no attempt to leave the city until the afternoon of the
next day. Then he went up the east side, intending obviously to make a wide circle around the British army which
was still encamped on the high ground lying to the south of
the Hollow Way, in the neighborhood of the spot where
Grant's Tomb now stands. He had apparently encountered
little difficulty in getting out of town, for he had gone as far
as what is now East 111th Street when he was seen by Captain
Quarme, a British naval officer, who was being rowed ashore
from a gunboat anchored behind Randall's Island. Quarme
drew a gun on him and placed him under arrest.

He was passed along from one hand to another and did not
reach headquarters until after night had fallen. Then he
was taken to the old Beekman mansion, a fine old colonial
house facing the East River at East 51st Street, and brought
up before Sir William Howe himself. There was no trial.
Howe looked at the evidence, which by this time had been removed from the prisoner's shoes, and asked him who he was.
Hale readily admitted his identity and his rank, and Howe
ordered him to be hanged.

A British officer who was present at the interview wrote
that Hale's "manly bearing and the evident disinterested
patriotism of the handsome young prisoner, sensibly touched
a chord of General Howe's nature; but the stern rules of
war concerning such offenses would not allow him to exercise
even pity." Howe may have been touched, for he was a
kindly, amiable man, but in a letter written the next day to
Germain he did not even mention the incident.

In the *Orderly Book* under date of September 21, 1776,
written in a bold hand with many flourishes is the following
entry: *

A Spy from the Enemy (by his own confession) happrened last
Night was this day Executed at Eleven oclock in front of the
artillery park.

* MS. *Orderly Book,* W. L. Clements Library.

Nathan Hale beyond a doubt, but of so little moment was the execution of a spy that the clerk who made the entry did not even take the trouble to put down the name. Nor is any mention made of the victim's alleged complicity in the plot to burn the town.

The prisoner was thrown into an outbuilding said to have been used for a green-house, and given until morning to make his peace with his God. In this he was evidently successful, for he was the calmest man in the execution party the next morning. From all accounts he was rather brutally handled by the provost-marshal, a burly Irishman who was to find out for himself, some years later, how it felt to dangle from the end of a rope. The name of William Cunningham, as this provost-marshal was called, was long a symbol of brutality among the patriots. There was doubtless good reason for it, but one can hardly expect sympathy and understanding from a hangman.

The complaints against Cunningham at the time of the Hale execution were that he refused the condemned man a clergyman, and denied him even the use of a Bible for which he had asked. The hangman was also accused of tearing up letters of farewell that had been written by the prisoner to his mother (who is known to have been deceased at that time), and to his sweetheart. As the story goes Hale was led up on a ladder while the rope was tied to the limb of an apple tree in Colonel Rutger's orchard. Then the ladder was wrenched from under him.

It is still something of a mystery just where Colonel Rutger's orchard was, though the spot of Hale's execution is now marked as being near the corner of First Avenue and 55th Street. Here, we may believe, the young patriot turned as he stood on the ladder and left as his legacy to posterity the noble sentence, "I only regret that I have but one life to lose for my country." In quite another vein were the last words of a young British spy condemned to death at the instance of

Washington a few months later. The execution of Major
André was not so summary. He had been given an almost
elaborate trial, and though Washington found it the most
difficult task of his entire life, he sent him to the gallows.
André was executed with a little more style. In the first
place he was hanged to a scaffold. And he was permitted to
stand on his coffin which was mounted on the tail of a cart to
give him height while the rope was adjusted. When the cart
was driven out from under the task was regarded as complete.
Asked if he had anything to say Major André replied, "I request you, gentlemen, that you will bear me witness to the
world that I die like a brave man."

The sweetheart, to whom Cunningham refused to send the
letter from Nathan Hale, must have been quite youthful at
the time, for we are told by Benson J. Lossing * that when
she had recovered from her grief she married another man
and was left at eighteen a widow with one child. After a
little she remarried, and was again widowed. She did not
try the venture a third time, but lived to the ripe old age of
88, and died with the words on her lips, "Write to Nathan!"

Probably no figure in American history has so fired the
imagination of the American youth as did young Nathan
Hale by his life and his death. Though perhaps it was the
famous poem by Francis M. Finch first read to the Linonian
Society of Yale College at its centennial anniversary in 1853
that brought him to the attention of the rising generation.
For seventy-five years this poem has stood the test of time, and
it seems today as popular as ever.†

* In his little book, *Two Spies*, published in 1886.

> † To drum-beat and heart-beat,
> A soldier marches by;
> There is a color on his cheek,
> There is courage in his eye;
> Yet to drum-beat and heart-beat
> In a moment he must die.

And so on, for many stanzas that would make any youth yearn to die a
noble death.

CHAPTER VIII

THE WAR MOVES TO WESTCHESTER

FOR A MONTH the two armies faced each other on the highlands of what is now Riverside Drive. Howe kept his troops from becoming bored by furnishing them with picks and shovels and laying out a very elegant set of entrenchments. The American shovelmen could probably have duplicated these in three or four days had there been any occasion, but there was none, and the work served to keep the British soldiers occupied.

Meanwhile Sir William was busying himself over the exchange of prisoners. With the two generals he had captured at Long Island he thought himself in a position to do some shrewd bartering; but the Americans were not overanxious and he finally consented to exchange Lord Stirling for a Royal Governor who had unfortunately fallen into the hands of the Americans; and General Sullivan after the failure of his mission to negotiate a peace brought no more than a brigadier who had been captured by Montgomery at Montreal.

From his position on the heights Washington viewed all this shoveling with a suspicious eye. He was sure that the British were preparing for a trick manœuvre that would take him unawares so he tried to watch in all directions at once. The fortifications on the heights were heavily manned, and his line reaching back to Kingsbridge was on the alert for any attempt to cut his communications with the mainland. But Howe was planning no swift coup at this time as his letter to the Ministry plainly shows:

New York-Island, September 25, 1776

MY LORD:

Upon the present appearance of things, I look upon further progress of this army for this campaign, to be rather precarious, an attack upon *Rhode Island* excepted, which I would willingly defer for a short time in case it should be thought advisable to employ our whole force together. The duration of the campaign must be short, and the second division of *Hessians* not arrived; nor have I any dependence upon General *Carleton's* approach, to act with influence this year, upon the main Rebel army, opposed to us, though it is reported today by the deserters, that General *Burgoyne,* with a large corps of troops and *Indians,* is advancing fast to *Albany,* by way of the Mohawk River. If he gets possession of *Albany,* it will no doubt, facilitate General *Carleton's* movement to that place, and will be attended with favorable consequences. But in my situation, I presume, I must not risk, as a check at this time would be of infinite detriment to us.

The enemy is too strongly posted to be attacked in front, and innumerable difficulties are in my way of turning him on either side, though his army is much dispirited, from the late success of his Majesty's arms; yet I have not the smallest prospect of finishing the contest this campaign, not until the Rebels see preparations in the Spring, that may preclude all thoughts of further resistance. To this end, I would propose eight or ten line-of-battle ships, to be with us in *February,* with a number of supernumerary seamen for manning boats, having fully experienced the want of them in every movement we have made. We must also have recruits from *Europe,* not finding the Americans disposed to serve with arms, notwithstanding the hopes held out to me on my arrival at this port.

Finding the Hessians averse to having their accounts methodized, in the manner observed by the British regiments, I have given them money on account, taking care, that the sums advanced are sufficiently within the whole pay due to them by treaty, to answer for their stoppages of provisions. . .

I have the honor to be, etc., etc.,

W. HOWE

If Howe had really wanted to bag Washington's army the trick was absurdly simple. A quick movement of troops across the narrow neck of land lying to the north in co-operation with a few gunboats of the fleet along the Hudson and in East River, and the army of Washington would have been in the sack. Howe must have known this. It was the current talk of the day, the obvious, the almost inevitable move. And as Washington lingered on the heights that bear his name a number of the patriot leaders of New York went so far as to write to Colonel Tilghman of Washington's staff suggesting that General Mifflin or General Lee might point out to the Commander-in-Chief the precariousness of his situation.

Tilghman loyally replied that Washington would be ready for any move the British might make. But General Lee, when he arrived in the North after his repulse of the British at Charleston was not so considerate of the feelings of the Commander-in-Chief. For he advised Washington to withdraw at once to White Plains where he would be out of reach of the guns of the fleet, and from which place he could easily retreat if Howe should launch an overwhelming attack against him. Although Washington did not follow this advice in its entirety he did hold his troops in readiness for a quick withdrawal. It is well that he did; for when Howe was ready to go he moved quickly and with the touch of a real soldier. He sent Lord Percy up from the city to make a feint against Fort Washington while the main body of British troops was hurried aboard the ships and carried quickly up East River through a fog so dense that the patriot army did not know the enemy was on the move until he had already landed at Throg's Neck.

Curiously enough this fog has never been set down by historians as in any way providential. It is admitted that the fog arrived at the very moment when Howe desired to move his army, and that it completely shrouded his movements from the prying eyes of the patriots until the last man and the last gun had been set down on the Westchester shore. But for some reason not now available it was regarded as having none of the earmarks of the more or less miraculous manifestations of the weather that was accustomed to come to the rescue of Washington when he was hard pressed.

Wrapped in their mantle of fog the British seamen succeeded in making their way through the tortuous passages of the East River; they slipped unobserved past Blackwell's Island, Ward's Island, Randall's Island, and Riker's Island; they found Hell Gate and passed out into the Sound. Up to this point their movements have every indication of being of a providential origin. On reaching the Sound, however, they seem to have been deserted by Providence; for instead of disembarking on the mainland, they were landed on Throg's Neck, a marshy point of land jutting out into the Sound that was virtually an island at high water.

For six days Howe lingered here landing his ordnance and equipment and organizing his units. Then on the night of October 18th he swiftly transferred his army to Pell's Point, a portion of the mainland lying to the east, and began his march towards White Plains.

Historians have long persisted in regarding this landing at Throg's Neck as a blunder on the part of Howe that cost him a long delay and permitted Washington to escape from the trap. It has been ascribed to ignorance of the shoreline, lack of accurate information, bad maps, over-cautiousness, poor management, and one thing or another. The skill with which his seamen brought their magnificent flotilla of more than 140 sail through the treacherous windings of the East River channel in a dense fog without a grounding should be a sufficient answer to the charge of lack of information and bad maps. And the swift efficiency with which Sir William lifted his army from Throg's Neck and set it down on Pell's Point in a single night should be a conclusive answer to the charge of poor management. Howe could move

with catlike precision when he wished.   So there must have
been some other reason.

Looking back the Tories saw a mysterious halt before the
entrenchments on Brooklyn Heights which made possible
the "masterly withdrawal."   They saw another mysterious
delay at the Murray Mansion while the bewildered rebel
army was making good its escape from the town of New York.
And now this unaccountable wait at Throg's Neck while
Washington was withdrawing his slow-moving army from
Harlem to White Plains.   Were these delays accidental?
Were they merely characteristic of a dilatory temperament on
the part of Sir William?   Or were they, just possibly, part
of a definite plan?   Was the General bungling, or was he
playing an adroit political game?   He was, they remembered, still a Whig Member of Parliament as well as
Commander-in-Chief of his Majesty's forces in America.

The landing at Pell's Point, though executed with precision and dispatch, and under cover of darkness, was not entirely unexpected.   Colonel Glover of Marblehead, with a
force of 750 men and three field pieces, was on hand to greet
the British.   He was so well posted and gave them so warm
a reception that he kept them pinned to the shore for an entire day, during which Washington managed to drag the last
of his army out of danger.

The two armies now moved slowly along the opposite
banks of the Bronx River, which from the effectiveness with
which it kept them apart might have been a river the size of
the Hudson (as it was thought in England to be, the War
Office having ordered the navy to sail up the Bronx and clear
it of any American shipping found there) instead of a creek
that was fordable at any point without danger of wetting the
knees, and could be crossed in places with dry feet by hop-
ping from stone to stone.   At White Plains, however, they
could no longer keep apart; for when the head of Howe's

column reached the town he found Washington's army drawn up across his path. Even now the British general who had won renown by his wild and desperate charges dallied for three days before ordering his bugles to blow for a general engagement. This delay was what Washington most wanted and needed. He had not planted his army in front of the on-coming British because he was anxious for a battle, but simply to delay their advance until he could remove his accumulated stores into the Northcastle Hills.

The Battle of White Plains was at best a confused engagement. Washington, though he had the advantage of selecting the field, had not disposed his forces for an effective defense, and at the first charge of the British a large number of the Americans broke and ran. There was however a sharp engagement on Chatterton Hill which the British captured after a stubborn resistance by General McDougal. This was the most difficult part of the position. The rest would have been easy for Howe — if he had only pressed the attack. His reinforcements had arrived, his men were eager for battle, and the Americans were terrified by the cavalry which the British were now using for the first time in America. In addition to this the main body of Washington's troops had been severed from the detachment that was holding Fort Washington. All communications had been cut, and Howe's army was between the two pieces and in a very agreeable situation to deal with them one at a time.

Here was Sir William's chance. A brisk drive would have scattered the patriots into the hills. They might never have come together as an army again. The prestige of Washington as a general would probably have been lost by so crushing a defeat — even as the prestige of Gates was lost by his defeat in the South after all the acclaim he had received as the victor at Saratoga. Having dealt with the army in the field, Howe could, at his convenience, have turned his attention to Fort

Washington and afterward to Fort Lee, its feeble brother on the farther side of the river.

But Sir William did not follow up his chance. After the brilliant work of the British on Chatterton Hill he called a halt. For several days he dallied at White Plains while Washington threw up log fortifications and took all sorts of fantastic precautions to keep Howe from out-flanking and surrounding him. Then Sir William drew off and made his way back to Manhattan where at his convenience he took Fort Washington by storm, and narrowly missed capturing along with it the entire staff of the Continental Army including the tall Virginian in whose honor the stronghold had been named.

The ease with which he had taken Fort Washington was impressive but it did not satisfy the hue and cry raised by the Tories over his failure to thrust home a decisive victory at White Plains. The question came up again in 1779 when Sir William as a Member of Parliament was delivering before a committee of the House a narrative of his conduct of the American war. When asked why he had not pressed his attack on the precarious American position he said:

An assault upon the enemy's right which was opposed to the Hessian troops, was intended. The committee must give me credit when I assure them that I have political reasons, and no other for declining to explain why that assault was not made.

Cornwallis, present as a witness, testified to the same effect. When questioned on the subject, he said:

From political motives it is impossible for either the General or myself to explain these reasons.

Historians and commentators have for a century and a half been casting about for the reason for Howe's failure to drive his victories to the clinching-point. They have ascribed it to licentiousness, to cowardice, to indolence, to military incompetence, even to shell-shock received at Bunker Hill. It seems never to have occurred to them to take Howe's own word on the subject. That when he said it was because of political considerations that he refrained from striking the final blow at an all but defenseless opponent, he may possibly have been telling the truth.

This explanation fits in perfectly with what has gone before, and it fits perfectly with what is to follow after. The Whigs were bitterly opposed to the war. They regarded the trouble with America as a dispute in which the patriots as well as the Crown were entitled to certain inalienable rights. The Whigs had no desire to crush the patriots simply because they had the manhood to fight for these rights. And if by an overwhelming show of force Sir William could bring the Americans to their senses, if he could impress the country with the fact that a military victory for it was out of the question, he might bring about a conciliation and a voluntary submission. This would have been a tremendous victory for the Whig party that might easily have swept it into power and surely would have written the name of Howe in bold-faced letters on the pages of history.

It was a mighty conception and well worth striving for. There is only one difficulty with the acceptance of it: it removes most of the mystery from the strange conduct of the General and his brother the Admiral during their conduct of the American war.

If, with these considerations in mind, we look back at Sir William's letter of September 25th (supra) we find it taking on a new significance. He speaks of the *influence* of Carleton's approach on the main Rebel army, and the *favorable consequences,* not the military advantages, that would attend upon his possession of Albany. He has not the smallest prospect of finishing the *contest* (not the war!) this campaign, not indeed *until the Rebels see the preparations in the Spring, that may preclude all thoughts of further resistance.* And to the end that they may be properly overawed he proposes eight or ten line-of-battle ships with supernumerary seamen. All this is being planned, not for the purpose of killing the enemy, but with the idea of making an impression on their politicians.

Just what Sir William had in mind when he started this drive into Westchester is still somewhat shrouded in doubt. Some historians maintain that it was the initial step of a much larger campaign; that it was undertaken as the beginning of a thrust up the Hudson, long contemplated by the Ministry, for the purpose of bisecting the Revolution and isolating the trouble-making New England colonies from the rest.* It seems more probable that it was the belated attempt of an indolent commander to bottle up the Americans in a corner where he could deal with them at his leisure — and perhaps renew his proposals of peace; but that Howe did not see the importance of the bottling-up strategy until he was too late to make a success of it.

In either case he encountered difficulties that had not been foreseen. He found his equipment ill-suited to use in rough country, and after he had gone a few miles inland he was ready to admit that he was facing some of the roughest country he had ever seen. If it was the thrust up the river, Howe soon realized that he could not put it through with the equipment he then had. If it was the belated attempt at bottling-up, it could not succeed so long as Washington kept just ahead of him. It is barely possible that the sudden withdrawal from Westchester and the attack on Fort Washington may have been a ruse to lure the rebel army back into a position where the bottling-up tactics could be used. If so, the movement of Washington's army over into New Jersey must have been a disappointment to the British high command.

* The letter of September 25th seems to put at rest any possibility of regarding the Westchester campaign as part of an up-river thrust. In Howe's situation, he "must not risk" a check at this time.

The decision to pursue Washington's army into New Jersey is easier to trace. There is little room for doubt that this was the result of the earnest solicitation of Cornwallis, though, as we shall subsequently see, the pursuit was not always prosecuted as vigorously as Cornwallis would have liked.

Sir William's withdrawal from White Plains baffled Washington almost as much as it has been baffling the historians ever since. That the General had a reason, and a good one, he did not doubt; but he found it difficult to figure out just what it was. He finally concluded that Sir William was bent on one of two courses: the seizure of the Hudson valley and a conjunction with the British forces in the North, or a swift drive on Philadelphia. For a few days he watched his antagonist carefully, and was unable to tell which way he was going to jump. So Washington divided his army three ways.

He left General Lee at White Plains with seven thousand men to intercept the British if they should attempt to go up the river, while Washington himself with a force of about four thousand crossed over into New Jersey in the ambitious hope of stopping an army six times the size of his own in case the British should be intending to move on Philadelphia. The rest of the patriot force was given to Heath for strengthening the highlands of the river.

Meanwhile Howe was slowly closing in on the three thousand patriots cooped up in Fort Washington. The garrison could easily have been withdrawn, for the Admiral was paying little attention to the river. Washington and his staff passed freely back and forth between the fort and his camp in New Jersey. Indeed, only half an hour before the actual storming of the stronghold had begun, Generals Greene, Putnam, Mercer, and Washington had assembled for a conference there. Washington was inclined to abandon the fort, but Greene could not conceive it to be "in any great danger." This was probably the worst mistake Greene ever made.

The conference was still in session when the assault actually began. The generals managed to escape across the river, and Greene lived to write:

> There we all stood in a very awkward situation. As the disposition was made, and the enemy advancing, we durst not attempt to make any new disposition; indeed, we was nothing amiss. We all urged his Excellency to come off. I offered to stay. General Putnam did the same, and so did General Mercer; but his excellency thought it best for us all to come off together, which we did, about half an hour before the enemy surrounded the fort.*

Alexander Graydon, who was a member of the garrison, makes the escape of Washington even narrower. "It is a fact," he writes,† "not generally known that the British troops took possession of the very spot on which the commander-in-chief, and the general officers with him, had stood, in fifteen minutes after they had left it." And Joseph Cheesman of his Majesty's ship *Galatea* wrote a letter home in which he told how Washington had lost an arm in the battle.‡

The report spread among the British that Washington had been captured and when at length the surrendered garrison marched out they were beset by a parcel of soldiers' trulls and others who came out to meet them, as Graydon tells it, and kept asking, "Which is Washington? Which is Washington?"

Trevelyan writes of a colonel of the Guards who had been invalided home within a few days after White Plains, who told his friends in London that the country was so hilly, and the rebels such excellent marksmen that it was almost impossible to catch them. He also tells of an English officer who had made a special study of the marksmanship of the Americans in the war and claimed that in a good light with

* *The Campaign of 1776*, H. F. Johnston.
† *Memoirs of A Life*, Alexander Graydon.
‡ *Farley's Bristol Journal* for 1776.

their "cursed twisted guns" they could hit a man's head at two hundred yards, or his body at three hundred, with great certainty.*

The drive into Westchester was the first real taste that the British had experienced of campaigning in the wilds. And though their letters home were filled with thrilling accounts of their doings in the forest primeval a feeling of depression had come over their ranks. Moving their wagons and their heavy ordnance over the hills and through the swamps without the benefit of roads took the heart out of them, and they were doubtless glad to get back to Manhattan. But their general did not allow them to rest there for any length of time. Fort Lee was still in the hands of the patriots, and over beyond Fort Lee on the plains between the Hudson and the Hackensack rivers the patriot army led by General Washington was encamped. It was towards this army that Sir William now turned his eyes.

* *The American Revolution,* Vol. II, p. 321.

CHAPTER IX

HE CAPTURES ANOTHER GENERAL

MILITARY men have long persisted in treating the campaign in New Jersey as one of the mysteries of the age. This is no doubt because they look at it from a purely military standpoint. Viewed thus it quickly becomes almost as much of an absurdity as a mystery. If, however, we examine it as a bit of political strategy the mystery and the absurdity immediately vanish.

Since quitting Massachusetts (which he had found hopelessly rebel) Howe had been in the midst of Loyalist territory. His success at Long Island had given great aid and comfort to all the loyal subjects on the island, and by ridding Manhattan of rebels he had brought the most populous city in the colonies back into the fold. The hugely successful though scarcely decisive expedition into Westchester must have cheered the large Loyalist population, who were asking nothing from the Revolution except to be left alone. Howe would have been glad to call it a campaign and to go into winter quarters at New York after the capture of Fort Washington. He had more or less laid the foundation for this in his letter of September 25th, but, alas, the army of Washington was running loose in Loyalist New Jersey insulting and intimidating friendly subjects of the king, and perhaps attracting to the rebel cause people there who had not hitherto taken sides.

Something had to be done. The Loyalists must be protected, and those who were not out-and-out rebels must be approached with tact and friendliness. They must be reassured. They must be impressed or re-impressed with the might and puissance of his Majesty's arms. They must be given an opportunity to renew their pledge of allegiance. New Jersey must be patted and pacified; it must under no circumstances go over to the rebel cause. Fort Lee, across the river from Fort Washington, the only stronghold in New Jersey still in the hands of the rebels, was the first logical objective.

This the British captured without firing a shot. They simply scaled the Palisades, dragging a few heavy guns up behind them, and planted a battery on the high ground overlooking Fort Lee and the adjacent encampment. The appearance of the British in this position was a complete surprise, and General Greene who was in command of the fortification moved out with the utmost haste,* leaving behind him in addition to practically all the artillery and a thousand barrels of flour, the tents and personal baggage of the men who took with them nothing but their muskets. The sudden dash of Lord Cornwallis across the river with 4500 men would have caught a less wary general than Greene who was never so effective as when he was conducting a retreat.

Greene managed to join Washington at Hackensack, and though Cornwallis was doing his best to bottle them up between the Hudson and the Passaic rivers, they made their way across the Passaic and went into camp at Newark where they remained until word was brought that Howe was planning to land a detachment at Amboy to attack them in the

---

* Howe wrote to Germain that their tents were still standing and their kettles on the fire. Letter Nov. 30, 1776.

rear.   On the 28th of November the Americans marched out
of Newark, and it was well for them that their departure was
not delayed; for, as Washington wrote, "our force was by no
means sufficient to make a stand, with the least probability
of success, against an enemy much superior in numbers, and
whose advanced guards were entering the town by the time
our rear got out."

The Americans went through Springfield and Elizabeth-
town and took up a position at New Brunswick on the further side of the Raritan river.   But for the action of General
Howe they would not have reached the far side of the Raritan intact.   Cornwallis was in earnest about running them to
earth, and he drove his army over the heavy roads so rapidly
that he had come up to the quarry while the rear guard was
in the act of crossing the river.   He was about to hurl his
superior force on the enemy now in the greatest confusion
when a messenger from General Howe came dashing up to
inform him that any further movement of aggression was to
be deferred until the arrival of the General himself with re-
inforcements.

The General arrived a week later with a single brigade.
Meanwhile the army of Washington had passed out of the
danger zone.   What Cornwallis thought of the situation does
not appear.

Washington's army was dwindling fast.   The militia had
almost entirely melted away and the regulars were deserting
in squads.   With those who were left he limped towards the
Delaware.   Howe had given him a full week to make his
escape, but so slow was the movement of his forces that the
rear guard had not yet quit Princeton when the British entered the town; and the last of Washington's soldiers had just
shoved off their boats to cross the Delaware as the Redcoats
came puffing up.   Washington had been taking his time in
getting his army across the river, but he had done a thorough
job while he was about it, and had taken possession of all the

boats on the river for many miles in both directions. In keeping with their usual practise the British had brought no pontoons.

"How provoking it is," Colonel Enoch Markham is quoted as saying, "that our army, when it entered the Jerseys, was not provided with a single pontoon ! . . . If we had six flat-bottomed boats we could cross the Delaware."

Six flat-bottomed boats !   And within a hundred yards of the British headquarters in Trenton was a well-stocked lumber-yard, and if any ironwork was needed, the town boasted of four blacksmith shops.   Trevelyan's excuse for not building the necessary boats is that "our soldiers were un-skilled, and our commanders helpless, in front of an obstacle which they all pronounced insurmountable." *   In the same breath he admits that there was hardly a brigade in Wash-ington's army that would not have furnished the necessary artificers.   All these difficulties vanish, however, when we take the view that Howe did not want to cross the Delaware. He was glad to have Washington out of the way.   His so called "mysterious delay" at Princeton could so easily have been for the sole purpose of allowing Washington to make good his escape.   Stedman, an officer in Howe's army, writes: "General Howe appeared to have calculated with the great-est accuracy the exact time necessary for the enemy to make his escape."

General Howe not only appeared to have calculated; he undoubtedly did calculate.   And now that he had Washing-ton out of the way, temporarily, at least, Howe went about

---

* The American Revolution, Vol. III, p. 22.   Judge Jones (I, p. 128) goes a little more into the particulars.   "There was a board-yard entirely full and directly back of the house in which the Commander-in-Chief had his head-quarters and which he must have seen every time he looked out of his window. Besides there were in Trenton a large number of barns, and store houses, built of boards, out of which rafts might have been made in the space of two days sufficient to have transported the whole British army, with their baggage across the river.   But it seems the American War was not yet to end.   This was but the first real campaign; the General's favorites were not yet sufficiently en-riched; the rebellion was to be nursed, the General to continue in command, and his friends, flatterers, mistresses, and sycophants, to be provided for."

the real business that had brought him to New Jersey: he issued a proclamation signed by himself and his brother, the Admiral, promising a free pardon and the assured enjoyment of liberty and property to all who would sign a declaration of loyalty to his Majesty within sixty days. The offer included even those deluded mortals who had borne arms against the most gracious king.

New Jersey rose to this bait almost en masse. The province had from the first been strongly Loyalist. "Infamous," Washington called it in a letter to his brother. "Instead of turning out to defend their country, and affording aid to our army, they are making submissions as fast as they can. If the Jerseys had given us any support, we might have made a stand at Hackensac, and after that at Brunswick; but the few militia, that were in arms, disbanded themselves and left the poor remains of our army to make the best we could of it."

General Greene remarked that if New England had been the seat of the hostilities, the Provincials would not have been under the necessity of retreating more than six or seven leagues, and added that in a rearward march of over a hundred miles across New Jersey the army of Washington did not attract more than a hundred recruits.

New Jersey did not share the revolutionary enthusiasm of New England, perhaps because the inhabitants did not have the Adams cousins to arouse and instruct them, and it went flocking to sign on the dotted line at all the places designated by the delighted Commander-in-Chief of the British arms. When Howe saw that the thing was a success, he adjourned the war supposedly for the winter, and scattered his army in cantonments up and down the Delaware in a way that was calculated to impress Washington and to keep him in his place on the other side of the river.

As one misfortune after another had happened to the American army the prestige of Washington had gone steadily downward. Even the General himself was disheartened. "I am worried almost to death with the retrograde motion of things," he wrote to his brother. "Nothing in this world would contribute so much to my health and happiness as to be once more fixed in the peaceable enjoyment of my own vine and fig-tree." He was disheartened, but he had no thought of giving up. Washington was not one who gave up easily, though a grinning fate was waiting for him just around the corner with another blow: the almost grotesque capture of General Lee.

Charles Lee had been watching the discomfiture of his superior officer with a very definite sense of satisfaction. He had felt all along that Washington was not big enough for the job he was holding. Indeed, in Lee's opinion there was only one man in the country who was big enough for that job, and that was General Lee. It must be remembered that Lee had advised the abandonment of Fort Washington, and after the disaster there he was not long in reminding his General that he had "told him so."

Washington took this calmly; Lee *had* told him so. Lee, however, did not wait for the formal displacement of his leader before taking matters into his own hands; and when Washington in his retreat across New Jersey wrote Lee requesting him to move his detachment across the Hudson and join the rest of the colonial army, Lee totally disregarded the letter and stayed where he was. Instead of moving he wrote to the President of the Massachusetts Council that there was grave danger of an invasion of New England, which Washington would not be able to oppose, and urging Massachusetts to raise an army of her own in spite of the regulations of Congress forbidding independent armies. Nor was this all; he entered into a correspondence with Washington's own adjutant-general, Joseph Reed, seeking to undermine the chief. Fortunately, or unfortunately, as the case may be, this correspondence fell into the hands of Washington. Reed resigned, but Washington, who loved and trusted him,

GENERAL CHARLES LEE

persuaded him to reconsider, and afterwards made him a general.

Washington repeated his appeals to Lee to join him with all haste, predicting all sorts of dire consequences if his coming was delayed a great deal longer, and at last the unwilling subordinate got under way. Washington, in a frenzy, was sending a daily dispatch to Lee urging haste; but nine days passed before Lee accorded him the courtesy of an answer — and what an answer !

I could wish you would bind me as little as possible, not from any opinion, I do assure you, of my own parts, but from a persuasion that detached Generals cannot have too great latitude, unless they are very incompetent indeed.

Just what occurred to the famous Washington temper on the receipt of this epistle history fails to relate. If, however, the stories of Washington's profanity are entirely fictional, this situation would have been a good one on which to hang a tale. But at any rate Lee's army was on the move. That must have been some comfort to Washington in spite of the snail-like pace at which it was coming. It had been so long, however, in getting under way that even the deliberate Howe began to be worried; he was afraid that a plan was afoot for Lee to leap on the rear of the army of Cornwallis. Indeed, something of the sort was in Lee's mind. He refused to be hurried and assured Washington that he could do more good by hanging on the British rear than by obeying orders. He even intimated to Washington that he might attack them if he should see a propitious moment. But perhaps the most despicable thing Lee did was to detain, and then to attach to his own forces, the reinforcements hurried down the river by General Schuyler at Washington's frantic request for men to relieve the situation on the Delaware. These reinforcements were as useless with Lee's command as if they had remained at Albany. For the disobedient general, however, the day of reckoning was at hand.

Ten days after receiving a positive order to move, Lee had lingered at White Plains making leisurely preparations to start. Once in motion he had made an average of six miles a day for a week. Finding this too fast, he had cut down his speed to three miles a day. By the 12th of December the army had reached Vealtown and gone into camp. Lee did not lie with his troops, but went on some three miles further to Basking Ridge that he might sleep in the tavern there, taking with him only a small escort and the large pack of hounds which were always at his heels.

For days Washington had been pestering his recusant subordinate with letters and messages urging haste, but without apparent effect. He had finally sent Lord Stirling out with written instructions to "Repair with all possible expedition to Genl. Lee's Camp. — Know his Situation, Numbers, &ca." Cornwallis had also become nervous about Lee's whereabouts. He did not relish the thought that the army of Washington was in front of him, and the army of Lee behind him where it might watch for a chance to pounce on his back when he was least expecting it. At last the suspense became so great that Cornwallis sent Lieutenant-Colonel Harcourt out with a patrol of thirty dragoons to locate Lee's command. Harcourt did more than merely to learn the situation of Lee's corps; for he was told, probably by a Loyalist who had recognized General Lee, how to get to General Lee's headquarters. When Harcourt discovered that the reckless Lee was sleeping outside his own lines, he dashed in with his thirty troopers and captured the General.

Lee had been awakened by his servant to receive a message brought from General Gates by Major Wilkinson. He was in a bad humor, but he had invited Wilkinson in and had conversed with him while breakfasting. Breakfast over, he had seated himself and written a few lines of his reply to Gates when Harcourt and his thirty troopers had come thundering up and were pounding at the door. They caught him in his dressing-gown and slippers and without giving him a chance to dress bundled him on to Major Wilkinson's charger and whisked him away. They had need for haste for they had thirty miles to go, and the roads were rough and heavy. Then, too, their coming had been observed by a number of rebel sympathizers who were waiting in ambush with squirrel rifles for them to return.

A number of shots were exchanged with the local population as the cavalcade went thundering along the country roads, but only one dragoon was picked off. This was the cornet of the detachment, whose body was buried by the roadside, and from whose grave regimental buttons of the 16th British Light Dragoons were removed as recently as 1891, according to Trevelyan, who gives no authority for the statement.

Sir William reported the raid in a letter written December 20, 1776:

> During Lord Cornwallis's stay at Pennington (near Trenton), a patrol of thirty dragoons from the 16th regiment was sent out to gain intelligence of a corps under the command of General Lee, reported to be in Morris County on their way to cross the Delaware at Alexandria. Lieutenant Colonel Harcourt desired the direction of this detachment, and learning, as he proceeded, the situation of this corps, consisting of 2000 men, and of General Lee's headquarters, he contrived by infinite address and gallantry, to get to his house undiscovered by the guard, surrounded it, and overcoming all their resistance, made the General a prisoner.

The news of General Lee's capture was received in England with the greatest glee. The British had not captured a general since the Battle of Long Island; but that was not all. Lee had formerly been in the British army, and was taken by men of his old English regiment; and it was something to have made a prisoner of the general who was second in command of the American forces. There is a story to the effect that after he had been captured Lee sent for a tailor to mend his clothes, but "not a man in the regiment would work for so great a rascal." George III was so pleased by Lee's capture that he is reputed to have exclaimed, "I shall take care of Colonel Harcourt; leave his future to me." Whether or not the story is true, he did take care of Colonel Harcourt, for in due time he made Harcourt a field-marshal. The little village of Tring in Hertfordshire is said by the Evelyns to have declared a holiday in commemoration of the "takin of General lee, when their wil be a sermint preached, and other demonstrascions of joye, after which will bee an nox roosted whole & everery mark of festivity." *

Washington, who always managed to put the cause above the plane of personality, was able to write:

Our cause has also received blow in the captivity of Gen. Lee. Unhappy man! Taken by his own imprudence, going three or four miles from his own camp, and within twenty of the enemy, notice of which by a rascally Tory was given a party of light horse seized him in the morning after travelling all night, and carried him off in high triumph and with every mark of indignity, not even suffering him to get his hat or surtout coat.

Indignity, indeed! Were the British, far from their own lines and almost within the lines of the Americans, to wait while a rascally rebel made his toilet, even if he was a general? No doubt Washington wrote the proper and needful thing, but down deep in his heart, far beneath his rules of conduct, there must have been a vast amount of relief to have got rid of the troublesome Lee so neatly.

General Sullivan, who had been in command of the troops sent down by Schuyler, hearing of Lee's capture, at once assumed command of Lee's entire force. Nor did he delay in getting them across the Delaware as rapidly as possible, taking good care to make a wide circuit around the British. He crossed over at Easton, some forty miles above Trenton and on the 20th of December in a blustering snowstorm came

* *The Evelyns in America.*

marching into Washington's camp and turned over his command.

So Washington had Lee's army, and the British had Lee. The capture of the lanky general was extremely gratifying to Howe. It was a sweet-sounding note on which to end the campaign. The ragged colonists had been fairly run off their feet. Many of them were actually without any shoes at all, and the toes of those who were fortunate enough to have shoes were not entirely invisible. Nor were their bodies any too well protected from the wintry blasts that now went whining down the valley of the Delaware. Few of them had overcoats, and the uniforms of those who were lucky enough to have uniforms were in tatters. If Sir William had set out to make the colonist army look ridiculous he had certainly succeeded. The spectacle of the patriots shivering over their campfires on the further side of an ice-filled river like a gang of hoboes must have warmed the cockles of his heart, especially when he looked for a contrast at his own well-fed, warmly-clad, and thoroughly-contented soldiers comfortably quartered in the houses of citizens throughout all the larger towns in the neighborhood.

Howe must have looked with especial satisfaction at the blustering snow that was coming down. If that was a fair sample of the weather in those parts there was no telling what would become of the poor devils on the other side of the river by the time that spring had arrived. But western New Jersey was no place for the Commander-in-Chief. New York for him. Before retiring to the urban delights of Manhattan, however, Sir William felt that he must dispose his troops for the winter. It seemed like a simple problem. The advance posts must be so located as to assure the safety of the east bank of the river, while the communicating posts protected the section of New Jersey through which the armies had passed.

The chain of cantonments as finally placed extended from

Burlington to Perth Amboy with concentration camps at
Bordentown, Trenton, Princeton, and New Brunswick.
The camps at Trenton and Bordentown were small, and were
six miles apart. Both were on the river. Twelve miles inland on the road to New York lay Princeton. Cornwallis is
said to have advised the placing of these camps, and he always
maintained that they were in all respects adequate and would
never have been molested had his orders for the fortification
of Trenton been carried out by Colonel Rall who was in
charge of the Hessians cantoned there.

Howe seems to have been a bit shaky on this point, for on
December 20th, a week before Washington's descent on Trenton, we find him writing to Germain:

> The chain (of cantonments), I own, is rather too extensive;
> but I was induced to occupy Burlington, to cover the county of
> Monmouth in which there are many loyal inhabitants; and,
> trusting to the general submission of the country to the South-
> ward of this chain, and to the strength of the corps placed in the
> advance posts, I conclude the troops will be in perfect security.

Howe simply could not conceive that the ragged Continentals on the further side of the raging Delaware could ever
get themselves in shape for a coup against his well-ordered
forces. He little reckoned on the spirit that animated those
shivering patriots. It had probably not occurred to him that
all had deserted who were going to desert, and that those who
were left had in them the making of real fighting-men.

Colonel von Donop who was in command of the cantonments facing the river, had a strange prescience that all was
not well. He protested that his forces were too scattered for
an adequate defense in case of attack, and urged that they
should be massed to insure their safety, but was voted down
by Howe and Cornwallis.

Having established these small cantonments in New Jersey Sir William sent the main body of his army, thirty thousand strong, into New York for the winter. This was crowd-

ing matters a bit. The soldiers far outnumbered the civil population of the city, and after all the available houses had been occupied the army overflowed into the churches and public buildings. The burned portion of the city had not yet been rebuilt.

While chasing Washington across New Jersey Sir William had suddenly come to the conclusion that the time had arrived for a move in another direction. He had accordingly dispatched General Clinton with some six thousand troops to seize Newport, which because of its easy access from the sea was regarded as a desirable port of call for British shipping. Clinton begged to be sent against Philadelphia instead, but Howe was firm. He had no idea of letting Clinton walk off with a prize of so much importance as Philadelphia. He intended to handle that for himself, though he had not at this time made up his mind how to go about it. It may have looked well at the end of the campaign to say that the splendid harbor of Newport was now in the hands of the British, though the seizing of this undefended port brought the conflict in America no nearer to a conclusion. The Newport campaign did dispose of Clinton for the time being, which is probably the main reason why Howe insisted upon it. He was tired of Clinton.

Clinton in Newport, and Von Donop on the Delaware, Sir William mounted his charger, summoned his staff, and rode by easy stages back to New York, with the units of his army that were to winter in New York trailing along behind him. When these fortunate troops had finally reached their destination they found that the General had set aside a period of ten days for a grand celebration of the successful campaign. What this celebration must have been in a city where the military population outnumbered the civilians by about two to one can only be imagined.

Food and drink were plentiful, and everything pointed to a pleasant winter ahead. Society began to buzz. Sir Wil-

liam was known to be fond of all sorts of social doings, and
great expectations were in the air.   Balls were planned and
dinners arranged, and doubtless there was some refined an-
gling among the society folk for invitations to the brilliant
banquets, routs and parties that were to culminate in the investiture of Sir William as Knight's Companion of the Bath,
since the honor granted after the Battle of Brooklyn had not
yet been formally conferred.

These things were not unknown or unappreciated by the
little patriot army encamped on the farther side of the Delaware.   The tall Virginian in command there was in his small
way planning some festivities of his own.   What he had in
mind, however, was not a ball, or a banquet; it was somewhat like a surprise party — only different.

CHAPTER X

A CHRISTMAS SURPRISE

IN THE four months since landing his army on the south shore of Long Island Sir William had not done so badly. He had defeated the enemy soundly every time that he had been able to get him into a position for battle; he had worried him from New York to White Plains, and from White Plains had run him across the province of New Jersey and had driven him out of bounds beyond the ice-choked Delaware. The tattered colonial army was now shivering somewhere in Pennsylvania — what there was left of it; for the militia had quit and gone home almost to a man, and such of the regulars as had any place to go, had to all appearances, started for it. This might be the beginning of the end of the Continental army.

The British had captured nearly 4500 prisoners, including four generals. They had taken 235 iron cannon, 12 pieces of brass ordnance, nearly 24,000 shells, 17,000 iron cannon-balls, 2684 double-headed shot, 2800 muskets, 400,-000 cartridges, 500 entrenching tools, 200 hand barrows, 52 mantelets, 81 cheveaux-de-frise, and huge supplies of flour and stores, to say nothing of the kettles captured on the camp-fires at Fort Lee.

In the matter of territory regained they had also done very well. New Jersey was practically clear of rebels. So was the whole of Long Island. New York City and Newport were in

the hands of the British. Scattered American forces were
stationed at various points in rural New York, New England,
and other out of the way places, it is true, but these detachments were so insignificant as to be almost negligible.

Then, too, the British had accomplished something else.
They had disturbed the serenity of the Continental Congress to such an extent that the lawgivers had fled precipitately from Philadelphia and taken up their temporary quarters at Baltimore, though it is doubtful whether, even by
Christmas time, they had as yet felt enough security from
pursuit to unpack their bags.

Sir William was in high feather. He now had a vision of
finishing the war within another year "by an extensive and
vigorous exertion of his Majesty's arms" as he wrote to Germain on the 30th of November. The details of the plans
set forth in this letter are not without interest:

1st. An offensive army of 10,000 rank and file, to act on the
side of Rhode Island, by taking possession of Providence, penetrating from thence into the country towards Boston, and if
possible to reduce that town: 2000 men to be left for the defense
of Rhode Island, and for making small incursions, under the protection of the shipping, upon the coast of Connecticut. This
army to be commanded by General Clinton.

2d. An offensive army in the province of New York, to move
up the North river to Albany, to consist of not less than 10,000
men, and 5000 for the defense of New York and adjacent posts.

3d. A defensive army of 8000 men to cover Jersey, and to
keep the southern army in check, by giving a jealousy to Philadelphia,* which I would propose to attack in autumn, as well as
Virginia, provided the success of other operations will admit of
an adequate force to be sent against that province.

South Carolina and Georgia must be the objects for winter.
But to complete this plan not less than ten ships of the line will
be absolutely requisite, and a reinforcement of troops to the
amount of 15,000 rank and file, which I should hope may be had
from Russia, or from Hanover, and other German states, particularly some Hanoverian chasseurs, who I am well informed
are exceedingly good troops.

* Perhaps it was a jealousy that had caused the Congress to vacate in so
great a hurry.

By this calculation, the army in the southern district would consist of 35,000 effective men, to oppose 50,000 that the American Congress has voted for the service of next campaign.

The enemy, though much depressed at the success of his Majesty's arms, are encouraged by the strongest assurances from their leaders of procuring assistance from foreign powers, for which end it is understood that Dr. Franklin is gone to France, to solicit aid from that court. I do not presume to point out a way of counteracting him; but were that effected, and the force I have mentioned sent out, it would strike such terror through the country that little resistance would be made to the progress of his Majesty's arms, in the provinces of New England, New York, the Jerseys, and Pensylvania after the junction of the northern and southern armies.

An ambitious program indeed! And to what end? To *"strike such terror* through the country that little resistance would be made to the progress of his Majesty's arms." Always Sir William is making his plans to strike terror. His idea at this time seems to be to frighten the colonies into submission; and at the moment of penning this letter it seemed to him that he had made enough substantial progress to warrant a few bank holidays for himself and his brother islanders, and a bit of a Hochzeit for the German mercenaries who were out in Jersey holding the line.

But the revelry by night was rudely interrupted by the arrival of a man on horseback, a dispatch-rider on a foam-flecked steed, who brought the paralyzing news that Colonel Rall with his entire brigade had been "Surprised, Attacked, Defeated and taken Prisoners" * by the tatterdemalion army from beyond the Delaware. The Americans had crossed the river under cover of darkness and had swooped down on Trenton at daybreak the day after Christmas, and had captured the garrison almost before the slumbering Germans could get the sleep out of their eyes. Rall had been mortally wounded, and the invaders had recrossed the river with a thousand prisoners in addition to such munitions and sup-

* *Archibald Robertson's Diaries* (N. Y. 1930).

plies as had been left there by the British for the winter.

Sir William was more annoyed than alarmed. It was certainly provoking to have his well-earned holiday disturbed by the bushwhacking tactics of a handful of ragged fanatics; for after all it was not a very important foray. Perhaps the most serious feature of it was the detrimental effect it might have on his discipline in western New Jersey. Having taken the trouble to win over the people of that locality he felt that he must now take the further trouble to keep them in line. Another disadvantage of losing Trenton at just this time was that he did not care to close a thoroughly successful campaign on the dolorous note of a defeat, no matter how inconsequential. That would be unfair to himself and to his men. Trenton must be regained — and the loss of Rall's brigade must be avenged.

The Commander-in-Chief was unwilling, however, to have his own holiday disturbed by the administration of suitable reprisals. So he sent Cornwallis. This must have been a blow to the Earl who was already aboard his ship and on the point of setting sail for a winter vacation in England. But Cornwallis was a good soldier. Without a word of complaint he sent his portmanteaux, his boxes, his ditty-bags, and his rug-rolls back to shore, laid away for the moment the gorgeous parade uniform in which he was preparing to travel, donned his well-worn regimentals and started for western New Jersey.

Howe's report of the affair at Trenton is characteristically brief. On the 29th of December 1776, he wrote to Germain:

On the 25th instant, in the evening, a party of the enemy attacked an outguard from the post of Trenton, where Colonel Rall commanded with three battalions of Hessians, fifty chasseurs, and twenty-eight light dragoons, having with them six field pieces; which party was beaten back. On the succeeding morning at six o'clock the rebels appeared in force with cannon, evidently intending to attack the post. Colonel Rall, having received intelligence of their design, had the troops under arms, and detached his own regiment to support an advanced picket: this picket being forced and falling back on the regiment, threw it into some disorder, which occasioned them to retire upon the other battalions; no advantage being taken of this, they recovered themselves, and the whole formed in front of the village.

The rebels without advancing, cannonaded them in this situation, and Colonel Rall moved forward to attack them, with the regiments of Lossberg and Rall; in which attack Colonel Rall was wounded, and the regiment made prisoners. The rebels advanced to the regiment of Knyphausen, and also made that corps prisoners.

Some few officers, and about 200 men of the brigade, with the chausseurs, and a party of dragoons, retreated to Colonel Donop's corps at Burdenton, six miles distant. Several officers were wounded, and about forty men killed and wounded.

This misfortune seems to have proceeded from Colonel Rail's quitting his post, and advancing to the attack, instead of defending the village.

The rebels recrossed the river Delaware immediately with the prisoners and cannon they had taken.

This sounds very pretty, and doubtless Howe believed it to be the truth when he wrote it; but the fact is that the expedition against Trenton was a real surprise attack. Colonel Rall was in bed and asleep when a startled sentry came running into town crying that the enemy was upon them. The Colonel had been celebrating Christmas the night before, and had done a very thorough job of it. He had gone from one house to another playing cards and checkers and drinking Yuletide toasts with his friends. The disturbance made by the raiding party early in the evening had been a real annoyance to him, for he had turned out the garrison and made ready to put up a stiff defense, whereupon the raiders had disappeared into the night. Rall had gone back to celebrating, but he was in no mood to be disturbed by any more rumors or false alarums. It was for this reason that his servant had refused to admit a certain Loyalist who had made his way across the treacherous river to report the movement of Washington and his army.

Howe was technically correct when he says in his letter that Rall had "received intelligence" of the rebels' design. For, upon being refused admittance to Colonel Rall's presence the Loyalist informer had written and sent in to him a note telling what he had observed at the ferry on the other side of the river. Rall had received the note, for it was afterwards found in his pocket, but he did not read it. When he saw that it was in English he stuffed it into his waistcoat and went on with his game and his cups. Just before daybreak Rall went back to his quarters where he flung off his clothes and tumbled into bed — without giving another thought to the precious document in his waistcoat pocket.

Cannonballs were ricochetting down the street before Rall could be awakened and aroused to his senses. Once outside in the street he grasped the situation and rallied his men for an attack, but it was too late. The Americans were charging in from all sides with drawn bayonets, and those whose powder was still dry were making havoc among the German officers, with the "queer twisted rifles" they knew so well how to shoot. Rall was wounded, but continued to try to rally his men. Then two bullets found him at almost the same time and he fell from his horse.

He was carried into a nearby church, and afterwards was taken home on a church-bench that was used for a litter. As he was being undressed the warning note fell from his pocket. It was picked up and read to him. He groaned. "If I had read that at Mr. Hunt's, I wouldn't be here !" he muttered in German.

That was the way that Colonel Rall had "received intelligence" of the design of the enemy to make the attack.

As to another statement in his letter Howe is even more inaccurate. The "misfortune" did not "proceed from Colonel Rall's quitting his post, and advancing to the attack." It proceeded rather from Rall's disobedience of Von Donop's orders to fortify the place and throw up certain redoubts with flanking angles for the cannons at the junction of roads just outside the town. Though perhaps for the real cause of the disaster we must go back to Cornwallis who was responsible for laying out the chain of cantonments.

It may have been the haphazard methods of the British that had lost Trenton for them; but there was nothing haphazard about the plans they made for the retaking of the place. Their finest regiments were pushed towards the Delaware as fast as they could be put in marching order, and when Cornwallis joined his troops at Princeton on the first day of the New Year he found himself at the head of 8000 picked men keen for reprisal. He lost no time in getting them under motion, and though he had been in the saddle all the day before on the journey from New York, he started the advance towards Trenton before daylight on the 2nd of January.

Washington, who had learned from experience that Trenton was not an easily defensible post, had come out to meet the British and had disposed his army in a long line on the south side of the Assunpink Creek; a field, so we have since been told by military experts, that although of his own choosing was badly selected. If Washington had fought the Battle of Assunpink Creek that now seemed imminent we are assured that he would have been beaten, and that in all probability the Revolution would have been lost. But fate, or Providence, or perhaps it was only luck, decreed that the Battle of Assunpink Creek was never to be fought. As always, the army of Washington moved slowly, and in order to get all his units in their places he sent General de Fermoy up the Princeton road to harass and delay the British until suitable preparation for their reception should be completed. These harassing troops gave so good an account of themselves that the British were all day in marching the eight or nine miles that lay between Princeton and the banks of the

Assunpink. When finally the two armies were facing each other on the opposite banks of the stream the day was done and twilight was upon them.

A brief glance at the lay of the land was enough to show Cornwallis that the Virginia farmer on the other side of the creek had not yet learned the lesson of the Battle of Long Island. He had again placed one of his flanks on an unnavigable stream, and left the other up in the air. A heavy thrust against the exposed flank would crush the line in upon itself — and the disaster of Brooklyn would repeat itself. Cornwallis saw his chance, but he was loth to run the risk of bungling it by having the battle called on account of darkness. Washington had taken a week to pick his field, and the Earl thought it unlikely that having finally selected it the American would run off at the last minute and try to select another.

So the army of Cornwallis rested on its arms and licked its chops in anticipation of the morrow. If the British commander had his dreams that night about "bagging the old fox" and ending the war single-handed, so to speak, and returning to England to stay, one could not have blamed him. The cards were on the table, and they were all his way. Cornwallis went to bed and slept, and as he slept the army of Washington stole away in the night, and when Cornwallis awoke in the morning — it was gone.

The "old fox" had been warned of his danger in the nick of time. To make a stand where he was would have been fatal. To retreat would have invited disaster; the army would have disintegrated under the disgrace of another retreat, even if it had succeeded in getting away from the British. The staff were about evenly divided. Some wanted to stay and fight it out; others were for risking a retreat down the river. Then came a bold suggestion: why not take the new road through the woods, the one that ran down from Princeton almost parallel with the road on which the British

had come, and make a countermarch upon Princeton?
They would thus strike the enemy's rear, and might, if successful, make a thrust against Brunswick where the British
magazines were and the royal treasure chest, and where General Lee was being detained.

Who it was that made this suggestion has never been
proved, but it was, as Greene says, the inspiration of true
genius.* Washington may not have devised the move, but
at least he recognized its worth and put it through with the
utmost skill and generalship. In the dark watches of the
night he sent the lumbering baggage train down the river
where it would be out of the way, and manœuvred his
troops at a rapid pace along the new road through the woods
that led down from Princeton. At daybreak Cornwallis was
awakened by a distant rumbling that he took to be thunder.
But it was not the thunder of the heavens: it was the thunder
of Washington's artillery at Princeton.

Had Washington been an hour earlier he would have
come upon the three British regiments at Princeton while they
were at breakfast. As it was he encountered them just as
they were leaving the town to join Cornwallis. He hurled
his army upon them and overwhelmed them after a sharp
engagement. Then his men gave out. They were too spent
to keep on after they had captured Princeton. The Americans pushed out the Brunswick road and were just free of
the town when the advance column from Trenton, driven at
full speed by the enraged Cornwallis, came fuming in on the
other side.

The British stores and the treasure chest of three hundred
and fifty thousand dollars at Brunswick must have been a
great temptation to Washington; but his men were falling
asleep on their feet. When they stumbled they went down,

---

* Washington himself never claimed credit for the idea, though it has been
ascribed to him by Bancroft, Trevelyan and others. Rupert Hughes in his
life of Washington, after a thorough review of the authorities, gives St. Clair
the credit, which is probably much nearer the truth.

and when they went down they did not get up again.   Nor
was he any too sure that if he got to Brunswick he would not
find Sir William there with the rest of the British army.   So
five miles out of Princeton he turned due north and left the
Brunswick road.   His army stumbled on to Pluckemin,
where, finding that it was no longer pursued it went into
camp for a long sleep.   Later it moved over into the Short
Hills of New Jersey and took up winter quarters around
Morristown.

Cornwallis, intent only on saving his supplies and his treasure chest, went racing on to Brunswick.   If he even noticed
that Washington had turned off he showed no sign.   Having
been tricked once by this fly-by-night opponent he was not
taking any chances, and did not slacken his pace until he had
reached Brunswick and seen with his own eyes that his treasure chest and his magazines were undisturbed.

With no further attempts at reprisal the British abandoned
the whole of western New Jersey to the rebels and went
sheepishly about the business of making New Brunswick and
Amboy so secure for their army of 28,000 men that the rascally rebels with their 6000 (which shrank before the winter
was over to only 3000) would not be tempted into any more
surprises.

Of this winter campaign during which the Americans had
destroyed three British outposts and had come dangerously
near capturing a fourth, Howe's early reports are somewhat
casual.   On January 5th he writes to Germain:

During the night of the 2nd the enemy quitted this situation
(on Assunpink Creek), and marching by Allen's Town, and from
thence to Prince Town fell in on the morning of the 3d with the
17th and 55th regiments, on their march to join Brigadier
General Leslie at Maidenhead.
Lieutenant Colonel Mawhood, not being apprehensive of the
enemy's strength, attacked and beat back the troops that first
presented themselves to him, but finding them at length very
superior to him in numbers, he pushed forward with the 17th

regiment and joined Brigadier General Leslie. The 55th regiment retired, by way of Hillsborough to Brunswick, and the enemy proceeding immediately to Prince Town, the 40th regiment also retired to Brunswick . . . Captain Phillips, of the 35th grenadiers, returning from hence to join his company, was on this day beset between Brunswick and Prince Town by some lurking villains, who murdered him in a most barbarous manner; which is a mode of war the enemy seem from several late instances to have adopted, with a degree of barbarity that savages could not exceed. . . Lord Cornwallis seeing it could not answer any purpose to continue his pursuit, returned with his whole force to Brunswick.

The brilliant coup of Washington thus becomes the mere "quitting of a situation," and his masterly stroke at Princeton is nothing more than "falling in" with a couple of regiments on the march. As for the pursuit by Lord Cornwallis, if it had been pushed with a little more vigor it might easily have answered the purpose of capturing or dispersing the crippled and exhausted army of Washington.

To others with a different perspective the exploits of the Americans were much more significant. Laurels rained down upon the tall Virginian. Legends sprang into being. Frederick the Great was quoted as the author of compliments that he never uttered, and was credited with having presented Washington with a sword that he never sent. Another Prussian, however, Von Bülow, pronounced the surprise at Trenton as "one of the best planned and boldest executed" military movements of our century, and adds that "it was, however, excelled by the attempt upon Princeton, and both events are sufficient to elevate a General to the temple of immortality."

Sir William himself within a fortnight after his first report of the matter had changed his tune completely. He writes to Germain:

It is with much concern that I am to inform your Lordship, the unfortunate and untimely defeat at Trenton, has thrown us further back, than was at first apprehended, from the great encouragement given to the rebels.

I do not now see a prospect of terminating the war, but by a general action, and I am aware of the difficulties in our way to obtain it, as the enemy moves with so much more celerity than we possibly can.

Nor can we hazard a march at this unfavorable season, with any hopes of making a stroke upon the enemy, in his present situation, that might turn the scale in our favor.

Concluding upon the certainty of another campaign, and confident I need not press your Lordship, to send us every reinforcement of troops for immediate service, that can be procured, 20,000 men would by no means exceed our wants, yet 15,000 will give us a superiority, that I should hope, may be materially experienced in the course of the campaign. Philadelphia now being the principal object, by the greater number, we should be enabled to detach a corps to enter the Delaware by sea, and the main body to penetrate into Pennsylvania, by way of Jersey: there would also in that case be a sufficient corps to act from Rhode Island. On the other hand, if the reinforcements are small, we shall be confined to act in one body in Jersey, leaving only a small corps at Rhode Island, and another of sufficient force for the defense of this island (New York) and its dependencies.

It must have been embarrassing to Sir William to receive some weeks later a letter written by Germain at almost the same time that Sir William was dictating the foregoing, in which the General was told of the "sincere satisfaction" of his Majesty and in which Germain found himself quite unable sufficiently to admire the "greatness and rapidity" of Howe's success. Germain further congratulates Sir William on the fact that his correspondence "during the whole course of the campaign has so constantly contained advice of some important advantage gained" or news of "some other welcome event." *

Sir William wrote again on the 12th of February of the return to New York of some of the forces from Rhode Island, and spoke in a rather vague way of a contemplated movement "when the weather proves favorable, against the enemy

* Letter of January 14, 1777.

still remaining at Morris Town." The weather, however, never proved favorable enough to lure Sir William away from the delights of New York. It is doubtful whether he had even when writing the letter any serious intention of attacking Morristown. At any rate he never did attack it.

CHAPTER XI

HE DONS A RED RIBBAND

CORNWALLIS, having accomplished exactly nothing in his late sally into New Jersey (if we except the opportunity he had given the rebel general to make a hero of himself, and the abandonment of all that part of New Jersey lying to the westward of New Brunswick) resumed his belated vacation and sailed for England. General Robertson also ran across for his winter holiday. General Clinton, too, had asked and received from the Commander-in-Chief permission for a furlough in England. But General Clinton was not going home for a holiday; he was going on business. He felt himself deeply aggrieved by some of the things Germain had been saying about the way he had conducted his military activities in America, and was going home to straighten out the record by challenging Germain to a duel.

Sir William slyly mentioned in one of his letters that General Clinton "being gone to England," Lord Percy had succeeded to the command at Rhode Island. This was enough to put Germain, who had no taste for duels, on his guard. He accordingly had a messenger at the dock to meet and pacify the irate Clinton with all manner of apologies and promises. Clinton received the messenger, but was hard to pacify. He was out for blood and was not to be easily dissuaded from performing a task that promised so much pleasure to a num-

ber of others as well as to himself. He accordingly rejected
the friendly advances of the spokesman for Germain, and
cried so loudly for blood that Germain was driven to the
extremity of offering to procure for him a red ribband if he
would let bygones be bygones, and return to America and
go on with the war. The offer of a British knighthood was
too much of a temptation for the son of an ex-officer in the
colonial civil-service. So Clinton sheathed his sword, doubtless with the feeling that he ought not to be doing it, and
returned to his command in America with his ill-gotten red
ribband dangling from his sturdy neck.

While all this under-cover negotiating and bargaining had
been going on in England, the investiture of Sir William as
Knight's Companion of the Bath had been showing the budding democracy of the new world the sort of entertainment
it would deny itself should it succeed in its effort to banish
royalty from its shores. The original dispensation had come
to Sir William in a letter from Germain written at Whitehall, October 18, 1776,* immediately after the receipt in
England of news of the Battle of Brooklyn. It read:

SIR: It is impossible that any person who has duly attended
to your military conduct, and found it from your entrance into
the army invariably directed by an unintermitted ambition to
serve your King and country, can imagine that your meritorious
behaviour has been unnoticed by his Majesty, or that his gracious
approbation has not been frequently communicated to you by
his Ministers in their respective dispatches.

His Majesty, however, being desirous that the high sense which
he has of your successful endeavors to serve him should be still
of greater notoriety, has thought proper to afford you a more
public testimony of his Royal favor, and has, therefore, out of
his special regard to merit, wherever it is found, been graciously
pleased to nominate you for one of the Knight's Companions of
the most honorable Order of the Bath.

* The New York *Gazette* for January 20th 1777 carries under a London date
line of October 18 the note: "Yesterday the lady of Sir William Howe was introduced to their Majesties at St. James's and most graciously received." And
the next day he was knighted. This was not long after John Adams' ill-consid-
ered remark that the Howes "have not very great women for wives."

You will accordingly receive herewith the proper insignia, together with a dispensation for wearing them, and also the statutes of the order.

I have likewise the honor to transmit to you a letter from Lord Viscount Weymouth addressed to Vice-Admiral Lord Viscount Howe, which you will please to deliver to his Lordship.

You will learn from the enclosed copy thereof, that the King has been pleased to direct his Lordship to perform the ceremony of investing you with the ensigns of the order.

You will do me the justice to believe me sincerely happy in conveying to you this additional mark of his Majesty's increasing approbation of your conduct, and will give me leave to offer you my most unfeigned congratulations upon this unsolicited accumulation of your honors.

This letter had been received by Sir William in December, transatlantic mail service being what it was, and he had replied to it in a very humble tone on the 18th.

The King's most gracious approbation of the behaviour of his officers and soldiers, British and Hessians, is received by them with a sense of gratitude, equal to that zeal which they have demonstrated, and, I make no doubt, will continue to exert upon all occasions for his Majesty's service. The testimony also, which your Lordship has done me the honor to convey, of his Majesty's condescension in taking notice of my humble endeavors, to discharge the duty I owe to my Royal master, being the height of my ambition, I humbly beg your Lordship will do me the honor to express my most grateful feelings for such unmerited goodness. . .

There were other things in the letter, but they were not related to the matter in hand. Moreover Sir William was at the time of writing very much engaged in discharging the duty he had mentioned owing to his Royal master; for his armies were at the moment chasing the disorganized Continentals across the province of New Jersey largely for the entertainment and reassurance of the Loyalist population, to be sure, but it was a matter that required no small amount of stage-managing, and only two days after he had penned the rather prolix letter of acknowledgment for the coveted red ribband we find him writing Germain that upon the approach of the van of Lord Cornwallis's corps to Brunswick, by a forced march (this had occurred on the 1st of December) the enemy had fled most precipitately to Princeton. He adds:

> . . . and had they not prevented the passage of the Raritan, by breaking a part of the Brunswick bridge, so great was the confusion among them, that their army must inevitably have been cut to pieces.
> My first design extending no further than to get and keep possession of East-Jersey, Lord Cornwallis had orders not to advance beyond Brunswick, which occasioned him to discontinue his pursuit; but finding the advantages that might be gained by pushing on to the Delaware, and the possibility of getting to Philadelphia, the communication leading to Brunswick was reinforced, and on the 6th I joined his Lordship.

Has Sir William forgotten (in the three weeks that have passed between the event and his recital of it) that it was his own messenger who came dashing up with orders to stop, rather than the broken bridge that halted Cornwallis on the hither side of the Raritan? And what communications those must have been covering the eight or ten miles between Amboy and Brunswick after Sir William had spent an entire week reinforcing them against an army that was running away from him! The advantages that subsequently *were* gained by pushing on to the Delaware turned out to be very much of a boomerang, and it is hard to believe that Sir William had any very serious idea of getting to Philadelphia at this time. That the allusion to Philadelphia was no more than a handsome bit of alibi is suggested by the fact that on the day that he wrote of it (December 20th) we find him also writing of the chain of cantonments in Western New Jersey, where he concludes the troops will be in "perfect security" through the winter. This view is further supported by a second letter written on the same day, in which he is propos-

ing further plans for the spring campaign.   It is addressed
to Germain and reads as follows:

> In my separate letter by the *Tamer,* No. 32, I mentioned my
> ideas for the several operations in the course of the ensuing cam-
> paign, and proposed a defensive corps in Jersey, for the early
> part of the year: but the opinions of people being much changed
> in Pensylvania, and their minds, in general, from the late prog-
> ress of the army, disposed to peace, in which sentiment they
> would be confirmed, by our getting possession of Philadelphia, I
> am from this consideration fully persuaded, the principal army
> should act offensively on that side, where the enemy's strength
> will certainly be collected.
>
> By this change, the offensive plan towards Boston must be de-
> ferred until the proposed reinforcements arrive from Europe,
> that there may be a corps to act defensively upon the lower part
> of Hudson's river, to cover Jersey on that side, as well as to
> facilitate, in some degree, the approach of the army from
> Canada.
>
> The arrangement I would humbly propose for the execution
> of this plan is, that only 2000 men should remain at Rhode Is-
> land, with a proper number of ships, 4000 men on York Island
> and posts adjacent, and 3000 men on Hudson's river, which will
> leave about 10,000 men for Pensylvania, including, on a rough
> computation, that the extent of our strength at the opening of
> the campaign will not exceed 19,000 men.
>
> But as those operations, perhaps of the last importance to the
> nation, may depend upon the exigencies of the moment, I re-
> quest your Lordship to point out any general plans that may be
> thought most advisable, both with respect to the present strength
> of this army, and on the event of reinforcements, remarking the
> periods of time in which these troops may be expected.   I would
> further propose, that every augmentation of troops should come
> to this port, in the first instance, from whence they can be readily
> disposed of, as may be found requisite.
>
> We must not look for the northern army to reach Albany be-
> fore the middle of September, of course, the subsequent opera-
> tions of that corps will depend upon the state of things at the
> time.

Already the brave plans of the letter of November 30th
are undergoing a change.   The offensive army of 10,000 that
was to move up the Hudson river has shrunk to 3000.   The

army of 10,000 that was to act out of Rhode Island is cut down to 2000. Instead of a defensive army of 8000 for New Jersey and 5000 for New York, the 4000 men left on York Island must look to the defense of both. All this because Sir William has heard rumors that the people of Pennsylvania are "disposed to peace."

This plan is not to be confused with the scheme afterwards submitted by General Lee. It is true that Lee had been in the hands of the British for a week when this letter was written, but he had been held in New Jersey and was not brought into New York until after the first of the year. It is doubtful whether Howe had even seen him since his capture. Moreover the present plan contemplated an invasion of Pennsylvania by land, whereas Lee's plan involved an expedition by water. No doubt the British had expected from the first to take Philadelphia when the proper time came, and perhaps the rumors of a change of heart may have convinced Sir William that by spring the proper time would have come. Meanwhile there were many other matters of interest and importance to claim his attention.

The holiday season would probably have been chosen for the grand ceremony of his investiture with the Order of the Bath, had not the untoward events in western New Jersey occurred just when they did. The "disagreeable occurrence" at Trenton (as Lord George had called it) had followed Christmas day, and the battle of Princeton had been fought on January 3rd. Sir William could with impunity have issued his invitations at any time after this, for the exhausted army of Washington had gone into winter quarters immediately upon quitting Princeton. It was not until January 20th, however, that the honor earned by Sir William's "unintermitted ambition" to serve his king and country, was actually conferred.

There is some confusion about the date. Judge Jones gives it as some time in the month of March, while the New

York *Gazette* for January 20th reports the event as having taken place on the 18th coincident with the celebration of her Majesty's birthday. Not that January 18th was actually the birthday of the Queen, who, it so happened, was born in the summertime. But the King was born in the summertime, too, and in order not to bring the two holidays too close together the celebration of the Queen's birth was arbitrarily changed to midwinter.

The *Gazette* reports that the guns as usual were fired at Fort George, and that his Majesty's Commissioners gave a "grand entertainment to the Governors and Officers of Distinction, both British and Hessian; and in the Evening a very splendid Exhibition of Fire Works under the direction of Col. Montresor, was played off at Whitehall, upon the occasion."

"In honor of the Day," the *Gazette* goes on, "the General was invested with the most honorable Order of the Bath, by Lord Howe, assisted by General de Heister, in the presence of a numerous assembly. Sir William Howe gave an elegant Ball and Supper in the evening. The Ball was opened by Mrs. Clark, and his excellency Governor Tryon." *

Judge Jones, in his *History of New York*, though he gives no details of the ceremonies themselves, remarks:

This month (March 1777) was remarkable for the investiture of General Howe with the order of the bath; a reward for evacuating Boston, for lying indolent upon Staten Island for near two months, for suffering the whole rebel army to escape him upon Long Island, and again at White Plains; for not putting an end to rebellion in 1776, when so often in his power; for making such injudicious cantonments of his troops in Jersey as he did, and for suffering 10,000 veterans under experienced generals, to be cooped up in Brunswick, and Amboy, for nearly six months, by about 6,000 militia, under the command of an inexperienced general.

* Parson Shewkirk says in his diary on January 14th, "At the request of Gen. Howe, we loaned several wagon loads of benches for the entertainment to be held on the Queen's birthday."

This is a rather stern indictment, but Judge Jones, in another place enlarges upon it by adding, "he might better have been executed." We must remember, however, that the Judge was a keenly disappointed Loyalist, and that in addition to this he had a private grudge against Sir William because of certain livestock sold to the British army while it was encamped on Long Island where Judge Jones maintained a rather elegant country home, and for which his honor was never able to collect any pay. This was a wound to his official dignity which continued to rankle even after the Judge had been driven out of America and had taken up his residence in the mother country.

Doubtless there were other Loyalists who were equally bitter over the turn events had taken to whom the elevation of Sir William to the knighthood of the Bath was as a draught of wormwood and gall. If so, they were keeping themselves pretty well in the background as the little town on the tip of Manhattan Island made ready to give the red ribband a good wetting.

The investiture of the Order of the Bath was not at that time so simple a proceeding as one might imagine. The ceremony is an ancient one, so ancient that historians are not in agreement as to its beginnings. It probably originated from the custom of kings who had long made a practise of creating a number of knights at the time of coronation, probably for the purpose of defraying the expenses of the coronation ceremonies. The order is known to have been in a flourishing state during the reign of Charles II but after his time it passed into a decline and was more or less of a dead letter until revived by the first of the Georges who made it over into a military order in about the year 1725. The statutes of the order printed at that time are very concise in the ritual prescribed.

While the Bath is not strictly speaking a secret order, some of the regulations are quite rigid. After the candidate has once entered the chapter room, for example, he may not emerge until the ceremonies are complete.   The first step in the ritual is to spread a blanket on the floor beside a bathing-vessel, after which the barber of the order publicly shaves the beard and cuts the hair of the candidate.   The Elected is then prepared for the bath by certain "experienced knights" sent in to "council him in feats of chivalry."   Having been duly counciled he is preceded by knights and esquires of the sovereign's household playing music and "making the usual signs of rejoicing," to the door of the Prince's chamber.

After the Prince has been informed, the candidate is required to be undressed by the esquires and put into the bath. "These grave knights entring into the Chamber, without any noise, shall severally, one after another, kneeling near the Bathing Vessel, with a soft voice, instruct the Elected in the nature and course of the Bath, and put him in mind, that forever after he ought to keep his body and mind pure and undefiled, and thereupon the Knights shall each of them cast some of the water of the Bath upon the shoulders of the Elected and then retire."   This having been done the esquires were to conduct him to his pallet-bed, which is required to be plain and without curtains, and put him to bed. Here the candidate is expected to rest himself for the rigorous duties of the coming night during which he must remain on watch throughout the night in the "Chappel" of the Prince with no other company than one of the prebendaries of the church to officiate, a chandler to take care of the lights, and the verger to perform any other duties that may arise during the dark watches of the night.

The costume provided for the night watch seems from this distance to have been designed with little thought of what the well-dressed night-watchman should wear.   There is a robe of russet with long sleeves reaching down to the ground.   It is "tyed" about the middle with a cordon of ash-colored and russet silk, with a russet hood "like to an

Hermit, having a white napkin hanging to the Cordon or Girdle." In this regalia the Elected is left to his vigils throughout the night. The next morning he is again taken to the chamber of the Prince where he is put into bed. A coverlet of gold is laid over him, and he is supposed to sleep.

After a time he is awakened by the sound of music and is acquainted by the esquires with the fact that it is "a convenient time to rise." And here one of the most interesting parts of the entire ceremony occurs — the restoration to the Elected of the clothing of which he has previously been divested. First the "most antient" of the knights presents him with his shirt, the next hands him his breeches, the third his doublet, and another brings him a surcoat of red tartarin, lined and edged with white scracenet. Two others lift him from his bed and put on his boots while a third is busy looping him with a white girdle. Another pair comb his hair and deliver to the Elected his coif or bonnet. The candidate is now ready for the mantle of the order, a garment of silk the color of the surcoat which is thrown about him and made fast at the neck with a "lace of white silk having a pair of gloves hanging at the end thereof." On the left shoulder of the mantle is emblazoned the ensign of the order, three imperial crowns surrounded with the motto of the order "on a circle Gules, with a glory or rays issuing from the center." The motto adopted for all this gorgeousness is a simple one. It is, *Tria Iuncta in Uno.*

The Elected is next given his sword and spurs, whereupon his Majesty or his representative proceeds with the accolade, dubs him, kisses him, hangs about his neck a red ribband to which the golden badge of the order is affixed, and directs him to proceed to the chapel for the administering of the oath. The Elected raises his right hand and the oath is administered:

You shall honor God above all things; you shall be steadfast in the faith of Christ; you shall love the king your Sovereign Lord, and him and his right defend to your power; you shall defend Maidens, Widows, and Orphans, in their rights; and shall suffer no extortion, as far as you may prevent it; and of as great honor be this order unto you, as ever it was to any of your progenitors, or others.

This oath is very impressive, or would be, were it not for the fact that the Elected, immediately after he has taken it, is confronted by the sovereign's Master-Cook armed with a huge chopping-knife who warns the newly made Sir Knight that if he fails to keep his obligation the Master-Cook will be compelled by his office to hack the spurs from his knightly heels. It is delightful the way these knights and nobles take the servants into their revels.

Even after taking the oath, however, the Elected is not fully invested with his knighthood until he has paid the following fees:

£138	to the Great Master of the Order
22.6.8	to the Dean of the Order
22	to the King of Arms
22	to the Register
22	to the Genealogist
22	to the Secretary
22	to the Usher
18.13.4	to the Messenger, and an endless number of lesser fees.

The Elected does get for all this, however, a collar of gold of thirty ounces troy weight composed of several imperial crowns of gold tyed or linked with gold knots enamelled white representing the white laces used in the ceremonies, the collar of gold having a badge or symbol of the order pendent. This he is required to wear at all public ceremonies.

Just how much of this ancient ritual was employed by the Admiral in investing his brother with the ancient and honorable Order of the Bath does not appear in any of the contemporary writings that have yet come to light. The statutes of the Order as published in 1725 completely fill a stout octavo volume, with many opportunities for hilarity in the performance of the ritual, as we have already seen. The Admiral, however, being a sober-minded fellow no doubt injected a certain amount of solemnity into the occasion. He may, as the representative of the Sovereign, have abridged the ceremony of investiture to the simple act of hanging the red ribband round the neck of his brother and dubbing him Sir Knight with a brotherly kiss. What the light-hearted members of the social set not so restrained in their quest for amusement and relaxation may have done to add to the gaiety of the occasion could have been something quite different.

Nor was the spirit of festivity confined exclusively to the social register. The soldiers were released from their barracks and the sailors from their ships. There was dancing on the streets and merriment in public as well as private places. There were sleigh-rides out into the country towards Greenwich and Haerlem, and skating on the ponds and waterbrooks with which the island abounded. There was laughter, and singing, and the jingling of sleighbells, while Colonel Montresor was "plaining off" his magnificent exhibition of "Fire Works." If a good time was not had by all, surely this was through no fault of Sir William who, next to having a good time himself, most loved to see other people enjoying themselves.

CHAPTER XII

SIR WILLIAM CHANGES HIS MIND

THE OUTLOOK for the British at the opening of the campaign of 1777 was promising in the extreme. At the centre of the theatre of operations lay General Howe with a splendid army of twenty-five thousand. He had ample supplies on hand and sufficient transport facilities to insure a steady flow from the home base. His artillery train was all that could be asked for. Only in cavalry was he deficient, and this deficiency was pretty well offset by the fact that the American armies had practically no mounted forces at all. Up in Canada lay another perfectly equipped army under the command of Gentleman Johnnie Burgoyne, ready to start southward at the opening of spring on an expedition that was intended to effect a conjunction with the forces of Sir William, and to open a line of communication between Montreal and New York by way of the Hudson valley, that would cut the colonies, and thus the Revolution, into two distinct parts that could be dealt with one at a time. The control of the sea was, with the exception of some small privateering and blockade-running, entirely in the hands of the British.

In 1776 Admiral Howe had with his immense flotilla of transports, troop-ships, packets and other non-fighting vessels some fifty-six men-of-war. In 1777 the number was increased to eighty-one. It has been suggested that with this fleet at his disposal he could have stationed his fighting-craft in sight of one another in a line that would have extended along the coast from Boston to Charleston. Although the original plan had been to blockade the Hudson, the Delaware, and the Chesapeake with the larger vessels and leave the rest of the fleet free to patrol the coast, the Admiral never attempted an effective blockade of any of these great waterways unless he happened to be occupying it. Any blockading he may have done was incidental to some other business that he and Sir William were undertaking at the time.

Washington had spent a busy winter trying to assemble an army that would be able to stand up to these very formidable forces from beyond the sea, but the spring found him with no more then 7000 troops, many of them raw recruits totally inexperienced in facing gunfire. He probably did not have in his entire army a regiment that would today pass muster as shock-troops. General Putnam who was in command of the highlands of the Hudson some forty or fifty miles north of New York, where the patriots had stored their surplus supplies and munitions for safe-keeping, had only a nominal force at his disposal. Had the British felt inclined to go either up or down the river he could have done little to stop them. At Ticonderoga, the outpost of the Americans, was General St. Clair with a little army of 3500 that was supposed to turn back Burgoyne if he should attempt to pass that way. In the matter of arms, clothing, and equipment, the Americans were sadly lacking. They were still short of food. Their prospects looked pretty dubious. A military victory, if the British were really serious about it, seemed to be theirs for the asking.

Military commentators, who have devoted much thought to the situation, would have had the British open the campaign from their base in New York and first establish a strong communication with Canada by means of the Hudson and Lake Champlain. This should have been easy with the overwhelming superiority in numbers and their splendid fleet. Had Sir William advanced from the south as Burgoyne came down from the north nothing could have prevented the severance of New England from the rest of the colonial landscape. This highly important amputation having been completed, Sir William should next have turned his attention to the patriot force under Washington and drawn it into a pitched battle; or, if Washington had declined the honor of meeting the flower of Britain on the field of honor, Sir William should have pursued a policy of following him up to the point of extermination, scattering and dissipating his forces wherever he could find them. Had Washington succeeded in escaping him by retreating with his armies into the fastnesses of the West, Sir William, with the aid of his brother the Admiral, could have starved him out by seizing and holding the strategic points along the coast and maintaining a really effective blockade.

This is all very plain and very clear and very military. The Americans, on the other hand, being outclassed and outnumbered and having no foothold on the sea, were, if they were to make the most of their very unfavorable situation, necessarily confined to a sort of guerrilla warfare that would consist of the surprising and destroying of segregated or exposed detachments — such as the sortie on Trenton and the brilliant coup at Princeton.

According to the laws of military science this is what the two armies should have done. What they actually did do was something quite different. "It was a campaign," says Charles Francis Adams, at the risk of offending both the Sons and Daughters of the American Revolution, "of consecutive and sustained blundering" on both sides.

If Sir William had been really interested in the destruction of Washington's army he could with the overwhelming forces at his command easily have surrounded it in its winter camp at Morristown long before the spring in the North had advanced far enough to tempt Burgoyne and his army into the field. Or, if he had preferred to make a conjunction with Burgoyne before turning his hand to the forces of Washington, he could have made an early thrust up the river, so that Burgoyne, when he was able to move, would have had a clear path before him.

These considerations are, however, of a purely military nature; and it must by this time be obvious that the considerations by which Sir William was guided were not always military. Quite the contrary. His two campaigns in America had not changed his attitude towards America to any great extent. He was still as hopeful as when he had written to Grocer Kirk that the colonists on being relieved of their "grievance" would return to all due obedience of the laws. The only difficulty was to find a way of relieving them of the grievance that would be satisfactory to both parties. The Independency issue had by this time arisen to plague him, though he still regarded this as the handiwork of a few frantic insurgents and did not doubt that upon a proper show of force it would be abandoned. All along Sir William had been well aware of the difficulty with which the army of his opponent had been held together. This led him to believe that the Revolution lacked spontaneity and was being kept alive by artificial respiration, and convinced him that, given time, it would die a natural death.

Had another admiral been in charge of the fleet, or had Lord Howe been less ardent a Whig than the General, either Sir William would have had to put up the appearance of a fighting-man, or resign the command. But the Admiral was no less pacific in his attitude towards the colonies than the General. He had figured prominently in the numerous overtures for peace, and may indeed have been the one to originate them. So the plans of Sir William were in no way impeded by a navy that was spoiling for a fight.

Up to this time the Ministry had been eminently satisfied

with the humane and pacific campaigns of Sir William. If there was any hope of a voluntary submission by the colonies the ministers were only too willing to avail themselves of it. As time went on, however, without any definite accomplishments in this direction, they became politely impatient and began to suggest as modestly as possible that they would be glad to see a little more action. These suggestions, which Sir William regarded as "ambiguous hints and whispers across the Atlantick, to be avowed or disavowed at pleasure," made but little impression on the brothers Howe. In the absence of any positive orders they naturally fell into the way of conducting the war according to their own Whig ideas, instead of the Tory ideas of the government that had sent them to America.

Sir William was in no hurry. He was willing to bide his time. So long as Washington was content to remain in winter quarters, the magnificent British army lay idle, its arms stacked, its artillery swabbed with tallow, its fighting-standards folded and laid carefully away where the moths could not get at them. The snows of winter melted and ran off down the little brooks of New Jersey with a pleasant gurgling sound. Wildflowers poked up through the leaf-mould and spread their pretty petals to the grateful warmth of the sun. The sap rose in the trees, the buds swelled. The birds came and mated and built their nests. But the armies of the King went not out to battle. Nor did the armies of the Revolution do any of the pouncing and surprising that the military experts have since declared to have been their logical move. Each was apparently watching for the other to do something. Howe said afterwards that he was waiting for the grass to grow so that he would have forage for his horses — a slender excuse with little to back it up.

Washington had some reason for not moving: he was still building up an army. From a strictly military standpoint Sir William had no reason at all — unless we take into consideration the fact that he was getting fat and lazy. He was now forty-eight going on forty-nine, and good living was beginning to tell on him. The fire that he had shown in Wolfe's famous scaling party at Quebec when a youngster of thirty had cooled considerably. He was no longer the irrepressible daredevil. He would much rather gamble or philander with the beautiful wife of his commissary of prisoners than embark on any of the forlorn hopes that had tempted him as a youth.

It was Washington who eventually made the first move. He notified Congress on the 28th of May that he was marching his army to Bound Brook. This brought Sir William out of his lethargy, for it was only seven miles from the British post at New Brunswick. The British general yawned, stretched, looked at the weather, and at last ordered the bugles to blow. The British line moved slowly out and took up a position between the army of Washington and the town of Princeton. Sir William boasted that he would be in Philadelphia in six days, though he did not mean it, nor did Washington believe that he meant it. Congress, however, took the boast literally. The pompous lawgivers flew into a panic and hastily summoned Benedict Arnold to protect them. They directed him to fortify the Delaware against the possibility of an attempt by the British to effect a crossing.

They need not have worried. Sir William had no intention of attempting to cross the river at this time. His only idea had been to draw Washington into an engagement, no doubt with the thought of making the Virginian and his army more ridiculous. But Washington was not just then craving a fight. He kept to the hills. Then came a period of shadow-boxing. Sir William marched and countermarched. He advanced and feinted, and withdrew as if in alarm. Washington watched all this with interest, but he did not come down out of the hills. If he had learned nothing else from his previous encounters with the British he had reached the sound conclusion that with his present army it would not be well for him to come to serious grips with them.

With all his marching and countermarching Sir William made no effort to reach Philadelphia by land, and when he found that he could not draw Washington into a battle he withdrew with his armies to Staten Island to try something else that he had in mind.

Sir William had made little success with his attempt to build up the shattered morale of the Loyalists of New Jersey. A thwacking victory over the rebel armies might have turned the trick. At any rate it was worth the trial. Perhaps Washington had seen through the ruse, or if he had not entirely read the mind of his opponent he was lucky enough to keep out of his way. Ill luck, bad breaks, and poor judgment, combined with the taking of some pretty long and desperate chances by his opponent had lost Sir William the loyalty and confidence of New Jersey; and now the adroitness of the enemy was keeping him from winning the inhabitants back.

The stupidity of Sir William in not taking care of the civil population in a territory that was friendly to him is almost unforgivable. The Hessians looted the homes of rebel and Loyalist alike wherever they went. A certificate of loyalty signed by Sir William and the Admiral meant less than nothing to them. They tore the papers up when presented, threw the pieces in the face of the one who had the effrontery to try to stop them with a scrap of paper, and calmly proceeded to walk off with the householder's goods, or with his wife or daughter if they happened to be in a mood for a bit of dalliance. The looting began as soon as the Germans had crossed the river into New Jersey, and continued unabated so long as a European mercenary remained in the province. They gutted the valuable library at Princeton. They stole or destroyed every volume on the shelves. They wrecked the college museum and carried off the exhibits and specimens as plunder. They smashed the mathematical instruments to get a few pounds of brass for the junkman.

"The fine settlements of Maidenhead and Hopewell," says a contemporary letter in the *American Archives,** "have been broken up. The houses are stripped of every article of furniture; and what is not portable is entirely destroyed. . . Every article of house-linen seized and carried away. Scarce a soldier but what has a horse loaded with plunder."

Sir Henry Clinton was not blind to the injury that was being done to the British cause by all this promiscuous plundering. "Unless we would refrain from plunder," he wrote, "we had no business to take up winter quarters in a district we wish to preserve loyal." That Sir William himself was not unaware of the plundering would appear from a letter written during the Jersey campaign in which he told Germain that "although the men behave with great spirit, yet the temptations of plunder are so great, that it is not in the power of a few officers to keep the men under restraint." To this end he asks for some additional officers of the guards. Further than this he appears to have taken no action to curb a practise that was driving the Loyalists away from him faster than he could recruit them with the most reassuring of promises and proclamations.

Washington, on the other hand, showed rare good judgment when after the capture of Trenton he invited the inhabitants of New Jersey, loyalist and rebel alike, to reclaim on proof of ownership the great mass of loot which the Germans had collected there. This simple act of justice did more to win his way into the hearts and confidence of the inhabitants of New Jersey than a dozen successful battles would have done.

Back in February Sir William had written for a second time of the plans of the Americans to increase the size of their army. He reported them as "most sanguine in their expectations" of bringing an army of 50,000 into the field,

* *American Archives*, Peter Force.

and as using "every compulsory means to those who do not
enter voluntary" into their service. In other words conscription. Washington would have been glad to know that his
efforts at conscription were making so favorable an impression on the enemy, for he was having a very difficult time in
getting together an army one-fifth of the size anticipated by
the credulous British commander. In March (1777) Washington's army mustered 4500 men, and by June it did not
exceed 8000.*

When Sir William had written on December 20th proposing that the main army should act in Pennsylvania in the
coming campaign he had not yet received an answer to his
letter of November 30th in which he had suggested a main
thrust up the Hudson valley. When in due time the answer came, it was of course favorable. Germain acknowledged the receipt of the "well drafted plan for the operation
of the next campaign" and said that it had been laid before
his Majesty who would send his sentiments thereon later.
As for the reinforcements and recruits, however, Lord George
was able to promise no more than 4000 Germans, 800 Hessian chasseurs, and 1800 recruits. This, according to the
figures of the Ministry, would bring Sir William's army up to
35,000 — a figure that would make any force the rebels had
as yet been able to put into the field look very puny indeed.
And Lord George regretted keenly that it would be possible
to send no more than 100 horses at the outside. Horses, it
seemed, were very scarce, and were extremely perishable en
route. The ten ships of the line for which Sir William had
pleaded were, he was told, being considered by Lord Sand-
wich who was in charge of that branch of the service.

With all this disappointing news came the very reassuring
intelligence that the Ministry had "great reason to believe"
that Dr. Franklin's secret errand to France would be without
avail, and that his mission to procure any open alliance with

* These are Stedman's figures.

LORD GEORGE GERMAIN
Courtesy of the W. L. Clements Library

the French court would meet with nothing but the most disastrous failure.

No doubt Sir William was glad to be relieved of any further anxiety over the possibility of a Franco-American alliance, but he was unable to refrain from expressing his disappointment over the very substantial reduction in the reinforcements he had requested. He writes with pique that now he will be compelled to forego a principal part of the plan previously submitted and adopt a new plan on a smaller scale. In his long letter of April 1st 1777, covering a multitude of subjects, he says, regarding the change of plan:

From the difficulties and delay that would attend the passage of the River Delaware, by a march through Jersey, I propose to invade Pennsylvania by sea; and from this arrangement we must probably abandon the Jerseys, which by the former plan would not have been the case. On the contrary the enemy's western and principal army would have been between the two corps defined for this service, and we should then have had the communication open for the Seneca Indians to have joined us.

He goes on to say that the Provincial troops under Governor Tryon will be employed upon the Hudson river or to enter Connecticut, as circumstances may point out, and warns the Ministry that the offensive army left in such posts as New York and Rhode Island will be too weak for any rapid success. "I shall hope," he says, "for the arrival of reinforcements in time to strengthen this (meaning the garrison at New York) as well as other corps; but I fear they will not be sufficient to cause any material alteration in the plan now proposed."

From these considerations, and the delays which may attend the evacuations of the Jerseys, from the vicinity of the enemy's principal force, it is probable the campaign will not commence so soon as your Lordship may expect; though we should not undertake anything offensive in that quarter, which I mean to avoid, unless some very advantageous opening should offer.

As we have already seen, no such advantageous opening did offer. Sir William did everything he could think of to get Washington's little army of 8000 to come out in the open where everything would be above-board and try conclusions with his army of 30,000, the winner to take all, no doubt. But Washington had meanly refused, and had continued to skulk in the hills. But the letter continues:

> I have reason to expect, in case of success in Pennsylvania, there will be found a considerable part of the inhabitants who may be embodied as militia, and some as provincial troops, for the interior defense of the province, which must be a great aid in the further progress of the war. . .
>
> Restricted as I am from entering upon more extensive operations by the want of forces,* my hopes of terminating the war this year are vanished; still I think it probable, that by the latter end of the campaign, we shall be in possession of the provinces of New York, the Jersies, and Pennsylvania, though this, in some measure, must depend upon the success of the northern army; for, notwithstanding it is my opinion the rebels will not be able to raise their army voted last autumn, yet they will have a numerous militia in the field, in addition to their standing force, with a tolerable train of artillery.

This sudden shift from an invasion of Pennsylvania by land to an incursion by way of the sea was not, as the casual reader might suppose, brought about by the failure of the Ministry to furnish the recruits and reinforcements that had been requested, and over the refusal of which Sir William was just now in a bit of a pet. His army had an overwhelming superiority in numbers without any reinforcements at all, and it had a superiority in arms and equipment, and a superiority in training and discipline. If Howe had seen fit to make an expedition against Philadelphia by way of New Jersey, it would have been beyond the powers of Washington and his Continental army to prevent. At one time his failure to co-operate with Burgoyne in the drive through the valley of the Hudson was ascribed to jealousy. He may have

---

* Lord George should have marked this for future reference.

felt some jealousy of Burgoyne, though Huddleston says that Howe's mind was "far too torpid to be moved by jealousy." It is his conclusion that Sir William lacked ideas, and at this particular moment somebody gave him one, and he jumped at it. The person who furnished him with the idea was none other than General Charles Lee, then in the hands of the British as a prisoner of war.

CHAPTER XIII

MR. LEE'S PLAN

LEE'S PLAN was entitled, "Scheme for Putting an End to the War, submitted to the Royal Commissioners, 29th March, 1777." It was endorsed by Sir Henry Strachey, secretary to the Royal Commissioners, as the brothers Howe had been calling themselves, "Mr. Lee's Plan, 29th March, 1777." *

The date is significant; for only two days later, on April 1, we find Sir William informing Germain that he had completely changed his plans and now proposed to invade Pennsylvania by sea.

Lee's plan is shrewdly drawn. It appeals to Sir William's well-known desire for a humanitarian victory, and it assumes on the part of the writer a well-founded knowledge of the conditions in Maryland and Virginia which Sir William did not possess. Nearly six pages of closely-written foolscap were required to state the scheme in its entirety, an extract of which follows:

As on the one hand it appears to me that by the continuance of the War America has no chance of obtaining the ends She proposes to herself . . . and as on the other hand Great Britain tho' ultimately victorious, must suffer very heavily even in the process of her victories, evry life lost and evry guinea spent being in fact worse than thrown away: it is only wasting her own

* *The Treason of Charles Lee,* by George H. Moore, N. Y. Historical Soc. Coll., 1874, Vol. IV, p. 406.

property, shedding her own blood and destroying her own
strength; and as I am not only perswaded from the high opinion
I have of the humanity and good sense of Lord and General
Howe that the terms of accomodation will be as moderate as
their powers will admit, but that their Successors (should any
accident happen) wou'd be vested with, I think myself not only
justifiable but bound in conscience to furnish all the lights, I
can, to enable 'em to bring matters to a conclusion in the most
compendious manner and consequently the least expensive to
both Parties . . . for if conditions were extremely repugnant to
the general way of thinking, it (meaning a military victory)
would be only the mere patchwork of a day which the first breath
of wind will discompose and the first symptoms of a rupture betwixt Bourbon powers and Great Britain absolutely overturn —
but I really have no apprehensions of this kind whilst Lord and
General Howe have direction of affairs.

This is a good Whig start. Little wonder that the Howes
fell so neatly into the trap. The captive general goes on to
presuppose 20,000 British troops ready for the field, and gives
it as his opinion that to "bring matters to a conclusion" it
will be necessary to "unhinge or dissolve, the whole System
or machine of resistance." This system depends, he thinks,
on the "circumstances and disposition of the People of Maryland Virginia and Pennsylvania — if the province of Maryland or the greater part of it is reduc'd or submits, and the
People of Virginia are prevented or intimidated from marching aid to the Pennsylvania army the whole machine is dissolv'd and a period put to the War, to accomplish which I
now take the liberty of offering. . . I have at the same time
the comfort to reflect, that in pointing out measures which I
know to be the most effective I point out those which will be
attended with no bloodshed or desolation to the Colonies."
Lee offers more than once to answer for the success of the
plan with his life (a phrase to be found in many of his letters
on comparatively trivial subjects) so positive is he that "all
the inhabitants of that great tract southward of the Patap-
sico and lying betwixt the Patomac and Chesapeak Bay and

those on the eastern shore of Maryland will immediately lay down their arms."

Howe thought Lee knew what he was talking about, that he had a real understanding of the people of Maryland and Virginia. And the picture Lee drew of the victory of mind over matter, and the colonies in a blissful state of friendly submission was just too much to be resisted.

Rupert Hughes charitably refuses to regard Lee as a traitor, and speaks of the attempt to brand him with treason as "a sad farce." In proof of the purity of Lee's motives he cites evidence that a scheme for an invasion of the colonies by way of Chesapeake had been laid before Germain the preceding fall and had received his approval, and Mr. Hughes doubts in a very positive way that Howe had been influenced one way or the other by Lee's plan, which he refers to as a promising scheme that was never put to the test.

Are we to believe that a scheme is any less traitorous because it had previously been considered? And does the fact that Howe never acted on it, which Hughes takes for granted, reduce the whole matter, as he says, "to a bugaboo"? Was Arnold any less guilty because the papers in Major André's boot failed to reach their destination? The treason arose from General Lee's offering the plan to the enemy, not from the enemy's conduct after he received it.

Charles Francis Adams, on the other hand, brands Lee as a traitor, and says that if his plan had been effectively pursued in 1777 "it could hardly have failed to work."

With his letter notifying Germain of his change of plan Howe enclosed a copy of a letter that he was just then writing to General Carleton in Canada. It was dated 5 April 1777.

SIR: Having but little expectation that I shall be able, from the want of sufficient strength in the army, to detach a corps in the beginning of the campaign, to act up Hudson's river, consistent with the operations already determined upon, the force your

Excellency may deem expedient to advance beyond your frontiers after taking Ticonderoga, will, I fear, have little assistance from hence to facilitate their approach; and, as I shall probably be in Pennsylvania when that corps is ready to advance into this province, it will not be in my power to communicate, with the officer commanding it so soon as I could wish; he must therefore pursue such measures as may from circumstances be judged most conducive to the advancement of his Majesty's service, consistently with your Excellency's orders for his conduct.

The possession of Ticonderoga will naturally be the first object; and, without presuming to point out to your Excellency the advantages that must arise by securing Albany and the adjacent country, I must conclude they will engage the next attention; but omitting others, give me leave to suggest that this situation will open a free intercourse with the Indians, without which we are to expect little assistance from them on this side.

Sir William goes on to say that the northern army will find the friends of the government in that part of the country so numerous, and so ready to give every aid and assistance in their power, that it "will prove no difficult task to reduce the more rebellious parts of the province." He then promises that he will "endeavor to have a corps upon the lower part of Hudson's River sufficient to open the communication for shipping through the Highlands, at present obstructed by several forts erected by the rebels for that purpose, which corps may afterwards act in favor of the northern army."

A curious letter. Sir William clears his skirts in the first sentence. It is the Ministry who are to blame for his inability to act up Hudson's River. Nor does he mince matters about the fact that Sir Guy's army is to have little assistance "from hence" as he will probably be in Pennsylvania when the Canadian Expeditionary Force is ready to advance into New York.

Sir William's letter with its important enclosure must have had an unusually rough passage, for Germain did not receive it until the end of March. Lord George promptly advised Sir William of his Majesty's approval of the "deviation from the plan" previously suggested, being of the opinion that Sir

William's reasons for changing were "solid and decisive." He then adds, "but I must inform you that his Majesty is also of the opinion that a warm diversion upon the coasts of Massachusetts Bay, and New Hampshire, would not only impede the levies for the Continental army, but tend much to the security of our trade." Germain makes no comment on the neat way in which Sir William had exonerated himself in advance. Perhaps the busy minister read Howe's letter hastily and did not catch its real significance.

On the 26th of March, four days prior to the acknowledgment of Sir William's letter containing the change of plans, Germain had written Carleton a long letter of instructions for the launching of the campaign of the northern army down the valley of Champlain and the Hudson, in conjunction with which a diversion on the Mohawk under St. Leger was to be made. The letter is a little mixed. Germain says that Burgoyne is sailing to take charge of the expedition and "force his way to Albany," though Sir Guy is nowhere instructed to put Burgoyne in charge. The nearest that he comes to this is where he says:

That you should detach Lieutenant General Burgoyne, or such other officer as you should think most proper, with the remainder of the troops, and direct officer so attached to proceed with all possible expedition to join General Howe, and to put himself under his command.

With a view of quelling the rebellion as soon as possible, it is become highly necessary that the most speedy junction of the two armies should be effected.

Further on in the letter he specifies the exact troops that are to be assigned to both St. Leger and Burgoyne. He brings the letter to the following conclusion:

I shall write Sir William Howe from hence by the first packet; but you will nevertheless endeavor to give him the earliest intelligence of this measure, and also direct Lieutenant General Burgoyne and Lieutenant Colonel St. Leger to neglect no opportunity of doing the same; that they may receive instructions from Sir William Howe.

But, alas, that letter by the first packet was never to come. The copy of the letter of March 26th from Germain to Sir Guy Carleton was sent to Howe, as Germain said in his letter of April 19th, "by the last packet," and was acknowledged by Howe in his letter of July 5th. But by that time the British army had been withdrawn from New Jersey after a little fray with the Americans who tried to harass the rear of Cornwallis's forces, and were boarding the transports at Staten Island. "The embarcation," wrote Sir William, "is proceeding."

The Canadian campaign was proceeding on the lines of Burgoyne's own plan. The British had long intended to seize and probably to hold the line of the Hudson valley, but it was Burgoyne's "Thoughts for Conducting the War from the Side of Canada" that had put the idea into definite form. There had been some discussion of the "Thoughts" and some slight alterations from the original suggestion, but in the main the plan was Burgoyne's. References to "acting up the Hudson's river" had been cropping out in the correspondence between Sir William and the Ministry ever since he had come on the American scene. He was perfectly familiar with the idea. He knew it was important, perhaps even vital, and more than once he had been on the point of doing something about it himself. Now, however, his interest in the subject is hardly more than academic. He may have been piqued to think that others had taken it in hand. His thoughts are all in another direction.

Sir William wrote again on the 7th of July 1777, observing to his Lordship that the war was now "upon a far different scale with respect to the increased powers and strength of the enemy, than it was last campaign, their officers being now much better, with the addition of several from the French service, and a very respectable train of field artillery."

He mentioned the fact that Clinton had arrived and would be posted at New York.

A week later he wrote of receiving a letter from Burgoyne reporting his army before Ticonderoga, and mentioned with some irritation the fact that the Americans had made a foray in Rhode Island, which, while it in no way endangered the garrison there, had resulted in the kidnapping of Major-General Prescott. On the following day, the 16th of July, Sir William sat down for a somewhat lengthy chat with Germain. The letter is dated at New York.

My Lord: By the movement of the enemy's army in Jersey towards King's ferry, upon the North river, since the embarcation of his Majesty's troops from Staten Island, he seems to point at preventing a junction between this and the northern army, which will no further effect my proceeding to Pennsylvania than to make a small change in the disposition of the troops.

For if the enemy should cross the North river before I sail from hence, or should approach it so near as to give me a prospect of reaching Philadelphia before him, I shall, in either case, strengthen Sir Henry Clinton still more than by the reserve which is already ordered to remain here, in addition to the troops, mentioned in the return, under Sir Henry Clinton's command. He will then have sufficient force to act on the defensive against the whole rebel army; but as these additional troops will not be wanted here, if General Washington should march to the defense of Pennsylvania, I shall, in such event, order them to join me in that province. The enemy's movements taking this turn, I apprehend General Burgoyne will meet with little interruption, otherwise than the difficulties he must encounter in transporting stores and provisions for the supply of his army.

On the other hand if General Washington should march with a determination to force General Burgoyne, the strength of General Burgoyne's army is such as to leave me no room to dread the event: but if Mr. Washington's intentions should be only to retard the approach of General Burgoyne to Albany, he may soon find himself exposed to an attack from this quarter, and from General Burgoyne, at the same time; from both which, I flatter myself, he would find it difficult to escape.

Under the circumstances I propose going up the Delaware, in order to be nearer this place than I should be by taking the course of Chesapeak Bay, which I once intended, and preferred to that of the Delaware, provided the enemy had discovered a disposition to defend Pennsylvania.

Sir William changes his plans so fast that the Ministry is quite unable to keep up with him. Hardly has Germain had time to secure the approval of Sir William's plan for an invasion of Pennsylvania by way of Chesapeake, before he is advised that the Delaware had been selected as a better vantage point. The letter written by Germain on May 18th sounds a little tired of all this re-arrangement and vacillation. He says:

As you must, from your situation and military skill, be a competent judge of the propriety of every plan, his Majesty does not hesitate to approve the alterations which you propose; trusting, however, that whatever you may meditate, it will be executed in time for you to co-operate with the army ordered to proceed from Canada, and put itself under your command. . .

I will not enter into a particular consideration of the advantages which may be expected from a successful execution of your present plan . . . but am inspired with no small degree of hope that this campaign will put an end to the unhappy contest. . .

His Majesty does not hesitate to approve the alterations, *but* he trusts that whatever his general may meditate, *it will be executed in time for him to co-operate with Burgoyne.* This was written in the spring, but the summer was far spent before Sir William was to make answer to it. Indeed, when he wrote his answer he was in camp at the Head of Elk River in Maryland. The date was the 30th day of August 1777.

Sir William notes with pleasure the king's consent to his last change of plans (he had since changed them again from the Delaware to the Chesapeake!), but says that it is with much concern that he is to answer that he cannot flatter himself that he will be able to "act up to the King's expectations" with respect to finishing the recovery of the province of Pennsylvania in time to co-operate with the northern army, as his progress, "independent of opposition from the enemy's principal army, must be greatly impeded by the prevailing disposition of the inhabitants," who, he is sorry to observe, seem to be strongly "in enmity" against the British, many having taken up arms, and by far the greater number having deserted their homes, driving off at the same time their stock of cattle and horses.

After what had happened on Long Island and in New Jersey this would seem to have been a wise precaution on the part of the Americans.

In ending his letter Sir William again complains that an adequate army was not furnished him as requested, adding with some heaviness of heart that he conceived such an army to have been necessary for bringing the war to a conclusion this campaign, which he now has "not the smallest hope of effecting" with his present force.

That Sir William was well aware of the earnest desire on the part of the Crown and the Ministry that he should co-operate with the army of the North cannot be denied. That he was well aware of the military value of the move is indicated by the statement of Sir Henry Clinton, who wrote: "I owe it to truth to say there was not I believe a man in the army except Lord Cornwallis and General Grant who did not reprobate the movement to the southward and see the necessity of a co-operation with General Burgoyne."

When Howe finally informed Clinton of his decision to go to Philadelphia by sea, Clinton refused to believe it. He thought it a feint to deceive the British as well as the Americans so that the news would not leak out. Among the *Clinton Papers* was found a memorandum addressed to Captain Drummond on which Sir Henry had written: *

By God these people can not mean what they give out they must intend to go up Hudson's river & deceive us all, if they do I for one forgive.

* W. L. Clements Collection.

That Sir William never received any positive instructions
to act up the Hudson in co-operation with Burgoyne is now
generally conceded. That Lord George intended to send
him such instructions is equally plain; but when one cold
day he stopped at the office to sign his dispatches on the way
to the country and found that the orders for Howe had not
been "fair copied" he blew up. Must his horses stand outside in the cold while he waited for such things to be done,
he demanded. D'Oyley, who handled the war business in
the office, said that he would send Howe the copy of the Burgoyne orders, so that his Lordship would not have to wait.
Howe's own orders could be attended to later. The copy
of the Burgoyne orders was sent, but the orders to Howe were
forgotten.

This explanation first appeared in the *Life of Lord Shel-
burn,* and has since been substantially corroborated by William Knox who was under-secretary to Germain.* Howe
himself when questioned in regard to the matter at his Enquiry before Parliament, said, "the letter intended to have
been written to me by the first packet and which was probably to have contained some instructions, was never sent."
Nor was Germain of the Colonial Office, or D'Oyley of the
War Office able to prove that any such letter was ever written.
The fact that Sir William never received the letter, however, does not exculpate him from the charge that he understood perfectly that the co-operation of his army up the Hudson was an integral part of the plan. And, knowing that it
was desired and expected by the Ministry, and that it was advocated by all of his staff except Cornwallis and Grant, he
must have had some very compelling reason for picking up
his army and starting off in the opposite direction.

It now seems highly likely that this compelling reason
arose directly or indirectly out of the plan submitted by
General Lee. It was such a plan as would appeal to the

* *Knox MSS.*

conciliatory Howe. Seize Philadelphia and save Pennsylvania from the encroachments of the rebels. Bring Maryland back into the fold. Keep Virginia from marching aid to corrupt friendly Pennsylvania — and the whole rebel machine is "dissolv'd and a period put to the war."

Without the accompanying intimidation of Virginia and the reduction or submission of Maryland, Lee thought the capture of Philadelphia unimportant. Sir William did not wholly agree with this. To him the taking of Philadelphia was the main theme with Virginia and Maryland as side issues. Once he had the city with the friendly people of Pennsylvania all around him, the timid Loyalists of Maryland, and even of Delaware and Virginia would have a rallying-point. To Sir William it was a splendid vision full of hope and promise of a bloodless victory.

Co-operation with the Burgoyne plan would have been an important step towards a military victory. It can scarcely be doubted that Sir William was well aware of this. The truth seems to be, however, that Sir William was not at this time any more interested in a crushing military victory than he had been at Brooklyn, or at New York, or at White Plains, or during the remarkable race across New Jersey. He was still chasing that will-o'-the-wisp, conciliation.

This may have been bad generalship. It may have been poor judgment. It may even have been very stupid from a political point of view. But at least Sir William can not in this instance be charged with inconsistency.

CHAPTER XIV

HE TAKES A CAPITAL

W HEN CHARLES LEE was fighting the French and Indians on the side of the British during the winter of 1755–1756 he took a great fancy to the Mohawks. The Indians reciprocated by making him a blood-brother and christening him with the delightful name *Ounewaterika,* which means boiling water. He was well named, for wherever he went somebody was in hot water. He had made no end of trouble for Washington before his capture, and was destined to make more for him at a later date. Just now he was turning his attention to Sir William.

After his capture he had been held at New Brunswick until the 13th of January 1777 when Sir William had ordered him taken to New York and confined in a room at the City Hall. The British had talked of trying him for treason, and General Howe had written to Germain for orders. Germain had promptly instructed Sir William to send the captive general to England by the first ship of war that he might be tried there; but Washington had raised so much of a to-do and had threatened such severe reprisals on the captured Hessian officers still in his hands, that Lee never was sent. He was at a later date exchanged. For the present, however, he was in a position to exercise his peculiar talents on Sir William, and his plan of the 29th of March had started things nicely.

During the entire period of Lee's captivity reports were everywhere spread in patriot circles of the cruelties and indignities heaped upon him. Lee himself must have heard of these stories, and though they were apparently made out of whole cloth it was a long time before he ever took the trouble to deny them. He no doubt enjoyed the role of martyr. The cantankerous Judge Jones is not so reticent, however. He tells us that General Lee was confined in the Council Chamber of the City Hall, "one of the genteelest public rooms in the City, square, compact, tight, and warm." A sentry, says the Judge, stood at the door. Firewood and candles were provided for the prisoner, and he had directions to order a dinner every day from a public house, sufficient for six people, with what liquor he wanted, and of what kind he pleased. He had the privilege of asking any five friends he thought proper, to dine with him each day. "This," exclaims the disgusted jurist, "was all furnished at the expense of the nation."

The fact that Lee was maintained at the public expense seems to have annoyed the Judge. He speaks of it more than once. He was also annoyed because Hull "who kept the City arms in New York" waited upon Lee at General Howe's orders every morning with a bill of fare from which Lee ordered his own dinner and his own liquors. "It was cooked at Hull's," he adds, "and always upon the table at the time appointed. His servant had free access to him at all times."

In spite of all these privileges and considerations Lee was not happy in his confinement. Perhaps he was unable to get hold of congenial guests to share his splendid dinners and choice liquors, for we find him writing to Washington:

I am likewise extreamly desirous that my Dogs should be brought as I never stood in greater need of their Company than at present.

After Lee's capture his dogs had been gathered up with his surtout coat and his other belongings and sent back to his home in Virginia, and Washington, who was himself fond of dogs and who always had packs of them around at home, replied with some feeling:

Your dogs are in Virginia. This circumstance I regret, as you will be deprived of the satisfaction and amusements you hoped to derive from their friendly and companionable dispositions.

Perhaps it was sheer ennui that drove the captive general to the drafting of plans by which the British might be able to bring the war to a favorable close.

That Sir William had the authority of the Ministry for the move against Philadelphia by sea cannot as we have already seen be questioned. He also had authority, if not pretty definite orders, to make a "warm diversion" upon the coast of Massachusetts Bay and New Hampshire, which he had promptly declined to undertake. Orders from the spineless Germain seldom stood in the way of anything Sir William really wanted to do. It is very doubtful if, feeling the way he did, he would have sent his army up the Hudson in response to the most positive orders from the Ministry. He had already told Carleton that the northern army could count on no help from him until it was ready to move on the highlands of the Hudson only a few miles above New York. Sir William's campaign of pacification and voluntary submission had nothing to gain from up-river New York, but it had a great deal to look forward to from an expedition into Pennsylvania by way of Maryland and Virginia.

General Lee had told Sir William what he most wanted to hear; and, having heard it, Sir William stopped his ears to all else. Clinton pointed out the military weaknesses of the southern expedition, and the folly of leaving Burgoyne to fight his way unaided through the difficult country that lay between Canada and Albany. Always General Clinton was pointing out some mistake or weakness to Howe, and always Howe was disregarding Clinton's advice to his subsequent

regret.   If Clinton's advice had been followed Bunker Hill
would probably have been taken by the British without the
loss of a man.   They had differed over the campaign in New
Jersey, and over the expedition to Rhode Island.   Indeed,
it is not unreasonable to suppose that Sir William sent Clinton on some, perhaps all, of those far off campaigns more
to get rid of him than anything else.   They used to admit to
each other that they had never been able to agree on a single
question.   Howe did not hesitate to say that it was impossible for them to live together in harmony.   Clinton hated
to serve under Howe, and Howe knew it.   And now Howe
was planning to take his splendid army on the greatest campaign that he had yet attempted — and leave Clinton behind
with an insignificant garrison to hold New York — and perhaps the sack.

The *Clinton Papers* * are full of the quarrel.   Clinton was
touchy.   He brooded for days over an imagined slight in a
careless remark of Sir William's concerning the move against
Rhode Island, and jotted down conversations and intended
conversations with his chief over an "unfriendly insinuation."
He was "picqued" and mortified over the "tweedledum business" of the landing at Throg's Neck where the enemy was
not near.   By "some cursed fatality" they could never seem
to draw together.   He thought he had reason to believe "by
some circumstances" that the General had intimated pri-
vately his disapprobation when he had given a public approbation.   Clinton was forever feeling hurt and aggrieved and
wanting to resign — though he never did it — and Sir William was lamenting that Clinton was determined never to
serve under him.

Then they would patch things up.   Sir William would ex-
press his high opinion of Clinton as an officer and a man, and
Clinton would go away mollified until the next time.   In
Clinton's minutes of their discussion of July 8th, 1777, Clin-

* W. L. Clements Collection.

ton notes himself as saying to his chief, "I was never fond of this War," and "was not a Volunteer at first." "I told him freely my opinion of this War; and his was that another Campaign would do it even with the present Army; I confess I doubted, and said no Rebellion could be quelled by Armies on the defensive." Sir William seemed to be "struck"; he thought if he could take Philadelphia, Jersey would fall. Clinton told him the "Government did not seem to hold that language," and declared freely "and too freely" he thought this must finish it. At this Sir William is reported to have stared.

Clinton went on to speak of the interposition of the French and gave it as his opinion that "more Troops would certainly be sent tho' late." The memorandum rambles on, and without any realization of the immense importance to posterity of what he is writing, Clinton puts down in a few brief lines the most revealing words he is ever to write concerning his superior officer. He furnishes the key to the mysterious campaign against Philadelphia. He tells why Sir William is willing to sacrifice Burgoyne, to risk New York, and to snub his second-in-command.

Sir Henry had remarked that it was a general idea that the British had no friends in America. He said that it was to be lamented if there were none, but he thought that there were. To this Sir William replied that he had every reason to believe that there were "in Pensilvania, & that they were tired of the war."

Clinton was skeptical. He reminded Sir William that he had thought the same of New Jersey. Sir William agreed, but owned that he had been disappointed. Then comes the all-important part:

he perfectly agreed, & said it must be flattering &c &c to a great Nation to conquer by its friends and keep with little Assistance afterwards, whereas the present plan seemed to be on false principles, that if he Conquered (which I doubted more and more every day) he must afterwards keep, which was impossible.

There is Sir William's policy in a nutshell.   He wanted to
conquer America by its friends, and keep it with little assistance afterwards.   He wanted, as he had always wanted,
conciliation and voluntary submission.   A conquest by the
sword from across the seas, which must afterwards be held by
the sword, seemed to him not only to be on false principles,
but impossible.   He has been told by General Lee, and perhaps by others, that there are hosts of loyal friends in Pennsylvania, enough to furnish the necessary nucleus for conciliation.   General Lee is so sure of it that he is willing to
risk his life on the outcome.   Why bother with battling his
way up the Hudson with so fair a prospect of voluntary submission calling to him from beyond the Delaware?

Clinton, little dreaming of the importance his notes will
have taken on a hundred years hence, writes prosaically on.
"His great hopes seemed to be the Arming of friends. . . I
told him with regard to his present plan I saw it a good one
upon the principle of raising friends &c, but I thought the
time of Year bad, and that the better Move would be to act
upon the Hudson's river, form if possible the Junction and
then the 4 Provinces were crushed . . . that I dreaded the
time of year and thought it better to close the Campaign by
that than begin it."

The memorandum rambles on as Clinton sits in an idle
moment making history.   "In proposing this I had no selfish
views, for in mine I could only act as a subaltern, in his I
should probably be in a degree independent. he agreed; I
lamented that he was obliged to act on the defensive in two
places to enable him to act offensively in a third . . . he
agreed but said he had sent home his plan, it was approved
& he would abide by it.   I said certainly that mine was not
exactly the same & reminded him of what I had proposed before I went to Rhode Island about Chesepeak &c. that in
Winter it would have done. he agreed."

Clinton's jealousy of Burgoyne comes into the memorandum. He is complaining that "so many things had been done" to mark his "insignificancy" that he felt himself hurt.

"I would not repeat them, the principal was however Burgoyne's being sent with a respectable Command, have the intire planning of his whole Operations, as it appears by Mr. Carleton's to him. he made answer it was my own fault, for I ought to have insisted upon that Command. I told him I had a delicacy upon those matters that would not permit me to do anything of the kind. that I had mentioned to my friends that I was satisfied. if I asked the Command of the Northern Army when it came in Communication with his, he would give it me. in answer to which he said he thought it right to tell me, having reconsidered it, that he could not give me the Command of the Northern Army this Campaign, for that would be disgracing Burgoyne. I told him I was much obliged to him for being so ingenuous with me, that I agreed with him in the Opinion, & wou'd not have put him to that difficulty by refusing me. . . I told him I thought Burgoyne would ever be the fitter person for that Command, that he must ever think so, at least my delicacy would ever make me think so, & prevent my asking it."

Clinton's delicacy was a great obstruction to his success. It kept him on the lookout for slights and injuries and in due time developed into a full-fledged complex of inferiority. He once jotted down in a cipher memorandum that he had served so well in all he had been given to do that Howe could not forgive it.*

Perhaps it is just as well for Clinton's subsequent career that he did not have the Canadian command; though it is very doubtful whether he would have received it even if he had been ever so insistent, for the Burgoyne command was a creature of the Burgoyne brain. There would probably have been no such command but for Gentleman Johnny's "Thoughts for Conducting the War from the Side of Canada."

Had Clinton but known it a very splendid command was coming to him at the termination of this expedition against

* *Clinton Papers,* Clements Library.

Philadelphia, but splendid as it was, he was not going to be any too happy to get it, and it was going to be his undoing. That, however, was some time in the future, and meanwhile the differences with his chief were keeping poor Clinton's nerves on edge. He protested that he was being left in New York to a "damned starved defensive." Sir William listened but his answer was short. He said that he could not spare another man.

Sir William tried to calm Clinton's troubled spirits. He said he was sorry to leave him so "intirely on the defensive, but lamented the necessity," and added that if Clinton saw an opportunity of acting offensively, he might, and promised that "if success where he was going was as much as he wished, but dare not expect" he should probably send Clinton "half his Army," and leave Clinton to act with it either at Rhode Island or in the Hudson River.

Even this did not satisfy Clinton. He thought the chances of such a success as Sir William had in mind altogether too remote, and tried to scare him with a spectre of Washington attacking New York. Washington would assemble ten thousand men in Westchester, he said, and would force a landing at Harlem Plains. The rebel general, he declared, would risk all to take New York.

Clinton was right about that. He had read the rebel general's mind with the utmost perception. Washington coveted New York. It was the apple of his eye. He never stopped wanting it above all things. For him the war was not over until the British were out of New York — and that was some two years after Yorktown. But just how Washington was going to be able to take or to hold New York without a single gunboat does not appear.

Howe stood firm. He said the rebels had no cannon. The memorandum continues: "I said that Washington had one of three things to do, — March in force against Burgoyne — Murder us in his (Howe's) absence — or meet the General at his landing, that I thought an attempt upon us most likely, as it was of the most consequence." Howe said everything to convince Clinton he would not spare him a man, and Clinton "therefore went on describing" his situation.

There was talk of making a diversion up the Hudson River, and they agreed that it ought not to be done until Howe had landed and could see what force was opposed to him, though they were agreed that the rebels would not "risk a Battle to save Philadelphia." Clinton was of the opinion that Washington had already detached a great force to meet Burgoyne, and Howe said he hoped Washington would go with his whole army, "for that he never could come back & could not live there." Clinton did not know whether he could come back, but he was sure Burgoyne "cou'd not come forward, upon which depended the whole Campaign." Howe said he hoped to see Burgoyne no further than Albany — a needless touch of jealousy perhaps.

Howe's guesses were both right and wrong. Washington did not go north to meet Burgoyne, but he did risk a battle to save Philadelphia. Clinton gave up, but he continued to bare his heart in his diary. "In speaking of my own force, I told him tho' reputed 7,000 Men, I was barely 5,000 effective. he thought it possible. I said further that half of it was Militia. that was too true. in short it is a damned starved defensive."

So Clinton was left to his damned starved defensive, and Howe's troops went on the transports. He had written July 5th that the embarkation was proceeding. He wrote again on July 16th that the troops were all on board, but that the fleet was still in port. Then came a long silence. The summer was drifting away, and the Ministry was without a word from the Commander-in-Chief. Fall came. The leaves were beginning to turn. Perhaps they had already fallen from the trees; for it was not until the 28th of October that Lord George received his next dispatch from Sir William. By that time the fleet had landed. The battles of Brandywine and Germantown had been fought. But the letter was not concerned with these matters; it was dated August 30, 1777, and was written from the Head of Elk, Maryland.

My last dispatches advised your Lordship of the embarkation of the army at Staten Island, from whence the fleet sailed on the 23rd of July, and arrived off the capes of Delaware on the 30th following; when, from information, I judged it most advisable to proceed to Chesapeak Bay; but meeting with constant unfavorable winds, we did not enter the bay until the 16th instant; from which time the winds proving fair, the fleet arrived at the mouth of the Elk River on the 22d, through a very difficult navigation; and the army landed on the 25th at Elk Ferry, the enemy's army being then in the neighborhood of Philadelphia. . .

The enemy's army is at this time encamped behind Brandywine creek, with an advanced corps at White-clay creek; their force consists of about 15,000 men, including militia; nevertheless I am of opinion, it will be a difficult matter to bring them to a general action, even though it should be in defense of Philadelphia. . .

P. S.   The enclosed Declaration I have published to endeavor to quiet the minds of the people at large in Pennsylvania and the counties to which it has relation, led astray by the leaders in rebellion, as well as with an intent to disunite their army. A Counter Proclamation is also ready to issue when expedient.

Sir William had not lingered off the Delaware Capes.   He had stopped just long enough to find out that Washington's army had not gone up the Hudson River.   This must have been reassuring; for if Washington had not taken the all-important step before this time it was practically certain that he never would.   The brothers Howe bobbed at anchor off the Capes and asked a few questions of Loyalist pilots and skippers in the neighborhood, and when they heard of all the shoals and tides and shore-batteries, and the rivers to cross before they could get to Philadelphia by way of the Delaware, they quickly decided to push on up the Chesapeake and to approach the capital by the back door.   Very little persuasion was necessary. Howe had from the first preferred the Chesapeake route, perhaps because Lee had preferred it, or possibly because of the favorable impression he hoped his amazing fleet of 225 sail would make on the inhabitants of Virginia and Maryland. There was no lack of accord between the brothers on this point, and when the Admiral was told by a naval officer that the Delaware route was not feasible because "the rebels had filled it with obstructions" Sir William was perfectly willing to go the longer way.

He had by this time ceased worrying about Burgoyne. Why worry when he was unable to do anything to help him ? Nor is he particularly worried about the fact that the rebel army is planted across his path. He still thinks that Washington will avoid a general action as he did during the Jersey campaign. Sir William seems to forget that the rebels, too, must occasionally play at politics. They could no more abandon Philadelphia to its fate without a fairly convincing gesture of defense, than they could abandon New York even after it was under the British guns.

And, true to form, here was Sir William with a Declaration of amnesty and forgiveness even before his feet had touched dry land.

DECLARATION

Sir William Howe, regretting the calamities to which many of his Majesty's faithful subjects are still exposed by the continuence of the rebellion, and no less desirous of protecting the innocent, than determined to pursue with the rigors of war, all those whom his Majesty's forces, in the course of their progress, may find in arms against the King, doth hereby assure the peacable inhabitants of the province of Pennsylvanis, the lower counties of the Delaware, and the counties of Maryland on the eastern shore of Chesapeak Bay. . .

Security and protection are likewise extended to all who . . . have acted illegally in subordinate stations (jurists, legislators, and the like are not to be firgiven!), and conscious of their misconduct, been induced to leave their dwellings; provided such persons do forthwith return, and remain peacably at their usual place of abode.

Leniency is extended to officers and men actually in arms against his Majesty who recant and desire to return to their due allegiance.   And a free and general pardon is promised to all such as shall come and voluntarily surrender themselves to any detachment of his Majesty's forces before the day on which it will be notified that said indulgence is to be discontinued.   The declaration is dated August 27th 1777, and is signed by the General alone.   The earlier proclamations had been signed by both the General and the Admiral.

Another forty days passed before Sir William again took his pen in hand to drop the Ministry a line to let them know what had been taking place in America since his last.   The letter, which is dated at Germantown, October 10, 1777 covers nine printed pages, and reports almost in diary form the movements and successes of the British troops on September   3–6–9–11–12–13–14–16–17–18–19–20–21–22–23–25 — and on up to October 4th when the Battle of Germantown was fought, and the last obstruction removed from the path to Philadelphia and to the hearts of the loyal Pennsylvanians on whose co-operation General Charles Lee had so extravagantly expressed a willingness to stake his troubled life.*

Two columns, one under Cornwallis and the other under Knyphausen, "fell in with a chosen corps of 1000 enemy advantageously posted in a wood, which they defeated."   One night the two armies slept only four miles apart, but attempted no surprises, and the next morning the enemy moved on, taking position on the heights east of the Brandywine. On the 11th, at daybreak, the army advanced in two columns, the right under Knyphausen arrived at Chad's Ford in front of the enemy, and the Queen's Rangers under Captain Wemyss "distinguished themselves in a peculiar manner." What the peculiar manner was is left to the imagination. Knyphausen, however, "kept the enemy amused in the course

---

* Montresor notes as to the Battle of Germantown, "During the action this day, the countenances and actions of many of the inhabitants were rather rebellious and seem to indicate their wish for the rebels to regain the city."

of the day with cannon, and the appearance of forcing the ford, without intending to pass it until the attack upon the enemy's right should take place."

How well Knyphausen kept them amused is now history; for the second British column under Cornwallis swung round in a wide enveloping movement, and suddenly General Sullivan who was in command of Washington's right discovered that the enemy were behind as well as in front of him. It was by this time a familiar feeling to General Sullivan. He had made the same discovery at Long Island, and it had led to his capture. He did not want that to happen again. Sullivan was in a bad fix. His line was stretched along a creek through the forest for some two miles and he had just learned that the enemy were marching towards him in a line parallel with his — and back of it. He must hastily draw in that two mile line. He must turn it at right angles to its present position so that it would meet the oncoming British column, and he must while shifting his men keep them in fighting formation as they were likely to collide with the enemy at any moment.

The news had been slow in coming in. Once again Washington's scouts had failed him. Word had been sent from the Great Valley Road lying off to Washington's right as early as eleven o'clock that a large body of British were marching that way. But Washington had misunderstood the movement. He thought it a scouting detachment, and ordered Sullivan to push across the Brandywine and cut it off. Sullivan investigated and did not find the British line; that is, not until two o'clock in the afternoon, and by that time it had him neatly outflanked.

It was the story of Long Island all over again. The British were in the rear of the Americans. The hammer was poised above the anvil. All Howe had to do was to strike the blow. If he had said, "Push on to the attack!" America might still be saluting the British Jack and uncovering at the strains of "God Save the King." But Sir William was not thinking of crushing the enemy at just that moment; he was thinking of his hungry men who had been on the march since daybreak and had with their arms and heavy packs covered seventeen miles of rough country. So he gave the order to halt for dinner.

At half past three, the British having dined and rested, resumed their flanking movement. Their delay had given Sullivan and Stirling time to get their forces into some semblance of a line of defense. Sullivan in his haste had left a gap of half a mile in the new line, and the British found it and were soon pouring trouble into his exposed left flank. The Americans broke. The line crumbled in on itself, and had it not been for the masterly withdrawal of Greene, who was in command of the left, when Knyphausen ceased his amusing and launched his first real attack there would not have been much of an American army left to be hidden by the mantle of the night which finally settled down upon the rout and the slaughter and the confusion.

Greene put up so firm a retreating front that he enabled most of the artillery to be saved. The Americans drew off in the direction of Chester — and Sir William let them go. It was freely said by military men at the time that if the British had pressed their advantage at Brandywine, Washington's army would have spoken no more. Howe excused himself in his letter to Germain on the ground that his men were exhausted with their long march and the exertions of the battle, but added that the enemy's army barely escaped a "total overthrow" that must have been the consequence of an hour more of daylight. The point is that the enemy's army did escape, and Sir William missed another chance to be a hero.

Lafayette had by this time arrived in America. He had wheedled a major-general's commission from Congress back in July, and Brandywine was his first appearance under fire.

At the heels of his idol, Washington, he had ridden into the hottest part of the fight when a bullet struck him in the knee. In all the excitement the young Frenchman did not even know that he had been wounded until a brother officer called his attention to the blood running out of his boot. This did not stop him, however, and he went on with the fight until the colonial army had succeeded in backing itself off the field before taking the time to have the wound dressed.

Washington had left the field at Brandywine in such haste and confusion that he had been unable to take care of his wounded, and the next morning we find Howe, who ought by all good military standards to have been up and on the heels of his adversaries at daybreak, writing a courteous note suggesting that surgeons be sent to attend them as the British would not be "so situated as to give them the necessary relief." But Howe was not fighting according to military standards. He had something quite different on his mind. He was now in the midst of the most strongly Loyalist territory that he was ever to occupy and he was getting some real enjoyment out of his role as saviour. He lingered at Brandywine catching his breath and communing with the Loyalists who came to pay their respects while his burial squads went about interring the dead rebels, whose bodies had, as Montresor notes, "become very offensive."

If Sir William thought that he was through with Washington after the debâcle at Brandywine he was greatly mistaken, and when his army again took to the march after a day of rest he found the Americans waiting for him near the White House Tavern. Howe glanced over the terrain, and with his usual skill in tactics seized the high ground near the tavern and made ready for battle when an unexpected reinforcement came to the Americans in the form of a severe rain storm which beat in the face of the British and put the flintlocks of both the armies so completely out of business that the battle had to be called on account of the weather.

For a day or two the hostile armies bivouacked in the rain; then Washington withdrew hoping for a better chance to get in a telling blow at the British. A surprise attack he had planned on Howe's rear with the design of cutting off his baggage train proved so much of a failure that the attacking party was itself surprised in the night and so terribly punished that the encounter has since been referred to as the Paoli Massacre. Up to this time Congress, as a gesture of confidence in Washington's army had, with some nervousness, it is true, been sticking to its post in Philadelphia. But after the bloody affair at Paoli the august lawgivers tumbled out of their beds in the middle of the night and escaped to Trenton. They did not long remain at Trenton, however, but pushed on to Lancaster, and eventually to York which seemed safer to them.

One might think that Washington would have had enough of the British by this time, but he was still itching for a fight, and on September 23rd wrote to Putnam to hurry forward 2500 men from the camp on the Hudson. "Send on this detachment with the least possible delay," he says. "It is our first object to defeat, if possible, the army now opposed to us." The next day he wrote Gates at Saratoga asking him to return Colonel Morgan and the riflemen Washington had loaned him for use against Burgoyne. The letter was twelve days in reaching Gates who responded with characteristic conformity to Washington's wishes that he could not spare them as the deadlock with Burgoyne had not yet been broken.

Sir William was able to move about, seemingly where he wished, and still a battle did not develop. He passed through Valley Forge on the 21st, and with what may have been an uncanny prescience, set fire to the town and burned it to the ground. On the 25th in a downpour of rain his army moved into Germantown and took possession. The next day he sent Cornwallis to make a formal investment of Philadelphia. Cornwallis marched into the city at the hour when banks are supposed to take down their shutters and the stock market opens the board for the day's transactions. Montresor describes his reception as the acclamation of "some thousands of the inhabitants mostly women and children."

All this time Washington had been waiting for his chance. He wanted another battle, but he wanted it on his own terms. What he had been hoping for was such an opportunity as had been presented at Trenton — and suddenly he thought that he had found it. An intercepted letter indicated that Howe was dividing his forces and sending a detachment across the river to make an attack on Billingsport in New Jersey. Another Trenton ! It was more than Washington could resist. But if it was to be another Trenton he must move quickly.

Washington's plan was simple in conception though rather difficult to perform. Four main roads led into Germantown, and he proposed to send a column down each of these roads — and have the four arrive at the same time after an all-night march. The attack proper was to occur at daybreak. In spite of the hasty preparation the instructions to officers were detailed and elaborate:

General Armstrong to pass down the Ridge Road by Levering's Tavern and take guides to cross Wissahiccon Creek about the head of John Vandeering's mill dam so as to fall in about Jos'h Warners new house.

Smallwood and Foreman to pass down by a Mill, formerly Daniel Moriss's and Jacob Edjes Mill into the White marsh Road, at the Sandy Run — thence to White Marsh Church — there take the left hand road which leads to Jenkin's Tavern on the old York Road, then keep down the old York Road below Armitages beyond the Seven mile Stone; half a mile from which, a Road turns off short to the Right hand fenc'd on both sides, which leads through Enemy's Encampment at Germantown Market House.

As we read we are led to wonder how in the darkness of the night any of the four columns managed to reach its objective. It so happened that General Greene was half an hour late, for not only had his route been four miles longer than that of the other columns, but he had lost his way, and when he did finally get into town his line was wrong end to and had to be countermarched before he dared to trust it to go into battle.

Sullivan — hard-luck Sullivan — was the first to arrive, though Conway was the first actually to engage the foe. When the British patrol first spied Conway the 2nd Light Infantry were sent out to meet him.   Immediately afterward the 40th regiment under Colonel Musgrave came up as a reinforcement to the Light Infantry.   Conway was in such a bad way that Sullivan had to stop his advance and go to the rescue.   He saved Conway, but came very near being flanked in the embroglio.   With the aid of Mad Anthony Wayne, Sullivan reformed his forces and pushed on.   But he was met by the British advance before he had come up to the main body of their troops.

Watson in his *Annals of Philadelphia* tells of an old resident of Germantown who claims to have heard Sir William exclaim, "My God!   What shall we do?   We are certainly surrounded."   In his *Narrative* Sir William denies that the British were surprised, and says that he had received early notice of the enemy's intention, though he had hardly expected the rebel army to approach "so soon after so recent a defeat."   General Hunter, one of Howe's officers in the advance, pictures his commander as in anything but a funk.

"By this time General Howe had come up," he says, "and seeing the battalion retreating, all broken, he got into a passion, and exclaimed, 'For shame, Light Infantry, I never saw you retreat before, form! form! it is only a scouting party.' " *

If Sir William did show the white feather on this occasion,

* Montresor who was also on the spot says the British were "almost surprised."

it was the only time in his life. He may have been lazy and indolent, he may have been loose in his morals, he may have been infatuated with the dice-box and intrigued by the turn of a card, but he was no coward. Like Washington, to whom his resemblance was more than once noted, he did not know what fear was. He soon found out, however, that his army was beset by more than a scouting party, and fell back on his main body.

Colonel Musgrave did not fall all the way back to the main body of British troops. With about 120 men he established himself in the brick house of Benjamin Chew which stood in a point of land at the junction of two of Washington's converging roads, and enfiladed the columns of the Americans as they swept past. This so upset the plans of Washington, and so disorganized his units as to enable the British to form themselves to repel a heavy attack. And the kindly Providence that had sent a fog to protect Washington on the retreat from Brooklyn now sent another fog to mislead and confound him.

In the uncertain visibility the rebel forces led by General Stephen collided with a force under Mad Anthony Wayne who was hurrying back to support Sullivan and was crossing a space that had already been cleared of British. After a sharp engagement both units broke and ran away from each other. A few moments later Stephen's men fled again from a number of British who were trying to surrender to them. The confusion of Wayne's detachment occurred at a vital moment. Greene's brigades when they did finally arrive struck the British line with such an impact that they completely turned the right flank. Sullivan pushed in on the other side. This was where Wayne should have come in. The British were in a vise and somebody was needed to turn the handle. But Mad Anthony was lost in the fog. And presently Sullivan's men began to run out of ammunition.

Those in front fell back, and those in the rear fell further back. The moment of victory had come. It had flickered with uncertainty for a brief space. And then it had passed. Once again Howe had won the day; and once again he made no effort to push home his victory. Washington had marched his army some twenty miles the night before to get at the British, and now he marched the jaded and broken men twenty-five miles back, all the way to Pennypacker's Mills before he dared to let them camp.

But he need not have been so cautious. Howe had no idea of following him. He had taken his "capital, as it were" and was now getting ready to march into it at the head of his splendid cohorts, after which he could be at home to the hosts of friends that he so firmly believed were awaiting his coming. He had been disappointed at the disposition of the inhabitants on his arrival at the Head of Elk.* Still, the Head of Elk was not Pennsylvania. Perhaps he had made a mistake not to have followed Lee's plan more literally. It might have been better if he had seized Annapolis, and if he had sent troops up the Potomac. Raising friends in Pennsylvania was the backbone of the plan, however, and here he was in Pennsylvania. Now he would see!

* Letter to Germain of August 30th.

CHAPTER XV

A SURRENDER — AND A RESIGNATION

MAD ANTHONY WAYNE was not the only one to get lost in that morning fog at Germantown. The confusion was so great that even General Howe's dog was unable to find his way around. He fell in with Washington's men and retreated with them all the way to Pennypacker's Mills before he discovered his mistake. After he had reached the American camp and his identity had been established he was haled before the Commander-in-Chief.

Washington could, according to the military code, have treated the captive as a spoil of war. But he was too fond of his own dogs to keep the pet of another, and with the thousand and one things of real importance that he had to do, he found time to write a note to General Howe, which he ordered to be sent back with the dog.

General Washington's compliments to General Howe, — does himself the pleasure to return to him a dog, which accidentally fell into his hands, and, by the inscription on the collar, appears to belong to General Howe.

This meant that somebody had to go back, presumably on foot, twenty-five miles with the dog, or at least to the nearest picket-line where contact could be made with the British. Then there must be all the bother of a flag of truce and a communication party hailing the foe and going forward un-

armed.   What the British sentries may have thought when
they saw the dog marching forward under the flag of truce
can only be conjectured.

Sir William's response, whatever it was, has been lost; but
we may be sure that the general who would invite the enemy
to send back surgeons to attend his wounded left on the field
after a battle, would not be lacking in his acknowledgment
of the return of a lost dog.   Surely there were gentlemen in
those days, and there were social amenities that must be observed even if the war had to be temporarily suspended in
the meantime.   Washington and Sir William had no small
amount of respect for each other as individuals though they
did not always agree on matters of generalship.   They
wrangled occasionally over the exchange of prisoners almost
to the point of heatedness, but it is safe to say that if Sir
William had been making a peacetime visitation to the provinces, instead of bringing war against them, Washington
would have been among the first to throw open the hospitable doors of his spacious home to the distinguished
visitor.

Washington was fond of cards himself.   He liked to place
a small bet on any game of chance.   His diaries speak frequently of his winnings and losses at cards, and even mention
little wagers that he placed on horse-races and cockfights.
Nor was he at all squeamish about taking a drink, if it was
good liquor.   Indeed, we have his own word for it that he
was still on his feet after some thirty-six toasts at an entertainment given to members of the first Continental Congress by
the city of Philadelphia.   And Sir William could not possibly have enjoyed dancing any more than the future Father
of his Country who had never been known to miss a ball,
and who in spite of his huge stature and his big feet, was,
according to legend, a model of grace on the ballroom floor.

The two had much in common, and if by the very nature of the situation they had not been aligned as enemies

they would undoubtedly have been friends. John Adams, on the other hand, could never have been Sir William's friend. John despised royalty, and was forever sneering at the aristocracy. He regarded himself as a great thinker. He took himself seriously. He permitted himself no frivolous side, and described the brilliant function at which Washington had drunk so many toasts as "a most sinful feast" with "twenty sorts of tarts, fools, trifles, floating islands and whipped sillabubs." He did admit, however, that the wines were "most excellent and admirable" and that he drank Madeira "at a great rate."

That is about as near as John Adams ever came to letting himself have a good time with the little things of life. He hated the Howes and never could see them as anything but a couple of big bullies or designing wretches who had come to America to frustrate the simple joys of a handful of settlers who were acting entirely within their rights. He speaks of Lord Howe as "that rare curiosity," and regards the attempts to make a peace at Staten Island as "a bubble, an ambuscade, a mere insidious manoeuvre, calculated only to decoy and deceive." The proposal of Lord Howe brought by General Sullivan to Congress is the "most insidious, tho' ridiculous Message which you can conceive." Without knowing anything about it John Adams does not hesitate to say that he believes the two Howes "have not very great women for wifes." He thinks that if they had, America would have suffered more from their exertions than it did. "A woman of good sense," he adds, "would not have let her husband spend five weeks at sea in such a season of the year. A smart wife would have put Howe in possession of Philadelphia a long time ago." The letters of John Adams would have had much more real worth if they had not so obviously been written for posterity. And in the case of the one last quoted it must be remembered that he was writing to his own wife.

Having captured Philadelphia, Howe would have been

glad to settle down there and take his ease while the vast loyalist population of the surrounding country came flocking in to sign their declarations of fidelity to the King and perhaps to enlist in the loyal militia that he was known to have in mind. He would undoubtedly have done that very thing if a certain matter of pressing importance had not been brought home to him: he and his army had to eat. Not that the British did not have ample supplies on their boats; but simply that the food transports could not be brought to Philadelphia so long as the patriots held the forts on the Delaware. Without the freedom of the Delaware, Philadelphia was no less than a death-trap for the British.

Had Washington comprehended the full importance of the situation Yorktown might have been anticipated by some four years. Until the capture of the forts on the Delaware the British in Philadelphia never had more than a week's supply of food on hand as all supplies had to be brought in by flatboats which ran the gauntlet of the forts by night. But Washington never realized the vital power that the possession of these defenses had placed in his hands. Instead of manning them and strengthening them, he paid no attention to them at all for two vital weeks after the Battle of Germantown, but hung around on the outskirts of the city looking for another chance to hurl his undisciplined men against the well-trained forces of the British now securely entrenched behind redoubts.

Howe, too, was taking his time. No doubt he had his eye on Washington, and at the first move to reinforce or rebuild the forts would have leaped upon him. "When at last," says Adams in his *Military Studies*, "a force of some two hundred men was thrown into Fort Mifflin (by Washington), it was found to be garrisoned by thirty militia only." In another place he describes these vital strongholds as "neglected, half-finished only, ill-garrisoned, unsupplied and unsupported," in spite of all of which they managed to hold out for six weeks; and General Greene afterwards gave it as the opinion of the best citizens of the city that if the forts had held out until the middle of the following week Sir William would have had to evacuate.

Meanwhile an event of primary importance had occurred in the rolling fields north of Albany. Burgoyne, outnumbered, surrounded, and cut off from supplies, had surrendered. This decisive event had taken place on October 17th though the official report from Gates did not reach Congress until October 31st. Even then it was not too late for a united patriot army strengthened by the guns and ammunition captured from Burgoyne to have rushed to the defense of the Delaware River forts. If Washington could have held them, the Americans might have had another surrendered army on their hands. But Gates, who had more personal ambition than patriotism, refused to let his armies go. He said that he was afraid that Clinton might dash up the river and capture the arsenal at Albany, and might possibly push on and recapture Ticonderoga. So the forts of the Delaware were lost, and Washington received the blame, which was, to all appearances just what Gates wanted.

It is true that Clinton had shown some inclination to go that way. He had received a number of frantic appeals from Burgoyne, though the two had found it difficult to get their letters through the rebel lines. Burgoyne's letters had an especially hard time. As Gates and Arnold tightened their strangle-hold on Gentleman Johnny he sent messenger after messenger to Arnold beseeching him for aid, or even for advice. But there was no answer. Among the letters from Clinton that did not get through is one written on August 10th that has since been much quoted by historians to show Clinton's state of mind at the time. It reads:

You will have heard Dr Sir I doubt not long before this can have reached you that Sir W. Howe is gone from hence. The Rebels imagine that he is gone to the Eastward. By this time however he has filled Chesapeak bay with surprize and terror.

Washington marched the greatest part of the Rebels to Philadelphia in order to oppose Sir Wm's army.   I hear he is now returned upon finding none of our troops landed but am not sure
of this, most part of his troops are returned for certain I am sure
this . . . must be vain to them.   I am left to command here,
half my force may I am sure defend everything here with as much
safety I shall therefore send Sir W 4 or 5 Bat'n.   I have too small
a force to invade the New England provinces, they are too weak
to make any effectual efforts against me and you do not want any
diversion in your favor I can therefore very well spare him 1500
men I shall try something certainly towards the close of the year
not till then at any rate, It may be of use to you to inform you
that report says all yields to you.   I own to you I think the
business will quickly be over now.   Sir W.'s move at this time
has been capital Washingtons have been the worst he could take
in every respect I sincerely give you much joy on your success
and am with great Sincerity

This letter has provoked no small amount of discussion,
especially the lines to the effect that Burgoyne wanted no diversion in his favor, and that Clinton thought the business
would quickly be over.   Only recently, however, in the *Clinton Papers* a mask was found through which the letter was
intended to be read.   Seen through the mask the letter reads
thus:

Sir
W. Howe
is gone to the
Chesapeak bay with
the greatest part of the
army.   I hear he is now
landed but am not
certain.   I am
left to command
here   with   a
too   small   a   force
to make any effectual
diversion in your favor
I shall try something soon
At any rate It may be of use
to you.   I own to you I think
Sr. W.'s move at this time
the worst he could take
uch joy on your

THE MASKED LETTER

Since Clinton had from the first believed that co-operation with the army from the north was a vital element to the success of the campaign as a whole, it was to be expected that he would do what he could to help Burgoyne. Sir Henry's hold on New York was none too secure. He was still left to his "starved defensive" with no more positive orders from Howe than the suggestion that if Clinton found that he could make "any diversion in favor of Burgoyne's approaching Albany without menacing the security to Kingsbridge," it was not necessary to point out the "utility" of such a measure.

With this half-hearted consent from Howe, General Clinton finally started up the river. He decoyed Putnam to the wrong side of the river by making a feint on Peekskill while he neatly captured forts Clinton and Montgomery even though the American General Clinton did put up a determined resistance. This cleared the river of American domination practically all the way up to Albany.

Sir Henry was astonished at himself. "Six days sooner or six hours later," he declared delightedly, "we should not have carried our point." This was probably true. Six days before MacDougall had been sent to Washington with 2000 reinforcements, and six hours later replacements sent by Governor Clinton might have arrived. In his enthusiasm Clinton began to see himself as something more than a stodgy garrison officer; it looked as if he might after all be the means of saving Burgoyne from his desperate plight, and might at the same time pluck off for himself the major part of the credit for having amputated New England from the rest of the colonies. But all this was a castle in Spain which vanished into thin air when Howe ordered the troops that Clinton had been using for his offensive operations to be sent to Philadelphia at once. Clinton blew up. "Good God!" he writes, "what a fair prospect blasted." It was the old Clinton jinx again. But Howe was the Commander-in-Chief. There was no appeal. So Clinton turned sadly back and

abandoned all that he had won.   He also abandoned Burgoyne to the tender mercy of an enemy who outnumbered
his army three to one and had him virtually surrounded.

Among the *Clinton Papers* is a memorandum in the hand-
writing of Clinton's secretary that bears all the earmarks of
having been composed by Clinton that reads:

> Had Sir Wm. Howe Fortified the Hills round Boston, he could
> not have been disgracefully driven from it: Had he pursued his
> Victory at Long Island, he had ended the Rebellion: Had he
> landed above the lines at New York, not a man could have
> escaped him: Had he fought the Americans at Brunswick he was
> sure of Victory: Had he co-operated with the Northern Army,
> he had saved it, or had he gone to Philadelphia by land, he had
> ruined Mr. Washington and his Forces; But, as he did none of
> these things, had he gone to the D—l, before he was sent to
> America, it had been the saving of infamy to himself and in-
> delible dishonour to this Country.

This may have been intended as a paragraph for Clinton's
book on his experiences in the war.   Or he may have written it merely to get it off his mind.   In either case it is a very
neat summary of the conduct of his superior officer, though
it gives no intimation of what Clinton thought to be the reason behind all these failures and shortcomings.

Sir William defended the Pennsylvania campaign very
spiritedly in his narrative before Parliament.   He disdains
to shelter himself behind the "complete approbation" as
well as the acquiescence of the Secretary of State, and proceeds to a full discussion of the merits of the proposed expedition into New England and up the Hudson River.   New
England he dismisses with a word.   It is too strongly rebel;
Washington would have had too much help from the country.   The Hudson River is different.   There Sir William
would have had to fight his way through the fortified highlands against the "entire force of his opponent," and, had he
been successful he would have "wasted campaign with a considerable army" merely to "insure the progress of the north-

ern army, which could have taken care of itself," provided he had made a diversion by drawing General Washington off to the southward. Then, too, his enemies would have insinuated that he had gone north merely to share in the glory that would otherwise have belonged to Burgoyne. And, last but not least, he had never received any orders to co-operate with Burgoyne. By going into Pennsylvania, on the other hand, he would be entering a country where Washington could count on little local assistance, and where at the end of the campaign the British would be in possession of not one, but three provinces, as well as the capital of Pennsylvania, "the capital, as it were, and residence of the Congress in North-America, situated in one of the most fertile provinces of that Continent."

At this distance the argument seems a bit fatuous. From a military standpoint the move against Philadelphia was a colossal blunder, a blunder that would have been fatal to Howe if Washington had not matched it with a series of blunders equally colossal.* That Sir William himself knew the expedition to be a failure is evidenced by the fact that before he had been in possession of the city for three weeks he had written to Germain tendering his resignation. He based his resignation on the ground that he had not the "good fortune to enjoy the necessary confidence and support" of his superiors because of the "little attention" that had been given to his recommendations since the commencement of his command. That may have influenced him in his decision, but it is significant that his resignation took place immediately upon his learning of the disaster to the Burgoyne expedition, and after he was convinced that the project of "raising friends" on which he had staked all, was doomed to failure.

Three days before writing his letter of resignation he had received a letter from Germain, written on the 6th of Au-

* *Studies Military and Diplomatic.*

gust preceding, in which his Lordship had stated that it had always been his wish and his "constant endeavor" that Sir William should be supplied with as many men as he could "possibly stand in need of."

You will have received every reinforcement of the artillery companies which could possibly be spared from this country, and I am much concerned to find that you have been in the least degree disappointed in your expectation of being able to raise men for that corps.

Sir William had evidently been brooding over Germain's letter when he sat down to his desk on October 22rd. His answer covers a wide range of subjects before it comes to the matter of resignation at all. It is almost as if the idea came to him after the letter was half finished. He begins with a discussion of the want of brigadiers in the line, and after that, gives an extended apology and explanation for the tardiness of his dispatches, which he assigns to a lack of safe communication with the shipping. Then he comes to the report of General Burgoyne's surrender. As to this he says:

The rebels having reported that Lieutenant-General Burgoyne's army has surrendered prisoners of war, will no doubt send such account to Europe; and I mention this circumstance to your Lordship with my opinion, that it is totally false: though I confess from the tenor of General Burgoyne's letters and messages to Sir Henry Clinton, I apprehended the account the enemy has published of his retreat to be true. (This refers to his retreat only, not to his surrender.)

I was surprised to find the General's declaration in his message to Sir Henry Clinton by Captain Campbell, 'that he could not have given up his communications with Ticonderoga had he not expected a co-operating army at Albany:' since in my letter to Sir Guy Carleton, a copy of which was transmitted to your Lordship in my dispatch of the 2d April, 1777, and of which his Majesty was pleased to approve, I positively mention that no direct assistance could be given by the southern army. This letter I am assured was received by Sir Guy Carleton and carried by him to Montreal before General Burgoyne's departure from thence.

After this Sir William indulges in a rather lengthy discussion of plans for the next campaign, "there being no prospect of terminating the war to the advantage of Great Britain" in the present one. He is doubtful about the next campaign "unless ample succours be sent from Europe." The armies in New England must be "very powerful," he says, not less than 10,000 men, and he estimates the force necessary to send against the south at not less than 15,000, in addition to the garrisons to hold New York and Philadelphia. It is easy to believe that there was a long pause at this point in the writing of the letter as the subject matter suffers a complete change.

I must now beg leave to add a few words relative to my own situation in the important trust I have had the honor to hold, and in the discharge of which I can confidently affirm, that my sole view has been invariably confined to the advancement of his Majesty's interests.

From the little attention, my Lord, given to my recommendations since the commencement of my command, I am led to hope that I may be relieved from this very painful service, wherein I have not the good fortune to enjoy the necessary confidence and support of my superiors, but which I conclude will be extended to Sir Henry Clinton, my presumptive successor, or to such other servant as the King may be pleased to appoint. By the return therefore of the packet, I humbly request I may receive his Majesty's permission to resign the command.

In the very letter in which he resigns because of the little attention given to his recommendations, we find him making more recommendations, and very considerable ones involving new armies of some 25,000 troops. But for these new recommendations his plea of non-support by the Ministry might have had a leg to stand on, although it would seem on going over the records that Sir William and the Admiral had both been very handsomely supported. It is hard to avoid the conclusion that in spite of Sir William's assertion that he believed the report of Burgoyne's surrender to be "totally false," he knew it to be true. And he must have realized that a large part of the blame would fall on him. This being the case, the rebels instead of being awed and impressed by him would hold him in contempt. The loyal colonists would not come flocking to him, and his usefulness in the role of Great Conciliator to the Colonies was over.*

Once again Sir William Howe moved quickly. He managed to get in his resignation before the news of Burgoyne's surrender had time to be confirmed.

He made no further mention of Burgoyne in his correspondence until his letter of November 29th in which he reported that "by Lieutenant-General Burgoyne's convention with Major-General Gates the troops included therein were to have embarked from Boston" but on account of the scarcity of shipping there, had gone to Providence instead. He hoped that the Americans would not regard this as a violation of the convention. The matter came up again in his letter of November 30th where he states that "in consequence of the misfortune that has fallen upon the troops of Lieutenant-General Burgoyne's command, a considerable reinforcement from General Gates's corps has joined General Washington." He reports the hopes of "the people" as being greatly raised, with no prospect of a successful termination of the war "unless a respectable addition to the army is sent." Still more recommendations! Thus does Sir William forget himself.

Germain had heard rumors of the Burgoyne disaster when he wrote Howe on December 11th. He mentions his "poignant concern and mortification" over the reports, and ventures to remark that if they should prove true in their full extent "a material alteration in the plan of carrying on the war" must necessarily take place. He highly approves Clinton's operations up the river and says that it is only to be lamented that Clinton was not earlier in a condition to un-

---

* The most that he can say is that an "equivocal neutrality" was all that he at first experienced after risking everything for the sake of taking Philadelphia, though his Majesty's revolted subjects in this neighborhood were induced at last to be "less reserved." The *Narrative*, page 32.

dertake the enterprise. He does not mention Sir William's resignation in this letter, but feels that he must write a separate letter of the same date on the subject. These letters were received by Sir William on February 27th. Regarding the resignation Germain says:

> I am to acquaint you, that I had the honor of laying before the King your separate letter of 22d October, wherein you desire his Majesty's permission to quit your command.
>
> His Majesty received your request with concern. But as the particulars of Lieutenant-General Burgoyne's situation are still unknown, and your own campaign is not finished, I am not authorized at present to signify his Majesty's commands upon that subject.

Sir William replied on March 5th regretting that he had caused his Majesty any pain, but insisting that in the present instance "conceiving the confidence of his Majesty's minister to be withdrawn" which, he had the presumption to believe he had once possessed, he considered it a duty he owed the King, the minister, the public and himself humbly to request his "dismission."

It was not until the 4th of February 1778 that Germain advised Sir William that his Majesty was graciously pleased to order him to signify to Sir William his royal acquiescence of the request for leave to resign the command. Sir William was to stay on, however, until Sir Henry Clinton, who had been decided upon as his successor, should be able to take charge. A few days later Germain was writing Sir William somewhat guardedly about certain "salutary measures" then under the consideration of Parliament of which he would be fully informed by separate letter.

The separate letter was a circular letter. Once more the Ministry were going to make a try for peace.

CHAPTER XVI

THE WINTER IN PHILADELPHIA

TALK OF AN alliance with France had been in the air since Lexington and Concord when letters from France had first told of a strong sympathy on the part of the French for the Americans. The subject was discussed in Congress that fall, and within a month or two after the Congressmen had begun to talk about it a Committee of Secret Correspondence was appointed to feel out the sentiments of France. The committee began its work of "impenetrable secrecy" with a letter written by Dr. Franklin to Dumas asking him to sound the ambassadors at The Hague to see if he could detect any interest on the part of any European power in an alliance that would carry with it a commerce of some seven million pounds sterling.

From this time on the market was flooded with rumors, some of which, no doubt, originated with that master of publicity — father perhaps of our present-day school of press-agents and public relations counselors — Benjamin Franklin. There was a tale of a French fleet that was being built by Sweden to insure the freedom of the seas for other countries beside Britain. A little later a story "leaked out" of a naval concord between France and Spain insuring a joint navy that would far outnumber all the ships that Britain could assemble within a year. Before long this imaginary fleet was lurking in the West Indies, waiting only for America to pass the Declaration of Independence before wiping the shipping of Britain completely off the seas.

So persistent, indeed, did these rumors become that in June 1776 the British Cabinet met to discuss the menacing reports that seemed to be emanating from the shores of France and Spain, and voted to increase the number of guard-ships and marines. But the British were not the only ones to take this flood of propaganda seriously. In America, too, as Van Tyne tells us, "much comfort was derived from embracing these delusive phantoms of hope."

The British pamphleteers in an attempt to fight fire with fire practised their art with great industry, and on one occasion flooded the colonies with an *Address by the People of Great Britain to the Inhabitants of America,* a pamphlet which though it purported merely to offer a bit of friendly advice, was reeking with hatred of the French and intolerance of the "papish superstition" said to be back of their alleged interest in America. Loyalist pamphleteers in America also rushed into print with their animadversions on the French and their arguments against an independence from Britain that should be purchased at the price of a slavery to a "foreign power." In spite of all of which the image of a French alliance continued to grow.

America talked of it by day and dreamed of it by night, and France, though slow to take official action, was not unmindful of the unparalleled opportunity that was knocking on her door. It was no small matter to become embroiled in a war with Great Britain, even though the British were permitting themselves the extravagance of a civil war beyond the seas. Many Frenchmen were already fighting in the armies of the colonists, but France felt that officially she must hold off until sure of her ground. Powerful influences were at work in France, however, through which clandestine contact was made with the congressional Committee of Secret Correspondence. An under-cover man known as Bonvouloir was sent to Philadelphia where he met the five members of the committee in the dark. He made no advances, gave no promises, offered no definite guarantees. The most he would do was to intimate that the selling of arms and munitions was after all a mere matter of trade that could be transacted between one business man and another without troubling with the machinery of state. As to the difficulty of getting such contraband on ships and out of a neutral port, he was sure that the port officials would look the other way at the proper time.

Bonvouloir did not pretend to have any rights or any powers. He had merely a suggestion to offer, a sort of flutter of the eyelid. But the secret committeemen were overlooking no chances, and a few months after the conference with Bonvouloir the Congress authorized the sending of a secret mission to Paris. Silas Deane and Arthur Lee were to go on ahead. Dr. Franklin was to follow later. Like most of the secrets of state the purpose of this mission was well known abroad even before the members had sailed; and when they arrived in Paris in July 1776 they found the British diplomats there ahead of them ready to counteract in advance anything that they should undertake.

Had the aid of the French been compelled to pass through official channels, the secret commissioners would have had a difficult time indeed. But it was, as Bonvouloir had intimated, a purely private matter. A newly organized business firm known as Hortalez & Company was willing to run the risk of selling things to the Americans and finding the bottoms in which to get them out of port. Then the stream of guns, ammunition, clothing, supplies and all sorts of manufactured goods began to flow to America.

Hortalez & Company, as we now know, was simply another name for Pierre Augustin Caron de Beaumarchais, without whose aid, both moral and material, the success of the American Revolution must have failed or at least have been indefinitely postponed. The aspirations of the Americans had caught the imagination of the big-hearted Beaumarchais, and he threw himself into their cause with all his tremendous power and resourcefulness.

Beaumarchais argued, he cajoled, he taunted, he pointed the finger of scorn — and at last he won Louis XVI over to the idea of giving secret aid to America. In the matter of selecting and dispatching the most needed supplies Beaumarchais found Silas Deane a tireless and able helper. That Deane was afterward an object of political intrigue and ingratitude is neither here nor there. Beaumarchais himself is better remembered as the author of *Figaro* and the *Barber of Seville* than as one who devoted his heart, his labors, and his strength to the rising republic in America.

Franklin, now in his seventy-first year, arrived and took France quite by storm. The coonskin cap he wore to keep his old head warm was soon a familiar sight on the hatracks of all the first families. It became to the salons of Paris the symbol of liberté, égalité and **fraternité**. Everywhere he went he was received with enthusiasm and affection. Without him the American mission must have failed. Aside from Franklin the personnel of the mission was far from impressive. Though Deane was in his element as a purchasing agent he was no diplomat. He was awkward and inept in high places. Lee was even worse. From this distance he seems to have been a rather despicable person. Not only did he fail to inspire any confidence on the part of the French, but he indulged in such slanderous recriminations against his fellow commissioners that but for the steadying influence of Franklin the Americans would undoubtedly have gone home in disgrace. So the aged Franklin was burdened with the double duty of keeping the peace on his own commission while he tried to convince the reluctant Louis that it was to the interest of France to take a hand in the American war.

In spite of all Poor Richard's subtle blandishments, however, the French monarch held off until after the Battle of Saratoga. So it was, after all, the ragged Continentals instead of the sagacious Franklin who furnished the clinching argument.

The news of the Burgoyne disaster did not reach London until the 2nd of December, although Gentleman Johnny had laid down his arms and signed the famous Convention of surrender on October 17th. Within a month after the receipt of the dispatches from Saratoga both France and England were in a ferment. An open breach between the two countries, cabinet ministers were forced to admit, was a matter of days, or perhaps hours. It was, as Trevelyan says, a season for strong measures and strange proposals. England would have been glad if she could have forgotten America for the time being and devoted her attention to France. But things had gone too far for that. If she let up the pressure on America she would at once find the Americans on the side of France. Britain could not let go, nor could she hang on without burning her fingers. The only course that remained was for her to make peace with her colonies without delay. This, she was to find out, was something that was not so easy to do; it takes two to make peace just as it does to make war.

France had been watching events in America as closely as England. With one ear to the ground and the other turned towards the capable Franklin she was well aware of what was going on; and when Jonathan Loring Austin came dashing up with news of the Battle of Saratoga she knew that the time had come to throw her hat into the ring. Two days after the gentleman from Massachusetts, Mr. Austin, had arrived, M. Gerard, secretary to the king's council, called on

Franklin to offer his congratulations and to hint that Count Vergennes, the shrewd and all-powerful Foreign Minister, was in a receptive mood. A few days later the negotiations began. They were still in progress at the turn of the year, and even then the end was not in sight.

Britain heard rumors of what was going on in France and realized that if her proposals of peace were to have any chance of success they must be made before France could conclude an alliance. France on the other hand was well aware that if she was to catch Britain off her guard she must forestall any possible proposals of peace. It was a race for a tremendous stake — but a race between tortoises.

The persistence of the rumors from France whipped Britain into action, but with all the speed at her command the middle of February had passed before the Ministry was ready to put before the House its scheme for a reconciliation with the colonies. We are told in the *Annual Register* for 1778 that "a dull and melancholy silence for some time succeeded to this speech. It had been heard with profound attention, but without a single mark of approbation to any part, from any description of men, or any particular man, in the House." But the bills were immediately passed and received the royal assent, "to the surprise of all," says Stedman, "and to the no small mortification of those who had hitherto zealously supported" the administration.

"Never perhaps," Stedman continues, "was there a moment during the whole of British history, in which the nation had greater cause of mortification than at the time of passing these acts: And it will be difficult to defend the ministers of that day against imputation of either want of wisdom or want of firmness. If what was now proposed was a right measure, it ought to have been adopted at first, and before the sword was drawn."

Two months more were to pass before the peace commissioners were to receive their orders and instructions. After that, another six weeks would elapse before they would have arrived in America on their all-important errand.

In the meantime Franklin and his quarreling commissioners had been threshing out the terms of an accord with France that would at once recognize the independence of the colonies and join with them in a defensive alliance against Britain. Would the British tortoise reach America first, or would it get there just in time to see the French tortoise walk off with the prize?

The orders and instructions of the royal commissioners form a curious document, prolix and verbose in the extreme and much too lengthy to quote in full. The preamble, however, is as follows:

St. James, 12 April 1778

GEORGE R.

Orders and Instructions to be observed by our right trusty and right well-beloved cousin and Councillor, Frederick, Earl of Carlisle, Knight of the most antient Order of the Thistle; our right trusty and wellbeloved cousin and councillor Richard, Lord Viscount Howe, or Our Kingdom of Ireland; our trusty and wellbeloved Sir William Howe, Knight of the most honorable Order of the Bath, Lieutenant General of our forces, General and Commander-in-Chief of all and singular our forces enployed or to be employed within Our Colonies in North America, lying upon the Atlantic Ocean, from Nova Scotia on the north to West Florida on the south, both inclusive; William Eden, Esq., one of our Commissioners for Trade and Plantations; and George Johnstone, Esq., Captain in our Royal Navy; being our Commissioners appointed by us with sufficient powers to treat, consult, and agree upon the means of quieting the disorders now subsisting in certain of our colonies, plantations, and provinces in North America. Given at our Court of St. James, the twelfth day of April 1778, in the eighteenth year of our reign.

As the head of an important commission Lord Carlisle was not impressive. He had been something of a scapegoat in his youth and London was not yet ready to take him seriously. It is as usual the clever Walpole who hits the nail on the head when he describes him as a "very fit commissioner for making a treaty that would never be made."

But whatever the faults of the Ministry may have been in the selection of their negotiators, they had learned a lesson from the conference at Staten Island. There would be no occasion for Lord Howe to return the commission and instructions as he had done in 1776 for enlargement of their scope; * for the powers of the commissioners were considerably broadened and a number of the stumbling blocks he had found in his way were considerately avoided.

The commissioners were now directed to address the Americans "by any style or title which may describe them," thus eliminating the necessity of using the troublesome "Esq., &c., &c." In other words the Ministry was now so anxious for peace that it did not shrink from addressing the American Commander-in-Chief as *General* Washington, if this should be necessary. Indeed, for some time past Sir William in his letters to Germain had been giving Washington the title of *General* instead of the conventional *Mr.* or *Esq.*, though doubtless this was the result of thoughtlessness. This instruction might have been stretched to the point of addressing members of Congress as *Hon.*, or even as *Gentlemen* in an extreme case.

And the "wellbeloved cousins" and others were now empowered to grant real pardons and arrange a cessation of arms, as well as to suspend until June 1, 1779, the operation of any act passed since February 1763, insofar as it related to America, and to make temporary arrangements for colonial governments in place thereof. They could even "conclude a treaty" in accordance with their instructions, although the biting quality of the word "conclude" was somewhat modified by a subsequent provision that rendered any such treaty inoperative until confirmed by Parliament.

* Letter of Lord Howe lately found in the *Germain Papers* in the W. L. Clements Library.

As an evidence of the honorable intentions of Great Britain the commissioners were instructed to remind the colonists that the mother country had "spontaneously passed" an act for removing all doubts and apprehensions concerning any past or future taxation of any of the "colonies, provinces, and plantations in North America," and for repealing (with a rather grandiose though somewhat dilatory gesture) the specific tax on tea that had done so much to get the fat into the fire. To show what great faith she had in the fair dealing of the colonies Great Britain had empowered her commissioners to say for her that she was even willing to forego a standing army in the colonies.

Nor had the little matter of the freedom of speech been overlooked. The widest possible latitude was to be allowed; indeed it was provided that after the commencement of the truce for the negotiation of peace, no person was to be molested in any of the provinces for declaring his opinion upon "any point of government" or for refusing to sign any test or association, or to take any oath. Political prisoners were to be released, and all forfeitures, confiscations, and sequestrations were to be surrendered.

Another matter on which the mother country was willing to be big-hearted, if necessary, was the selection of provincial governors. These governorships had in the past yielded some pretty desirable political plums, but the Ministry was not going to have them stand in the way of peace. The commissioners were empowered to allow each province to choose its own governor by election, and, if the colonists were insistent, the right of election was to be extended to the judicial and ministerial offices as well. Downright liberality, this!

As to the Declaration of Independence the commissioners were to tread lightly. This was a point on which one peace conference had already come to grief, and they were to treat the subject with the utmost tact and diplomacy. They were not to insist on a formal revocation (as my Lord Howe had so disastrously done!) since the Declaration itself and all acts arising from it, being in themselves quite illegal, would in effect be wiped out of existence by the conclusion of a treaty.   Indeed, the Americans had made so much of a shibboleth of the Declaration of Independence that the less the commissioners had to say on the subject the better chances they would have for reaching an agreement.   Here was a sleeping dog that the Ministry was not at all insistent upon arousing.

At the conclusion of the orders and instructions was a cautionary clause that the "negociations" were not to be broken off because of the absolute insistence of either party on some point that the other was not disposed to yield "provided the same be short of open and avowed independence." In case of such an impasse, proceedings were to be suspended until further orders could be obtained from the home office.

Never, it is to be believed, did a mission set out from a ministry any more desirous of coming to terms, or any more determined to make peace at any price.   That is, at almost any price; for anxious as Britain was to have peace with her colonies, she was not quite willing to lose them in order to gain their friendship.

It was, as the Earl of Chatham so often said, a delicate situation.   And if the Earl shook a trembling finger over the heads of his peers while he pictured France as a "vulture hovering over the British Empire and waiting only for the right moment to pounce," he is to be pardoned for his eloquence.   The situation was more than delicate; it was desperate, though the choice of his figure of speech might have been improved if the diet of a vulture is what we have been led to suppose.

The British commissioners reached Philadelphia on the 6th of June, only to learn that Silas Deane had preceded them by a full month with a treaty of alliance duly signed, sealed, executed and delivered by the treaty-making powers of France.   Deane had been a long time in getting to America, for the treaty had in fact been signed on the 6th of February — before the conciliatory bills had even been presented to Parliament!   The French tortoise had won, and now instead of having an insurrection on her hands Britain was facing a war.

Great Britain had moved as fast as she could.   She had been quite prompt about sending to America drafts of the conciliation bills as soon as they were authorized, hoping thus to smooth the way for her negotiators when they should arrive a little later on.   The bills were received in New York, and fell into the hands of Governor Tryon, that burner of libraries, who was hated and distrusted by the Americans. Instead of permitting these all-important preliminaries to emanate from Sir William and the Admiral, who, in spite of all that had passed were universally trusted and admired in the colonies, Tryon sought to gather a little of the glory for himself by having a large edition of the bills struck off and scattered throughout the confederacy.   The copies sent to General Washington with a polite request that he should aid in the work of distribution were forwarded to Congress. This gave Congress an opportunity to do some thinking in advance, and when the wellbeloved cousins and councillors did subsequently arrive they found themselves face to face with a unanimous resolution of Congress not to treat with the representatives of Great Britain until the British fleet and British armies had been withdrawn and the independence of the colonies had been duly recognized and acknowledged in positive terms by the British Ministry.

Lord Carlisle was surprised to find how closely the rebels hemmed in the British armies on all sides of Philadelphia. He was even more surprised to learn that his home office had issued orders to the army to abandon Philadelphia and withdraw into New York.   These orders had, in reality, been is-

sued some time before the departure of the peace commissioners from England, but Germain with characteristic lack
of frankness had seen to it that no inkling of the fact should
reach the ears of the commissioners before they had sailed.
But this was not all; Carlisle was chagrined and embarrassed when Washington refused to grant a passport to the
secretary of the commission to pass through the American
lines and present his proposals to Congress which was at that
time in session at York, Pennsylvania.

The mission, of course, came to nothing. Congress having just ratified a treaty of alliance with France was not at all
interested in any terms of peace within the power of the
Carlisle commission to offer. The proposals of the mission
forwarded to Congress by messenger under a flag of truce
aroused so little interest on the part of the august lawgivers
that Carlisle finally went off in a huff without waiting for an
answer.

Sir William and the Admiral do not seem to have had
much of a hand in the doings of the Carlisle Commission.
Doubtless they would have entered with energy into the negotiations for peace had proceedings ever advanced that far.
They had up to this time never failed to take advantage of
any straw that seemed to show a breeze, however slight, blowing in the direction of peace. They had tried to make use
of General Sullivan when he had chanced to fall into their
hands. They had even joined hands with General Charles
Lee while he was a prisoner of war in their custody, and before Lee had come to the conclusion that he could best help
the patriot cause by showing the Howes the proper way to
defeat it. Not more than a month after Lee's capture Washington was surprised to receive a letter from him asking him
to transmit to Congress a letter which was enclosed. The
enclosure urged the sending of two or three gentlemen from
Congress to discuss with the Howes a matter of the "Greatest
consequence" both to Lee and to the public. Congress had

rejected the proposal and another attempt at peace had gone for naught.

It now seems evident that upon the surrender of Burgoyne Sir William must have concluded that a peace by conciliation had passed entirely out of the range of possibility; that nothing could now bring the colonists to their senses but a conquest that should be brought about by bloodshed and slaughter.   He must have been even more firmly convinced of the correctness of this conclusion when he learned of the French alliance.   But he had sent in his resignation, and it had been accepted long before the alliance with France had been concluded.

All through the winter of 1777–78 Sir William sat snugly in his quarters at Philadelphia surrounded by his magnificent forces, while a few miles away over the hills of Pennsylvania the pitiful little army of Washington was wasting away from disease, desertion, and the lack of the barest necessities of life.   To have gone out and gathered them in should not have been an arduous task for the under-exercised armies of the Crown.   But Sir William could not bring himself to the point of making the necessary exertion.   So much adverse comment was made on this oversight that Sir William felt called upon to explain his reasons in the *Narrative:*

The entrenched situation of the enemy at Valley-Forge, twenty-two miles from Philadelphia, did not occasion any difficulties so pressing as to justify an attack upon that strong post during the severe weather, and though everything was prepared with that intention, I judged it imprudent, until the season should afford a prospect of reaping the advantages, that ought to have resulted from success in that measure; but having good information in the spring that the enemy had strengthened the camp by additional works, and being certain of moving him from thence when the campaign should open, I dropped all thoughts of an attack.

In another place he adds:

When I received my orders to return home, as soon as Sir Henry Clinton should arrive at Philadelphia, I confess I became

cautious of hazarding exploits which might have reduced the
army of my successor.*

It was not Sir William's enemies, but his friends the Tories
who invoked the muse that spring in an attempt to stir him
to action by singing:

> Awake, arouse, Sir Billy,
> There's forage in the plain,
> Ah, leave your little Filly,
> And open the campaign.
>
> Heed not a woman's prattle,
> Which tickles in the ear,
> But give the word for battle,
> And grasp the warlike spear.
>
> Behold each soldier panting
> For glory and renown,
> To them no spur is wanting,
> March, and the day's your own.

But Sir William did not march. He did not grasp the
warlike spear. He did not open the campaign. He did not
leave his little Filly. He did not arouse. In a military sense
he did not even awake. He did continue from time to time
to send in to the home office a recommendation calling for
more and more troops and armament. But this was not because he needed or expected them. It was rather with the
idea of having more unfilled recommendations in his files
when the day of reckoning should arrive. For Sir William
the war had come to an end with the acceptance of his resignation. It was understood that he was to remain until
Sir Henry should arrive to take over the command, but the

* Earl Grey, who was ever loyal to Sir William, said later that the British
never had the facilities for an attack on this entrenched camp of the Americans
in midwinter; while Rupert Hughes, after an extended review of the conditions
at Valley Forge, speaks of the impossibility of goading Howe into "taking his
big army out in the cold where Washington's almost helpless troops seemed
to be positively begging to be gathered in." *George Washington*, III, pp.
261–338.

arrangement did not provide that he was to fight any more battles. So Sir William put the war behind him and threw himself into the much more absorbing business of having a good time.

CHAPTER XVII

THE MESCHIANZA

IT WAS A winter of extremes. The Continental army at Valley Forge was starving and freezing, and slowly disintegrating from disease and desertion, while only a few miles away at Philadelphia the British were indulging in the most lavish extravagance. There was nothing new or unusual about this. One extreme has a way of producing the other. Sir William must have been fully aware of conditions at Valley Forge. He could not have helped knowing that the rebel army was in rags. He had seen the backs of the enemy often enough to know that most of them were naked almost to the point of indecency. No doubt he had heard the story of the sentry who was said to have been seen standing with his bare feet on his hat to keep them out of the snow. And he could not have failed to hear of the witticism of the rebel soldier, who, when told that buff had been adopted for the regimentals, said that it was a good thing as they would soon be all in the buff. Then, too, the story of the bloody footprints in the snow was all too true. Washington himself had seen them.

The British general never failed to have fairly accurate information of the condition of the troops facing him. It is true that in reporting the result of an engagement he sometimes overestimated the number he had killed or put to flight; but he was not without notable precedent in this respect. The only time when a soldier fails to overestimate the foe is when he is telling how many of them managed to get away. Estimating the numbers in an engagement is one thing; obtaining a fairly accurate count of an army cantoned for the winter is quite another, and with all the Loyalist information trickling in to him Sir William could hardly have been in ignorance of the true state of affairs at Valley Forge.

With this in mind it is not difficult to trace a connection between the hard times at Valley Forge and the free spending at Philadelphia. Here was a fine chance for a comparison. Valley Forge would show the Americans what they might expect from a rebel success, whereas Philadelphia would give them a fair idea of the prosperity that would follow the British flag. This coupled with Sir William's natural indolence, his social inclinations, and his love of high living lifted the lid and threw the town wide open.

The British army was then, as at a later date, a sort of social register. It was full of young blades from the upper classes who were keen for adventure and who were not in the habit of taking No for an answer. And when the work in the field was over for the season they were only too ready to stir up some other pleasant excitement. The more the merrier.

The Loyalist families of the City of Brotherly Love, moreover, were only too glad to open their doors to the handsome young British officers, most of whom, one may be sure, did not deny belonging to the aristocracy. A pair of epaulettes and a red coat were all that one needed for an introduction. These good Loyalists, who had long been put upon by the overbearing radicals, were overjoyed to think that at last their day had come. The social season inaugurated by the festive Sir William was hailed by them with delight. There was only one fly in the ointment — the too amiable lady that Sir William had brought with him from New York and Boston.

Vicious stories were being circulated around New York to the effect that Mrs. Loring had been left behind when the British commander sailed for Philadelphia. Had the first families of Philadelphia heard these tales they would no doubt have been much edified. The only trouble would have been that they would have known them to be false. For the dashing Mrs. Loring had put in an appearance at Philadelphia coincident with the arrival of Sir William himself. This was, of course, easily explainable: she had gone with her husband, and her husband being the commissioner of prisoners naturally went wherever the army went.

With this explanation sedate and strait-laced Philadelphia must have folded its hands and breathed a sigh of relief. It was something to have a certain amount of regularity about an affair that was causing so much whispering behind the old lace and the ostrich feathers of the Philadelphia fans. Any comfort that the elect of the City of Brotherly Love may have extracted from the presence of Joshua Loring quickly evaporated when it was given out that though he had a very positive distaste for social life of any form, he was not at all opposed to the social ambitions and indiscretions of his very giddy wife, and was quite willing to leave to others the little matter of providing her with an escort.

This, it turned out, was a matter to which the Commander-in-Chief was quite willing to devote his own personal attention.

The social season opened with a great burst of gaiety. To begin with, the taking of the "capital, as it were," must needs be celebrated with a magnificent series of balls, banquets and receptions which quite naturally revolved around Sir William and the members of his staff; and Philadelphia was not long in discovering that anything which revolved around Sir William and his staff also revolved around the charming Mrs. Loring; that she was, so to speak, the First Lady of the British

army.   It soon became apparent that any hostess who wanted
to have Sir William and the various other notables on his staff
in her receiving line must also make room for Mrs. Loring.

This was a bitter pill.   The first families of Philadelphia
were not accustomed to having as their Queen of the May a
lady of questionable character who was living more or less
openly in sin with an army officer — even though the army
officer did happen to be a member of the British nobility, a
Knight's Companion of the Bath, and heir-apparent to an
earldom.   Philadelphia society must have squirmed.   It must
have stormed behind closed doors.   Most assuredly it could
not approve; but there are times when it is best not to be too
squeamish — and with all the noble lords and earls and vis-
counts in her midst Philadelphia felt sure that this was one of
them.

So the first families shut their eyes and swallowed.   They
decked out their daughters and polished the family plate.
They threw open their hospitable doors.   And when the music
began, it was Sir William with Mrs. Loring on his arm, who
led the grand march.   Why allow a silly scruple to ruin a
brilliant social season ?   On with the dance !   Long live the
King !

With all the gold lace and red broadcloth that was about,
it must have been a difficult time for families with daughters
to bring up.   At last there were men enough to go round.
Indeed, women were at a premium.   Young things just coming into their teens were eagerly sought after by mature men
as companions for the dance or the amateur theatricals which
in the absence of the legitimate theatre had become all the
rage.   Hostesses of Philadelphia in order to provide partners
for their male guests went so far as to write to their rebel sisters
who had fled the city at the approach of the British, urging
them to come back for a visit and assuring them of the utmost
safety and an abundance of the most charming male escorts.
Some of these letters have been preserved, and though no ac-

ceptances have yet come to light it is highly probable that there were instances where patriotism was temporarily laid aside in the interest of a good time.

This gay winter brought upon Sir William a loud thunder of criticism. His philanderings were pretty well aired, and his taste for reckless gambling drew sniffs of disapproval or worse from loyalist and rebel alike. Hardly an elevating sight, they thought, to see a general gaming with his men. If they won, he was corrupting them with temptation; and if they lost, he was driving them to ruin and despair. How could he expect a young officer that he had robbed at the gaming table the night before, to risk his life in battle for him the next morning? But all the clucking and murmuring made little impression on the gallant Sir William. For him the war was over, and he saw no reason why he should suffer with boredom while awaiting the arrival of his successor. So he gathered his gay companions about him and went on with his winning and dining, and his gaming and daming.

That the fascinating devil did play havoc among his own officers can hardly be questioned. Following his example they gambled far beyond their means, and more than one who had risked his all and lost blew out his brains in the cold grey dawn of the morning after. Nor can it be said that all the motherly and fatherly warnings whispered into the shell-like ears of the fair daughters of Philadelphia were dutifully heeded. Wherever Sir William went he found a pair of beautiful eyes just turning away — invitingly. He could have had a willing successor to Mrs. Loring on every side. Rumor has it that he did. But Dame Rumor is not always to be trusted, so often does she mistake the will for the deed, and Mrs. Loring had long since demonstrated her ability to look to her own laurels. Sir William may have had other affairs during his stay in Philadelphia, but none of them was of sufficient magnitude to imperil the position of the Sultana, who maintained her supremacy to the last and occupied the seat of honor by his side at the extravagant farewell reception with which the army sent him off soon after the arrival of the belated Sir Henry Clinton.

If Sir William had been proceeding on the assumption that anything was to be gained by giving the poverty-stricken rebels on the outside a glimpse of the bounteousness that prevailed in Philadelphia he could not have succeeded any better than he did. His success was not confined to those on the outside, however. For his orgy of prodigality created in the minds of even the most frugal of Philadelphians a desire to get their hands on some of the easy money while the getting was good. Prices began to go up. The cost of foodstuffs soared. The city was dizzy with inflation. The price of labor arose to such heights that Sir William felt called upon to regulate it by military orders.

On the 13th of February 1778 we find him issuing a proclamation aimed at the draymen and porters, who by their exorbitant prices had caused "many inconveniences" and "great injustice" to the inhabitants of the city. The proclamation requires all porters and draymen to obtain a license, and fixes a scale of fees that must not be exceeded.

For loading, hauling, unloading & storing —

1 pipe of wine	7s	6d
¼ cask of wine	2s	6d
1 hogshead of rum or molasses	5s	
1 hogshead of sugar or tobacco	4s	

Barrels of beef, pork, gammons, beer, cider, pitch, tar, turpentine, oil, sugar, coffee, bread, flour, or any other barrels were to be handled at 15d per barrel. For tierces of rice or flaxseed the draymen were allowed 2s. Tea was 3s 9d per cask. Anchors were to be toted for 5s each, but for loading, hauling, unloading and storing a mill-stone the sweating roustabouts were allowed the munificent sum of 10s.

Sir William was a great believer in government by military order, and wherever he went he scattered proclamations right and left. If he was not inviting the unregenerate rebels to recant and be forgiven he was encouraging the culture of hay, grain, greens, roots, berries and other vegetables, and prescribing dire punishments for all who were rash enough to trample the gardens of the loyal subjects of his Majesty the King.

How effective the proclamation of the 13th of February may have been does not appear, though it is probable that it caused the draymen and porters some inconvenience. The drumhead was then as now a poor place for the quibbling of lawyers for the defense, and no doubt the pipes of wine came into the cellars of Philadelphia at the prescribed price of seven and six albeit with somewhat more than the usual amount of the profanity that seems to be necessary for the moving of heavy articles.

And Sir William dined and danced the winter into spring. The spring was well on the road to summer before Sir Henry Clinton arrived to take over the command. By this time Sir William was tired of Philadelphia and anxious to be on his way. Clinton arrived on the 8th of May 1778, and three days later Sir William wrote Germain that he would now delay his departure no longer than might be necessary to furnish his successor with "orders and other information of use to the service."

Just what these "orders and other information" may have been would be hard to say, for Sir William had hardly lifted a military finger since taking possession of the city. To communicate them to Sir Henry, however, required more than a fortnight and it was not until the 24th of May that the retiring general boarded the *Andromeda* and sailed away — leaving the fair Mrs. Loring to her complaisant husband or perhaps to the more inspiring companionship of other gentleman friends that she may have made during her very close association with the British men-at-arms.

Whether Sir William ever saw her again is not now definitely known, though Joshua and his errant wife did accompany the British army when it returned to England after the war. America would not have been a good place for the Commissioner of Prisoners just then. He and his jailer, Cunningham, had starved too many of the rebel captives to enjoy any great popularity in the victorious confederation. Little is known of the Lorings after they took up their residence in the mother country. One of the sons turned out to be a missionary. Another, John Wentworth, lived to become a Lieutenant-Governor of the Royal Navy. Just what influence was invoked to advance his preferment is not known. Up to this time no letters between Sir William and his fair inamorata have been found, nor have contemporary writings shed any considerable light on the subject. What may yet be found in the muniment rooms of England and in the huge unsorted collections of Revolutionary papers recently brought to America only time will tell. Whether the pretty romance that began in Boston and survived transplanting to New York and Philadelphia, actually put its roots into the soil of England after Sir William's return from America, is something that must be left for future historians to determine.

Sir William was 45 years old when he arrived at Boston. Burgoyne and Clinton, who were with him, were 52 and 38 respectively. Washington was 42. But Sir William outlived them all. Burgoyne died at 70 in 1792, and was followed three years later by Clinton who lived only to reach 57. Washington died in 1799 in his 68th year. Sir William lived on to see Britain engaged in still another war with America, and did not die until 1814 when he had reached the ripe old age of 85.

For all the criticism aimed at Sir William, for his blunders if he acted and his indolence if he did not, he always retained an immense popularity with his men. In spite of the ribald jokes that went around the barracks about his relations with the Sultana, in spite of his carousing and drinking with his

officers, in spite of the grafting that he overlooked on the part
of his favorites, and the money that he won or lost at cards,
his men had real affection for him.   They hated to see him
go, and as the time for his departure drew near they felt the
urge to show their loyalty to him by some outward demonstration of affection.   A set of resolutions accompanied by a
gold-headed cane or a watch and chain seemed somehow inadequate, and after many discussions the officers concluded
that the only way to give fitting expression to the sentiments
of one and all would be a farewell party in which practically
the entire army could participate.

Young John André, then a captain, who had been one of
the moving spirits of the amateur theatricals with which the
army set had helped to beguile their time during the winter,
was put at the head of the committee on arrangements.
The *Meschianza* * was the result.   André wrote it.   He directed it.   He produced it.   He designed the settings and
painted most of the scenery with his own two hands.   With
all this work to do it is not to be wondered at that he mis-
spelled the name of the production on the rather elaborate
cards of invitation that he designed for the occasion.

Judge Jones speaks of the affair as a "burletta" and adds
that it was "one of the most ridiculous, undeserved, and unmerited triumphs ever yet performed."   This perhaps was
because Judge Jones hated Sir William and disagreed with
him spontaneously in almost everything he did.   But young
John André loved him; and he wrote into his script all the
things that he thought would honor and delight the retiring
Commander-in-Chief, as well as his brother the Admiral who
was by courtesy included in the celebration although he had
not yet severed his connection with the war in America.

It was as if young John André had somehow stolen a
march on Fate.   He was never intended for the army, but
had gone into it only out of pique when a lady in the Mid-

* The correct spelling is *mischianza*.

land Counties had rejected his suit.   He would go off to the
wars and forget his broken heart.   The broken heart was
soon mended, and in the process of mending not only was he
able to forget one lady, but he learned to love all the rest of
them.   The jolly young clerk was not through, however,
when he had written and produced the *Meschianza*.   As to
him it was written that the sword should be mightier than the
pen.   The grim figure of Tragedy was already dogging
his footsteps, having reserved for the genial youth an all-
important niche in the hall of fame.

A quaint account of the *Meschianza* in André's handwrit-
ing is still in existence.   It reads as if it might have been
written for the home paper:

The Festival given in honor of Sr Wm Howe on the 18th of
May and stiled the Misquianza * began by a regatta upon the
Delaware; Four hundred persons were invited for all of whom
the most convenient accomodations were provided in Galleys and
Flat Boats: These were on the occasion lined with Cloth, covered with Awnings, and dressed out with Colors and Streamers
in full naval pomp.   The Embarkation took place at Knight's
wharf at the upper end of the City at 4 o Clock in the afternoon
and the Weather was as favorable as the preparations were
magnificent.

The account given in Almon's *Remembrancer* is a little
more journalistic though perhaps not quite so intimate in its
facts and figures.   It begins:

The army, anxious to give Sir Wm Howe the most public and
splendid testimony of the high esteem they entertain of him as
a general, and of the affection and attachment which his popular
conduct had secured to him from all ranks, both of officers and
men, prepared a magnificent entertainment to grace his departure; it consisted of a variety of parts and was therefore called
the *Mischianza*.

In designing his ticket of admission young Mr. André
depicted the sun verging towards the horizon beneath a huge

* Still another spelling !   Montresor spells it *Mischisanza*.

VIVE VALE

⁙⁙⁙ DISCE DENS ⁙⁙⁙ SPLENDORE RESURGAM

Ticket for the Meschianza.

THE ORIGINAL DRAWING BY JOHN (MAJOR) ANDRÉ

Courtesy of the W. L. Clements Library

wreath of laurel and an inscription which read: LUCEO DIS-
CENDENS AUCTO SPLENDORE RESURGAM. This must have been
a little puzzling to Howe, who, like another well-known
Englishman, knew little Latin and less Greek. A glimpse of
the sea was also shown, and a shield surmounted by the
Howe crest and the Howe motto *Vive Vale,* and encircled by
a chain of military trophies and ensigns. André's design was
greatly admired at the time, and when a few years later the
State of New York adopted a Great Seal it paid the young
playwright the compliment of unmistakable plagiarism,
though it eschewed the Howe crest and the varied assort-
ment of munitions employed in the original.

The fête began with a grand water carnival on the river,
and true to military tradition, advanced in divisions, each
consisting of a galley and thirty flatboats. The *Ferret* galley
led the way with several of the general officers and their
ladies, followed by three flatboats containing bands of music.
The *Hussar* came next. In this were Sir William and his
party. We may well believe that the eyes of all beholders
were focussed on his galley and its precious freight of important personages; for clustered about the General and the
Admiral and Sir Henry were the youth and beauty of Philadelphia — including the famous Mrs. Loring in person.
This was one of the last times she was ever to be seen in public with her distinguished lover, and doubtless she was making the most of it.   In fancy we see the tall General hovering
over her with the little attentions he knew so well how to render, and we see the beautiful though perhaps slightly wistful
Sultana helping Sir William to take his bows.

Down the river the flotilla slowly drifted to the tune of the
"loyal and inspiring ode *God Save the King,*" which, André
informs us, was "played and Chorussed." A salute of 19
guns thundered forth as the procession was passing the *Roe-
buck* and another 19 as it came abreast of the *Vigilant.*
And, to quote the author and producer once more, "the Bril-

liancy of the gay tribe which peopled the River made the whole uncommonly solemn and striking."

Opposite the Wharton house (the present site of the Pennsylvania Railroad station) the flotilla came to land after a two-hour cruise. Here a great amphitheatre had been laid out with triumphal arches at either end. To the amphitheatre the company made their way, passing through the Admiral's arch and between two solid files of grenadiers while "spectators not to be numbered darked the whole plain around," if we may rely on the words of young Mr. André again. A mock tournament followed.

At a trumpet call a mounted herald rode out from one end of the field to proclaim the supremacy of the Ladies of the Blended Rose in "Wit, Beauty and every Accomplishment" and to assert that should any knight be so hardy as to dissent he would have the Knights of the Blended Rose to reckon with. Quite promptly a bold young Knight of the Burning Mountain did dissent, and the battle was on.

The first joust was with the lance, then came the pistol, and after that the sword. But before there were any casualties the judges stopped the bouts and declared both sides the winner. Sir William must have appreciated this stopping of a battle in the middle. The tournament having been disposed of the entire company repaired to the house for dancing and supper. Led by the guests of honor the ticket-holders passed through an avenue 300 yards in length and 35 yards in breadth flanked with troops and decorated with regimental colors, and passed beneath the second triumphal arch.

On the pediment of this arch (which was intended as a personal tribute to Sir William) stood a living figure of Fame with a trumpet to her lips. This he must have understood and appreciated, though it is to be doubted whether he was able to make sense out of the long inscription in Latin that young Mr. André had painstakingly printed on the entablature. Perhaps Sir William was none the less grateful for the implied compliment to his learning. He was not yet done with Fame, however, for later in the evening the fickle goddess again appeared, this time in the form of fireworks, and blew in "letters of light" from the end of her trumpet the words, *Tes Lauriers sont immortels.*

She was still speaking to Sir William in a foreign tongue. But perhaps it was better so, for it seems to have been predestined that Fame should never speak to him in any language that he could understand.

At the proper moment the King's health was drunk, and there were numerous toasts to the General and the Admiral. "Very loud" acclamations were given, and persons who were near to Sir William could perceive a "generous emotion answering the undissembled testimony" of what young Mr. André describes as "our Love and Admiration." One more quotation from the author and we are done with him. "Freighted with new strangth and spirit," he says, "the whole repaired again to the Ball room * and day Light † overtook them in all the festive Mirth with which a youthful band could be animated."

But this was not quite all. There still remained the little matter of dealing with a supper which we are told consisted of a thousand and twenty-four dishes served by negroes in ornamental trappings with silver collars and bracelets.

With the exception of a Miss Achmutty (who was as a matter of fact Mrs. Montresor, wife of the captain) all the ladies in the cast of the *Meschianza* were Philadelphians. Captain André gives the names of the Ladies of the Blended Rose as Miss Achmutty, Miss J. Craig, Miss R. Chew, Miss N. Redmond, and Miss Bond. The Ladies of the Burning Mountain are given as Miss Franks, Miss N. White, Miss B. Bond, Miss B. Redman, Miss S. Chew, and Miss Smith.

---

* Which was painted to resemble Sienna marble and decorated with 100 mirrors in which the dancers might watch their reflection.

† He has Washington's habit of capitalizing a word in the middle.

Several blank spaces are left in André's copy, one of them occasioned, no doubt, by the withdrawal of Miss Peggy Shippen on whom André was a bit sweet at the time.   The charming Peggy * had expected to take part, and had practised with the others at a number of very jolly rehearsals; but when the day of the performance came, her father who had all along viewed the furor of dancing and gaiety with growing distaste, put down a parental foot.   And Miss Peggy, instead of dancing all night with the arm of a British officer about her slim waist, was sent to bed where she could weep undisturbed with her own pretty arm encircling a pillow of goose-feathers.

When the Americans reinvested Philadelphia a few weeks later and gave a grand ball in celebration of the event, the question of the propriety of inviting the ladies who had been at or in the *Meschianza* came up for some rather heated discussion.   It was finally decided that they should be included, largely on account of the scarcity of "eligible" women. They were marked, however; for as they entered the hall it was immediately noted that they were wearing the hair high after the English fashion, instead of low on the neck in the American mode.   An awkward moment followed.   There was danger of a great schism.   But just as all seemed to be lost, the orchestra struck up, the dancing began, and the high and low coiffures instead of dividing into hostile camps were happily intermingled.

Late stragglers from the *Meschianza* were just crawling into bed the next morning when word was brought into the city that Lafayette with a large body of soldiers was approaching, apparently bent on launching a surprise attack.   The truth was that the Frenchman had been dispatched on a secret mission to discover how far the British may have pro-

---

* The same Peggy Shippen who afterwards became the wife of Benedict Arnold, and who, only recently, was discovered to have been privy to if not actually involved in his treason. (Letters in *Clinton Papers*, Clements Library.)

ceeded with their intended evacuation. Just why Washington did not send out a spy for the purpose is not clear. If he had felt that a reconnaissance in force was necessary he should have provided the detachment with a cavalry support, for it was entering territory that was almost entirely hostile. But Washington had not yet learned the value of cavalry.

When Howe heard of the approach of Lafayette he was delighted. Here was a bit of sport that he had not been counting on. He quickly laid a trap for the distinguished visitor and invited friends to come in for dinner that night to meet "the Boy." Sir William was running true to form. He may have relinquished his command under circumstances that promised to involve severe criticism and possible disgrace, but he could not resist a last chance to snatch from the war some entertainment for his friends. He simply could not be glum with the ingredients for a good time in sight. The idea of bagging the Frenchman was irresistible.

He quickly dispatched Grant with 8000 men on one of the familiar encircling movements. Grey was to worry the left flank while Sir William and Clinton kept the young marquis amused on the front. As entertainment the affair promised to eclipse the *Meschianza*. But something went wrong. Grant came in too close in his enveloping manœuvre. The red coats of his soldiers were seen in time for the Frenchman to wade his men across the river and escape. So "the Boy" did not dine with Sir William that night, and Grant had to do a deal of explaining to head off a court-martial.

That was Sir William's last smell of powder in America. Within the week the *Andromeda* dropped down the river bearing him towards home.

CHAPTER XVIII

HE FACES PARLIAMENT

ON HIS ARRIVAL in England Sir William found his conduct of the war under a heavy barrage of criticism, and himself the target of no small amount of vituperation. His resignation at the psychological moment had given the Ministry an almost providential opportunity to unload the blame on an unsuccessful subordinate, and they were not long in taking advantage of it. There is nothing so necessary to the man of the street as somebody to be blamed when a war is being lost; and, led by the administration, the taxpayers of England were relieving their minds with more freedom than justice when the *Andromeda* came bellying into port on the 2nd of July.

Almon in his *Remembrancer* gives an extract of a letter written at the time:

This day Sir William Howe arrived in town from Philadelphia. He came in the *Andromeda*. He waited upon Lord George Germain next day, and the following day upon the King.

The packet that sailed for America February last, carried General Howe's leave to come home. That packet arrived at New York about the beginning of April.

His presence here will, no doubt, put a stop to the infamous abuse which hirelings of the Administration have for two years and upwards, been unceasingly circulating against him. There never was an instance in the English History, in which officers, in their absence, have been so villainously traduced, slandered, and falsified by the writers for the Government, as the two Howes, General Burgoyne, and General Carleton. These brave officers, whose characters were unimpeached, till a —— took the the lead, were called upon by an administration, whose ignorance and imbecility are without parallel, to perform impossibilities. Without any general plan or pervading system in the outline of their orders, each officer was left to himself; there was no perfection in any separate design, no connection between the component parts, no information, no ideas founded in truth; no general plan of operation; — how could such a conduct produce success ? If success, as a miracle, should happen, then it was to be ascribed to the merit and wisdom of the minister; but if defeat should happen, then the disgrace and censure were to be the lot of the officers. If any man of reflection were to ask this question, Why has the Minister acted in this manner ? . . . Such are the miserable effects of governing, or imagining to govern, by an administration who are all *obedience* in the closet; and who, being only third and fourth rate men, are for the emoluments of office, content to be the tools of a *secret, confidential junta,* consisting of certain low men, as despicable in understanding as depraved in principle. . . These creatures, or rather *upstarts,* are the authors of the public misfortunes. Nor is there safety or justice for any man, while the spies and emissaries of Lord Bute and Lord Mansfield are suffered to be about the King.

This was propaganda pure and simple. It was the first gun of the Opposition in the battle to keep the Ministry from shifting the burden of defeat from its own shoulders to those of its returning general. In the mad scramble to get out from under, the real facts of the case played very little part. For protection and exculpation Sir William threw himself into the arms of the Opposition, and the Opposition went gleefully to his defense.

To prepare the way for an enquiry anonymous charges against Sir William's conduct of the war were carried to Parliament by his friends. Thereupon the Gentleman from Nottingham, Mr. Howe, complained to the house that censures had been made against him to which the Ministry had remained silent. At this point the Opposition members set up a great clamor for a public enquiry. The Ministers tried

to stem the tide.　They used every means within their power
to prevent this public laundering of the Administration
linen, but without avail.　The Opposition jammed through
a resolution for the enquiry, the House appointed itself as a
committee of the whole to sit on the case, and fixed a date for
a public hearing.

But all this political plotting and manœuvring had taken
time, and although Sir William had reached London in July
1778 it was not until the 22nd of April 1779 that he stood up
in Parliament and read aloud the remarkable *Narrative* of
his conduct of the war.　By this time Sir William's teeth were
bad, and he was a bit paunchy with high living and a not too
moderate amount of drinking, but he must have made a
striking figure as he drew himself up to his full six feet and
rendered an account of his stewardship in the dominions beyond the sea.

He began with an apology for trespassing upon the indulgence of the committee, but passed quickly to the repugnance
of the Ministers to declare (in the house at least, he adds
slyly) any opinion concerning the transactions of the war during his command, although possessed of the necessary, and
only, documents upon which a judgment could have been
formed.　He calls attention to his correspondence with the
Secretary of State, but cannot flatter himself that the papers
have been considered with such minute attention that all the
circumstances of the American war have been invested with
even a partial view of clearing the conduct of the man who
commanded the army.　He had, he said, no intention of calling into question the justice or the policy of the war.　He
did not mean to challenge the expediency of measures which
had been framed, relaxed, or persevered in, by the councils
at home.　His sole object was the explanation of his own
conduct.　Those who could have done him justice, had been
silent: therefore to the judgment of the committee, and to
the impartiality of the country at large he was at last resort-

ing, flattering himself with the hope of an ample justification. Faults, he did not doubt, would be perceived, but none, he hoped, that could have been suspected of having arisen from want of zeal or from inactivity. "The happiest commander," he adds philosophically, "will be he who escapes with the fewest blots."

On a slip of paper that turned up among the *Germain Papers* is a memorandum evidently jotted down during the hearing, entitled "Some Heads of Sir William Howe's Speech April 22d 1779." Here we see this bit of philosophy in a slightly different form. "Faults, no doubt, must be perceived," it reads, "none however proceeding from a want of zeal. He is the happiest who commits the fewest." Perhaps this is the way Sir William said it before it was edited for publication as part of the *Narrative*.

That Sir William had the benefit of a number of collaborators in the preparation of his *Narrative* can hardly be questioned. In all probability as read to the committee of the whole it was the product of the best minds of the entire Opposition.

The defense of the speaker was divided into four principal parts:

1st. That he did not fail to furnish the Minister with ample information.

2d. That he did not fail to express an opinion of what appeared practicable to be done, with the succours required or expected, and with the force at different times on the spot.

3d. That his plans were carried into execution with as little deviation as could have been expected.

4th. That he had never flattered the minister with improper hopes of seeing the war terminated in any one campaign with the force at any one time under his command.

Having thus outlined his defense Sir William begged leave to trouble the committee with a narrative of such material operations of the war as might lead to an impartial judgment

upon his general conduct, and which might obviate misconceived opinions concerning particular events and elucidate
the truth of the facts premised.   There being no objection,
he spread out his papers before him and threw himself into
the task of elucidation with the industry and clarity not unlike that of the well-known ink-fish.

He began with the evacuation of Boston, which was disposed of in a single paragraph, and passed quickly on to the
Battle of Long Island.   This was the action that had wrung
from a delighted monarch the coveted red ribband of the
Bath.   But that was before his Majesty had heard the whole
of the story.   Sir William had undoubtedly had it in his
power to capture every man that Washington had brought
over from New York for his first pitched battle with the
British, and he had not captured them.   Stedman even denies Howe the credit of the encircling movement that had
brought the Americans to grief.   It was Clinton and Sir
William Erskine who suggested this particular bit of strategy
after reconnoitering the enemy, he says, and "this intelligence being communicated to Sir William, he consented to
make the attempt."   The question of credit, however, was
not brought up before the committee.   Howe admits the
ardor of his troops but he professes himself at a great rhetorical loss to know from whence it has been supposed that
carrying the lines would have been followed by the defeat of
the rebel army.   He then goes on to point out that any great
loss of his Majesty's troops could not speedily have been repaired, and he mentions some imaginary floating batteries by
which Washington could easily have covered his retreat —
and passes on to a consideration of his campaign against the
"island of New York."

The apparent inactivity of the British from the time of the
"masterly retreat" of Washington at the end of August until
the 15th of September, a delay that has been baffling military
commentators ever since, Sir William accounts for as having

been devoted to "the necessary preparations, and erecting batteries, to facilitate the landing upon the island of New York and battering the enemy's works at Horens-Hook." Two weeks for this, with the demoralized rebel army huddling on the tip of Manhattan just waiting to be taken !

The gorgeous spectacle of the Sunday morning attack on New York which might so easily have brought cheers and laughter from the house was boiled down to the brief statement that the "possession of New York was effected." Sir William might at this point have spared posterity a vast deal of speculation and argument if he had added another sentence to the effect that he did or did not stop at the Murray mansion for a glass of Madeira while the rebel army was making a bewildered escape from the trap he had set for it. But he evades this vital issue and goes serenely on to say that the following four weeks were employed in fortifying the heights from Macgowan's Pass to North River, in getting possession of Paulus Hook, and in making "enquiries respecting the face of the country to be possessed." The landing at "Frog's-Neck" which has always been regarded as one of Sir William's most inexcusable blunders is explained away by the statement that "going at once to Pell's Point" would have been an "imprudent measure, as it could not have been executed without much unnecessary risk."

What this risk was is left to the imagination of the committee. He is not much more specific as to the long-debated failure at White Plains, concerning which his detractors had been heckling him for some time. Even if he had made the assault and carried the lines, the enemy, he says, would have got off without much loss, the ground in their rear being such as they could wish for securing their retreat. Sir William realizes that his explanation is inadequate, that it is falling on deaf ears. For a moment he flounders. Then he comes out with a trump card. "The committee must give me credit when I assure them, that I have political reasons, and no other, for declining to explain why that assault was not made."

This explanation should have exploded like a bombshell in the face of the committee. Perhaps it did. It may have been followed by a momentous hush, such as history invariably reserves for incidents of the kind. We have no way of knowing. The *Narrative* makes no mention of any (laughter) or (applause) that it may have occasioned, but goes unemotionally on: "Upon a minute enquiry those reasons might, if necessary, be brought out in evidence at the bar."

They never were, however, as Sir William very well knew they never would be when he made this fortuitous statement. And the *Narrative* passes on to the campaign in the Jerseys that made the army of Washington so ridiculous for a time, and then, on a stormy Christmas night so neatly turned the tables. Two pages are required to place the blame for the loss of Trenton on Colonel Rall's disobedience of the orders to fortify this post. But Sir William cannot leave the subject of the Jerseys without a brief explanation of what he was trying to accomplish there. Protection of the inhabitants, conciliation of rebellious subjects, and prevention of the destruction of the country are among the objects he had in mind.

"Ministers themselves," he adds, "I am persuaded, did at one time entertain a similar doctrine, and from a circumstance not now necessary to dwell upon, it is certain that I should have had little reason to hope for support from them, if I had been disposed to acts of great severity. Had it been afterwards judged good policy to turn the plan of war into an indiscriminate devastation of that country . . . ministers, I presume, would have openly stood forth, and sent clear, explicit orders. Ambiguous messages, hints, whispers across the Atlantick, to be avowed or disavowed at pleasure, would have been paltry safeguards for the honour and conduct of a commander-in-chief."

This is strong language, but it is not wholly without justification. There can hardly be any question that when Sir William and his brother were first sent to the American sector they were to offer the olive branch with one hand while making significant gestures with the sword in the other. The futility of this method must soon have been apparent; for, as Fox pointed out in an address to Parliament, the Ministers began to write letters calling for more severity. But they were, as Sir William contends, not clear, explicit orders for him to crush the enemy at any cost. In his letter of March 3, 1777, after learning of the affairs at both Trenton and Princeton, Germain writes: "I fear that you and Lord Howe will find it necessary to adopt such modes of carrying on the war that the rebels may be effectively distressed, so that through a lively experience of losses and sufferings they may be brought as soon as possible to a proper sense of their duty, and in the mean time may be intimidated from oppressing and injuring his Majesty's loyal subjects."

Bancroft quotes from another letter of Germain, although he does not tell where it is to be found, urging Sir William to greater severity in order that the rebels "may not escape that punishment which is due to their crimes, and which it will be expedient to inflict for the sake of example to futurity."

And even as late as the 18th of February 1778 Germain is so mild in his communications to his commander-in-chief that he is able to give no more bloodthirsty instructions than the statement that the King has full confidence that while Howe remains in command he will "lay hold of every opportunity of putting an end to the rebellion and inducing submission to legal government."

As to his whispers across the Atlantic, his ambiguities and hints to be avowed or disavowed at pleasure, Sir William is

undoubtedly right. But did Napoleon or Julius Cæsar
wait for clear explicit orders from his ministers? Did Joshua
or Genghis Khan? Did Wolfe or Nelson or Paul Jones or
any other commander who was fighting away from home and
who was really bent on winning a war?

Sir William has by this time consumed one-third of the
space allotted to his *Narrative,* and has arrived at the conclusion of his first campaign using New York as a base. He now
enters upon a discussion of his plans for the future, his recommendations and requisitions for the building up of an
army that should be adequate for the accomplishment of the
purposes he had in mind, and the disappointing lack of co-
operation he received from the noble Lord in charge of the
conduct of American affairs, which eventually led to his request to be relieved of the command.* But on this point he
makes a showing that is far from convincing. Indeed, he
leaves the reader with the conviction that Lord George did
remarkably well by him; that, all things considered, the
home office backed up the man in the field far better than he
had any right to expect.

Germain in his memorandum, "Hints for the Management
of an intended Enquiry," found in the *Germain Papers* shows
that his expectation is that the "principal matter to be considered, and what should be carried constantly in View is
the Force or Numbers committed to the command of the
General, and the Force and Numbers in opposition to him,
from Time to Time." He believes that the difference in the
"Discipline and Appointments should also be attended to.
The one being composed of the best disciplined and appointed Troops and the other of new raised badly appointed
and undisciplined Men. The Numbers of the British

---

* Sir William had been a long time making up his mind to this, for in
June 1777 he had written to Germain that his Lordship's observations on the
most essential services to be drawn from the Indian allies, and the manner in
which they should be conducted, evinced his Lordship's "great judgment, and
attention to the most minute circumstances relative to America."

Troops above four and sometimes six Times the Numbers of the Rebels with those of the latter being ascertained by Proof will in a great Measure determine the Point in Question."

"This done," the memorandum goes on, "the Enquiry must descend to particulars and here the General must assign the Reasons in Vindication of his conduct." Which proves that Germain had the situation pretty well in hand, for this is exactly what happened. Sir William discussed at some length the plan for the invasion of Pennsylvania, and his reasons for his failure to co-operate with the ill-fated expedition of Gentleman Johnny Burgoyne. He is still convinced, as he has been from the first, that the invasion of Pennsylvania was right and the expedition up the Hudson River wrong. He calls attention to the noble Lord's approval of the Pennsylvania plan as "solid and decisive," and challenges Germain to produce any letter instructing him to go to the aid of Burgoyne. "The letter intended to have been written to me by the first packet," he says, "and which was probably to have contained some instructions, was never sent."

That was short and to the point. It has never been denied. It probably never will be. As to Sir William's military incompetence that is also supposed to be so firmly established by his conduct in this campaign, one cannot be quite so sure. It was obvious to everybody (that is, everybody but Howe and Washington) that if the Burgoyne expedition was a success the British could hardly help winning the war. It is equally obvious that only a slight co-operation on the part of Howe would have made the Burgoyne expedition a success. Howe was not stupid. He was, as a cursory examination of his military operations will quickly disclose, shrewd and clever. He easily out-manœuvred Washington whenever the two armies came to grips. He must have known that a man is easier to whip if he has one hand tied behind

him.   The conclusion is almost inescapable that if Howe
did not lift a finger to insure Burgoyne's success it was because he did not particularly want the Burgoyne expedition
to be a success.   He had admitted to Clinton that he did not
care to have Burgoyne come south of Albany.   He probably
did not want Gentleman Johnny on his hands.   If, however, Sir William had gone up the river and cleared the way,
and the Burgoyne expedition had come crashing down from
Canada and joined the main British force, nothing could
have saved the rebel army from defeat and eventual disintegration.   The British lion must have gobbled it up with a
prodigious licking of chops, while a Tory administration
patted itself on the back with one hand and divided the
spoils with the other.

There can be no question that the Howes were both capable fighters.   Sir William had fought for his country re-
lentlessly in the past, and the Admiral was in the not too
distant future to do some tall fighting on the deep to regain
for Britain the vaunted freedom of the seas.   But between
them they managed to divert the heel of the conquerer from
the neck of the colonies.   If we are to judge by the result
their method was effective whether it is to be ascribed to
military incompetence or to political expediency.*

"I have heard it has been said," the *Narrative* continues as
it draws near the end, "that my civil commission was inconsistent with my military command — and that my mind
was more intent upon bringing about a peace by negociation, than by force of arms.   Sir, thinking it my first duty, I
certainly should have preferred the former mode of conciliation, and my brother and I for that purpose did go to the
utmost verge of our very limited commission and instructions.   But our proceeding in the character of Commission-

* Sir John Barrow in his life of the Admiral quotes Lord Howe as replying
to Loyalists who had asked him for letters of marque to enable them to priva-
teer against the rebel shipping: "Will you never have done oppressing these
poor people ?   Will you never give them an opportunity of seeing their error ?"

THE

NARRATIVE

OF

Lieut. Gen. Sir WILLIAM HOWE, &c.

IF the peculiarities of my fituation be confidered, I fhall not be thought prefumptuous in defiring the indulgence of the committee during the trefpafs I muft this day commit upon their patience. The repugnance of his Majefty's minifters (in this houfe at leaft) to declare any opinion concerning the tranf-actions of the American war during my command, although poffeffed of all the neceffary, and only, documents, upon which a judgement could have been formed, impelled me to move, that my correfpondence with the Secretary of State for the American department, might be laid before you The moft material parts of my conduct, the reafons upon which I acted, the plans which I fuggefted and executed, appear in that correfpondence; and therefore to thofe who may have connected the whole in a re-gular feries of dates and events, the detail into which I propofe to enter may feem unneceffary. But I cannot flatter myfelf that the papers have been confidered with fuch minute attention, nor can I prefume to fuppofe, that all the circumftances of the American war have been invefted with the partial view of clearing the conduct of the man who commanded the army. And, Sir, it is with that partial view I now rife—for I mean not to call in queftion the juftice, nor the policy of that war.

B I mean

ers never for one moment suspended our military operations. . . And indeed those who are acquainted with my
commission and instructions, as a Commissioner of peace,
must know, that from the restrictions they contained, it was
next to an impossibility, that my military could materially
interfere with my civil duty."

If this sentence had been written by a Walpole it would
probably have been hailed as a sparkling bit of satire. Coming from the clumsy Sir William, however, it provokes (if
anything) no more than a smile behind the hand. The
speaker sets out to disprove the statement that his *civil* commission was inconsistent with his military command, and
concludes with the contrary assertion that it was next to an
impossibility that his *military* could materially interfere with
his civil duty — which is probably very much nearer the
truth. He nowhere denies the charge that his mind was
"more intent upon bringing about a peace by negociation
than by force of arms." Indeed, he admits it in so many
words.

"And Sir," he says in conclusion, "if the House of Commons, or any other individual member, shall have any charge
or accusation to make against me, I declare myself ready and
willing to meet it. The Committee is open for the reception of any other papers, and for the examination of any
other witnesses. My only wish is, that every possible light
may be thrown upon every part of my conduct."

If this statement had been taken at its face value, the future
hearings of the committee would have been much enlivened,
and posterity might have been furnished with a much clearer
picture of the alluring though somewhat shadowy inamorata
in whose company the General had beguiled so many hours
of his stay in America. But it was a time when the personal
liberties of a military man were more respected than they are
today, and though his enemies did on occasion throw out
veiled hints against his moral character, Sir William's repu-

tation as a gentleman came through with hardly a scratch.

He had sailed for America with a war chest of some £840,776, or something over $4,200,000, a treasure such as no commander in history had up to that time carried with him beyond the seas. A committee of investigation that was really looking for facts must surely have poked its finger into this pie. It was well known that this member or that of Sir William's administrative family had come out of the fray with a snug fortune tucked safely away. But the stigma of graft was never laid at Sir William's door. The Enquiry went down into history without bothering to rake his accounts over the coals.* This was not because of any inherent honesty on the part of Sir William, though it was freely said at the time that he came out of the war no richer than when he went in, but was probably due to the strategy of his political friends who managed to bring on the Enquiry in such a way that the Ministry rather than the General was the real prisoner at the bar.

Witnesses were called by both sides. Lord Cornwallis, General Grey, Sir Andrew Hammond and others testified on behalf of Sir William, and General Robertson and Joseph Galloway were called against him. There was some desultory cross-examination, but nothing was elicited that was new, or that was particularly damning either to Sir William, or to the Ministry. And when one day Sir William failed to put in an appearance at one of the sessions, the political gentlemen who had so neatly brought on the investigation arose in their seats and moved that since the hearing could not legally proceed without his presence, it was due and proper that the Enquiry should be dissolved. The motion was put and carried. The Enquiry was dissolved. And nobody had been hurt.†

* Sir Henry Clinton was not so fortunate — perhaps a neat bit of revenge on the part of Lord George Germain.

† *Cobbett's Parliamentary History of England,* Vol. XX, gives a full report of the proceeding which was productive of many pages of oratory and argu-

The cabal against Sir William now resolved itself into a battle of books. The *Narrative* with which the friends of Sir William had been delighted, had been put into print and immediately drew fire from Joseph Galloway who replied anonymously with his *Letters to A Nobleman,* a pamphlet which picked the *Narrative* pretty thoroughly to pieces and asked some embarrassing questions. To this Sir William replied in his *Observations upon A Pamphlet Entitled Letters to A Nobleman.* But Galloway was not yet done. He felt that he had been wronged and injured by Howe, and being of a religious turn of mind he thought that he owed it to himself to have an eye for an eye and a tooth for a tooth. He accordingly made a reply to the *Observations.** He also wrote a series of *Letters From Cicero to Cataline the Second,* in which he charges the Howes openly with having betrayed their country, and in which he accuses Sir William with having been the dupe of the "blackest of all traitors," Dr. Franklin.

Galloway, who was an American Loyalist, had served under Sir William first as an adviser and intelligence officer, and later as Superintendent of Police during the occupation of Philadelphia. He had been a person of some consequence in America, but in England his attacks were of little avail.

Sir William went his way, his skirts cleared, his head high. And the Ministers with rehabilitated reputation went on losing the war. Two years more of their blundering led to the surrender at Yorktown. Sir William was well out of it. He had relinquished his command just in time, and poor Clinton was reaping the whirlwind.

In 1782 Sir William was made Lieutenant-General of Ordnance. In 1790 he was given the command of forces that were mobilized for defense against Spain, though he saw

---

ment, and was not brought to an end until it threatened to drag in the Burgoyne campaign in the North and the wordy Gentleman Johnny who was spoiling for a chance to justify himself.

* *Reply to the Observations of Lieut. Gen. Sir Wm. Howe,* London, 1780.

no action in the field. Three years later his career was nicely rounded out by his promotion to the rank of full general. During the next decade he held various important commands, none of which took him away from his armchair, for by now he was getting along in years.

He was made Governor of Berwick-on-Tweed in 1795, and after ten years of this sinecure was transferred to the lucrative post at Plymouth which he held until July 12, 1814 when he died presumably of old age.

When the Admiral died in 1799, Sir William succeeded to the title and inherited the Irish earldom, but with all his energetic maleness and his philanderings on two continents he died, like Washington, without issue. With his death the line ended and the peerage lapsed.

CHAPTER XIX

SOME ESTIMATES AND AN OPINION

THE CHARACTER of Sir William was elusive. His men loved him. They would follow where he led, though they must have been baffled by his unaccountable fumbling at the moment of victory. They were, however, no more confounded than the enemy. To young Alexander Hamilton, who did not hesitate to criticize a general though he had himself won nothing but his chevrons as secretary to General Washington, he was such an "unintelligible gentleman" that no rule of interpretation could "possibly be found out by which to unravel his designs." In his letter using these words young Mr. Hamilton may have been reflecting some of the bewilderment of his chief who never was able to make head or tail out of the movements of his British opponent.*

He was not unintelligible to John Adams, however, who wrote to his wife that it was "impossible to discover the designs of an enemy who has no design at all." To the gentleman from Massachusetts the Howes were either fiends or blockheads according to his mood. But Israel Putnam was genuinely puzzled when after the Battle of Brooklyn he remarked that Sir William was either "a friend of America or no general."

To Joseph Galloway Sir William was nothing but a colossal blunderer. "Blunder upon blunder is incessantly rising

* Letter to Gouverneur Morris, July 6, 1777.

in its view," he says in his *Letters to A Nobleman*," and as
they rise, they increase in magnitude. . .   Blunders so gross
that their possibility almost exceeds the utmost extent of our
belief.   Blunders as fatal to this kingdom, as their cause is
inexplicable."   This is Galloway the pamphleteer thundering forth a denunciation and much more interested in making his point than in arriving at the truth.

Stedman, however, gives us quite a different picture.   Like
Galloway he was well acquainted with Sir William.   He had,
it will be remembered, fought under him in America, and,
writing in 1794 he had the advantage of fifteen years over
Galloway in which to reflect, and to study the American
campaigns.   "In reviewing the actions of men," he says,*
"the historian is often at a loss to conjecture the secret causes
that gave them birth.   It cannot be denied but that the
American army lay almost entirely at the will of the English.
That they were therefore suffered to retire in safety, has by
some been attributed to the reluctance of the commander in
chief to shed the blood of a people so nearly allied to that
source from whence he derived all his authority and power.
We are rather inclined to adopt this idea, and to suppose
motives of mistaken policy, than to leave ground for an imagination that the escape of the Americans resulted from any
want of exertion on the part of Sir William Howe, or deficiency in the military science.   He might possibly have conceived that the late victory would produce a revolution in
sentiment capable of terminating the war without the extremity which it appeared to be, beyond all possibility of
doubt, in his power to enforce."

In another passage Stedman undertakes to scold Sir William for his dilatory conduct, but he gives no further inkling
of the "secret causes" that may have given it birth.   "This
dilatory commander," he says,† "dragged out the winter

---

* *History of the American War*, Vol. I, p. 198.
† id., p. 310.

without doing one thing to obtain the end for which he was commissioner. Proclamation was issued after proclamation, calling upon the people of America to repair to the British standard, promising them remission of their political sins, and an assurance of protection in both person and property; but these promises were confined merely to paper. The best personal security to the inhabitants was an attack by the army, and the best security of property was peace; and this to be purchased by successful war."

General Charles Lee, who knew Sir William well, wrote of him in a letter to Benjamin Rush dated June ye 4th 1778,* "From my first acquaintance with Mr Howe I lik'd him I thought him friendly candid good natur'd brave and rather sensible than the reverse. I believe still that he is naturally so, but a corrupt or more properly speaking no education, the fashion of the times, the reigning idolatry amongst the English (particularly the soldiery) for every scepter'd Calf, Wolf, Hog or Ass, have so totally perverted his understanding and heart, that private friendship has not force sufficient to keep a door open for the admittance of mercy towards political heretics. He was besides perswaded that I was doubly criminal both as Traitor and Deserter — in short so totally was He inebriated with this idea that I am convinced He would have thought himself both politically and morally damn'd had he acted any other part than what He did — He is besides the most indolent of Mortals, never took farther pains to examine the merits or demerits of the cause in which he was engaged than merely to recollect that Great Britain was said to be the Mother Country, George the Third King of Great Britain, that the Parliament was call'd the representatives of G. Britain, that the King and Parliament form'd the Supreme Power, that a Supreme Power is absolute and uncontrollable, that all resistance must consequently be rebellion, but above all that He was a soldier, and bound to

* *Lee Papers*, Vol. II, pp. 397-9.

obey in all cases whatsoever — these are his notions, and this
his logic, but through these absurdities I cou'd distinguish
when he was left to himself rays of Friendship and good nature breaking out — it is true he was seldom left to himself,
for never poor Mortal thrust into high stations, was surrounded by such fools and scoundrels — Mc Kensey, Balfour,
Galoway were his Councillors — They urged him to all his
acts of harshness.   They were his Scribes; all the damn'd
stuff which was issued to the astonish'd World was theirs —
I believe he scarcely ever read the letters He signed — You
will scarcely believe it, but I can assure you as a fact, that
he never read that curious proclamation issued at the head of
Elk, till three days after it was publish'd — You will say that
I am drawing my friend Howe in more ridiculous colors
than he had yet been represented in — but this is his real
character — He is naturally good humor'd and complacent,
but illiterate and indolent to the last degree unless as an ex-
ecutive Soldier, in which capacity He is all fire and activity,
brave and cool as Julius Caesar — his understanding is, as I observed before rather good than otherwise, but was totally
confounded and stupify'd by the immensity of the task im-
pos'd upon him — He shut his eyes, fought his battles, drank
his bottle, had his little Whore, advis'd with his Counsellors,
received his orders from North and Germain, one more ab-
surd than the other, took Galoway's opinion, shut his eyes,
fought again, and is now I suppose to be called to Account
for acting according to instructions; but I believe his eyes are
now opened.   He sees that He has been an instrument of
wickedness and folly — indeed when I observed it to him,
He not only took patiently the observation, but indirectly as-
sented to the truth of it — He made at the same time as far
as his *mauvaise honte* wou'd permit an apology for his treatment of me."

It is apparent that Lee has not forgotten the consideration
with which he was treated during his detention in New

York. He was writing in a hovel at Valley Forge not long after his exchange, and as he looked back the apartment where he had been housed in the City Hall must have seemed good to him. There may even have been a thrill of gustatory recollection at the thought of the elaborate dinners and splendid wines that so rankled in the breast of the irascible Mr. Justice Jones.

Lee may not have penetrated to any considerable extent into the mental attitude of Sir William toward America and Americans, but his letter had done much to lay the ghost of a "sullen, hard, and cruel" personality ascribed to Sir William and others of his family in the introduction to the Charlestown *Orderly Book*. The authority relied on by the writer of the introduction is an unnamed "writer in the time of the Brothers Howe" who is quoted by John Barrow as saying that they had in common the "sullen family gloom," but that in one thing they differed; Sir William hated business and never did any, and the Admiral loved business, dwelt on it and could never leave it." To this is added the statement that their "uniform character was haughty, morose, hard-hearted and inflexible."

Sir William has been sharply criticized for permitting the mistreatment of his prisoners. No doubt his commissaries did keep the prisoners on short rations. Indeed the lot of a prisoner of war has never been a happy one. The suffering at Andersonville and Libby prisons is still remembered, and even in the World War prisoners were starved and mistreated. The conduct of Joshua Loring and jailer Cunningham was notorious in this respect. But the British prisoners in the American camps were treated just as cruelly. Washington was harshly censured for his treatment of prisoners taken around Boston, and the ill-treatment of the "Convention troops" captured from Burgoyne, during the winter they were incarcerated at Cambridge made a fine scandal at the time. Indeed, the idea of taking men prisoner instead of killing them, was that they might be used for slaves. And it was not until 1785 that the first treaty was made which provided for the kindly treatment of prisoners.*

Even Galloway, who after his migration to England spent most of his life yapping at Sir William's heels, is compelled to admit that the General was a liberal man, and that though he was a gambler by instinct and allowed "illegitimate" † opportunities to his favorites, he was not corrupt in money matters. In answer to the charge that Howe prolonged the war for the money there was in it, Galloway generously admits that the "love of money was the least of all his passions." He goes on to insist, however, that Howe did protract the war, but that this was out of loyalty to his political associates and in furtherance of the "dark and heinous conspiracy of the Faction with which the General was connected."

What his army thought of him may be gathered from the statement of Captain André, who wrote from Philadelphia, "I am just returned from conducting our beloved General to the water-side, and have seen him receive a more flattering testimony of the love and attachment of his army than all the splendour and pomp of the *Meschianza* could convey to him.‡ I have seen the most gallant of our officers, and those whom I least suspected of giving such instances of their affection, shed tears while they bade him farewell."

Judge Jones would have shed no tears had he been on hand to bid Sir William farewell. The mere mention of the General's name was enough to start him mouthing. We are indebted to the belligerent old Tory for the account of Howe's generosity to Lee while detaining him as a pris-

---

* Between the United States and Prussia.

† Galloway was an LL.D. (Princeton 1769).

‡ Montresor mentions the "great regret of this Army" at Sir William's departure, and a fortnight afterwards notes in his diary, "This army rather discontented since the Departure of Genl. Sir Wm. Howe and the new measures received from the ministry (referring no doubt to the peace proposals)."

oner of war in New York, though the tale is told more with the idea of hurting Howe's reputation than of helping it. We find the Judge complaining that Sir William was "extremely fond of liquors and intoxicated the greatest part of his time." In the same vein he says, "He then returned to New York, and after spending about a fortnight in dalliance with Mrs. Loring, while the troops were lying on board the transports crowded together in the sultry heat of summer, he went on board his brother's ship, and orders were given for sailing."

That the boats did not sail any sooner was, it has been shown, no fault of Sir William's, the delay having been caused by unfavorable winds, adverse tides, and other causes beyond the General's control. The dalliance with the fair lady was, it would seem, not the cause of the delay, but the result of it. But the old jurist continues to relieve his mind by describing Sir William as "feasting, gaming, banqueting, and in the arms of Mrs. Loring," and "lolling in the arms of his mistress, and sporting his cash at the faro bank." There is little doubt that these were matters of current hearsay, and were as truthful as current hearsay usually is.

In another place Judge Jones says, "Upon the close of the campaign, in 1776, there were not less than 10,000 prisoners (sailors included) within the British lines at New York. A Commissary of Prisoners was therefore appointed, and one Joshua Loring, a Bostonian, was commissioned to the office, with a guinea a day, and rations of all kinds, for himself and family. In this appointment there was reciprocity. Joshua had a handsome wife. The General, Sir William Howe, was fond of her. Joshua made no objections. He fingered the cash, the General enjoyed madam. Everybody supposing the next campaign (should the rebels risk another) would put a final period to the rebellion, Loring was determined to make the most of his commission, and by appropriating to

his own use nearly two-thirds of the rations allowed to prisoners, he actually starved to death about 300 of the poor
wretches before an exchange took place." Sir William
should have known about this, but *did* he?

To Judge Jones, Sir William was never anything more
than a lascivious incompetent so degraded that he did not
hesitate to sell his prisoners' food for the favors of a lady.

John Bernard, an actor, who visited America in 1797, was
told at the time that the reason for Sir William's fatal voyage to Philadelphia was that Mrs. Loring was in a condition
as critical as that of the country, and required the benefit of
the sea-air.   Such a bit of gossip was no doubt bandied about
at the time, but if it had been founded on fact Judge Jones
would not have overlooked it.   Nor would General Clinton
to whom Howe's decision to go south was little short of insan-
ity.   If Clinton could have based his General's most monu-
mental mistake on the pregnancy of a mistress, he would not
have gone about fuming over the subject as he did.

That Mrs. Loring did make the sea voyage with the fleet
is hardly open to question.   Surely she who had accompanied
her husband on the arduous journey to Halifax would not
balk at an easy run down to the Chesapeake in the same
pleasant company.   And soon after the arrival of the British
army at Philadelphia the Sultana was very splendidly established there in a "convenient" house called Stenton, which
was a fine mansion in the best colonial style.   Nothing was
too good for Mrs. Loring.*

Field in his *Battle of Long Island* contrasts the characters
of Sir William and the Admiral.   The younger brother, he
said, had acquired distinction by his services on the battlefield nearly equal to those which his Lordship had obtained
upon the sea.   His reputation for experience in the art of
war, and for ability as a soldier, was "equal to that of any general in the British service."   But while Admiral Howe was

---

* *First American Civil War*, by Belcher, Vol. II, p. 261.

remarkable for sobriety and abstemiousness, the General was noted for self-indulgence and sensuality. He goes on to say that the Admiral was "haughty and reserved, even to his friends, whereas the General was familiar and affable, even to those whom he held in contempt. The life of the viscount was pure and honorable, while that of the General was largely spent in gaming and debauchery."

But it was not alone the military reputation of the General, Field tells us, that had won for him the command in America. He acquired the high position of commander-in-chief "through the personal favor of the king, to whom his features bore such an extraordinary resemblance as to give color to the popular scandal of their common paternity." It is Field's judgment that while the General's ambition spurred him on to make "magnificent and brilliant plans of great military sagacity," his sensuality "lulled him into indolence" at the very moment his plans promised to ripen into success.

Field pays his compliments to Mrs. Loring and her penchant for the gaming-table, remarking that her losses could not have caused her any great inconvenience since her husband had been "purchased with an office, the emoluments of which were rated at thirty thousand dollars per annum." We are also told that the "foibles and vices of the commander did not, however, destroy the affection and esteem of his army; for his affability and kindness of manner won for him the first, while his ability and courage secured to him the other."

The idea that politics might have been a deciding factor in Sir William's conduct of the war, seems not to have entered Mr. Field's mind though he does not hesitate to say that Sir William obtained the command entirely through the "personal favor of the king." Field does not seem to have discovered that the personal favor of the king in this instance amounted to a command instead of an offer.

Sydney George Fisher in his *Struggle for American Independence* says of Sir William that he was, like the Admiral and the rest of the family, "quite easy-going and generous. His most conspicuous characteristics were great personal courage, and a certain contemptuous indifference, which enabled him to bear himself with great dignity and defend himself with great adroitness in the storm of criticism which came upon him for his conduct of the war." Perhaps we may not now question his dignity, but a study of the *Narrative* on which his defense was based, and the ease with which his detractors shot it full of holes disclose that it is hardly to be regarded as a perfect example of adroitness in defense. The political skill with which the Enquiry was brought on, and with which it was conducted and resolved into an exoneration of the accused, was much more adroit, but it was only in a very small part the adroitness of Sir William Howe.

As to the General's personal appearance, Fisher describes him as being large, of dark complexion like all the family, with heavy features and very defective teeth. In the portrait of Sir William that was painted into Benjamin West's "Death of Wolfe" now hanging in the Clements Library, the artist has depicted him as a young man tall and muscular. Only a partial view of the face is given, and that is darkened by shadow. Young Howe is shown as one of a group standing around the dying hero. He is dressed in a velvet coat of dark green which hangs down nearly to his knees, and is wearing moccasins and tight-fitting leathern breeches. Shot and powder horns hang on beaded straps from his shoulder and he has a beaded bandeau round his hat. His right hand is obscured from view by an Indian crouching beside him, but his left hand is pointing back to the victorious troops, perhaps the command he had just led up the heights.

It is this left hand that is in the main the portrait of Howe, for it is his dominating feature. West has painted it small, soft, and pink, the hand of a sensualist and a voluptuary. West went to London in 1763 though the picture was not painted until some four or five years before the Revolution. He knew Sir William and used to skate with him in Kensington Gardens, but whether the portrait was painted from life, or only from memory does not appear.*

The Corbett portrait made in 1777 depicts Sir William in a gorgeous full-dress uniform. He is wearing his red ribband, and the badge or symbol of the Order of the Bath is pinned to his left breast. The great height of the subject is obvious though the portrait is only three-quarter length. Both hands are visible, the right, large, veined, bony, and powerful, draped from a parapet. The left, though covered by a military glove, leaves little doubt as to its size and strength. It is such a hand as might be expected of a prize-fighter. There is little likelihood that Sir William's hands had grown and coarsened in the few years that intervened between the portraits. It is much more likely that Corbett was depicting the hands as he saw them, while West was stylizing them to fit them into his composition. All the hands in the West canvas were soft and sensitive, even those of the redskin.

The two portraits have one thing in common, however. They show Sir William as a man of vanity given to decking himself out in gay colors, for no other reason, we may be sure, than that which prompts the male of the feathered kingdom to preen and display his brightest plumage.

Van Tyne in his *War of Independence* says that Howe had shown the hand of a master in the perfection of the details of his strategy, and his resort to the Indian style of fighting from behind trees and stone fences, and the single file in the

---

* Dunlap in his *History of the Arts of Design in the United States* tells how West was one day skating in the Serpentine when he heard someone calling "West! West!" It was Colonel Howe (afterwards General) who said that he was glad to see West. "And not the less," he added, "since you come in time to vindicate my praises of American skating."

flanking march. He ascribes his downfall to women, wine and the card-table, which, he hazards, "seemed to have unnerved" him, leaving him "unequal to the emergency, when it was well to listen to Nelson's dictum that no victory was won as long as there was anything left to capture which might be captured. To lose nine thousand men who were to be had for the taking (he was referring to the Battle of Brooklyn) was enough to break the reputation of one greater than Sir William Howe."

Sir George Trevelyan in his *American Revolution* speaks of Howe as "an indulgent commander and a hearty companion; who lived and let live; and who, when off duty, was as genial to his followers, high and low, as on the actual day of battle he was formidable to the enemy."

An anecdote of Sir William's imperturbability under fire is given in a *Diary of the American Revolution* by Frank Moore. During the campaign around New York Sir William and Lord Percy entered into a dispute over the age of Percy's horse. A wager had just been made when a ninepounder came along and completely severed the nag's head, whereupon Sir William, instead of ducking for cover as a more prudent general might have done, with cannonballs coming so near, calmly picks up the head, counts the teeth, and wins the bet.

Rupert Hughes, in his life of Washington * devotes an entire appendix to Sir William, his views and those of others concerning him, which proves, he asserts, "that Howe was neither so purposeless nor so big a fool as everybody thought him," adding as a final word, "Perhaps nobody could have been."

The Howes were Whigs. They were friendly to America. They belonged to a party that was friendly to America. Their party was not in power, however, and the war was brought on by their political opponents. Sir William

* Vol. III, page 142, and Appendix III.

through no choice of his own was sent over to prosecute a war in which he did not believe.

There is a pleasant fiction in all popular governments that in time of war the army is an instrument without parts or passions put into the hands of the state to insure the will of God. The ancient tradition is that as soon as war is declared the army, from the commander-in-chief down to the most lowly buck private, shall cease to think for itself. All the thinking is to be done by the party in power. But America was far away, and the master's voice was feeble. The commands that reached the distant shores of the new world were "ambiguous messages, hints, whispers across the Atlantick, to be avowed or disavowed at pleasure."

Sir William was well aware of the ancient tradition of which we have been speaking. He may easily have meant to keep within it when he first took over the command. But as time went on and nothing but the ambiguous hints and whispers came to him, he began almost unconsciously to conduct the war on Whig principles instead of Tory. In the absence of positive orders his own convictions were certain to show him the way. While it can hardly be said that he entered the war with any great singleness of purpose, it cannot be denied that so long as he retained the command he kept hoping that somewhere somehow a peace by conciliation might be worked out. Upon Burgoyne's surrender, however, the futility of this hope became apparent, and his interest in the American contest faded away.

But all this time cause had been steadily piling up effect. Without the delay at Brooklyn there would have been no White Plains to explain away. Without White Plains the halt at the bridge of the Raritan would never have been necessary. Without Brunswick there would have been no Trenton, and no Brandywine.

Even so late as Brandywine there was still a chance for a really aggressive general to have won the war. The Americans were on the run; they were falling over each other in rout and confusion when Sir William called off his men. A determined pursuit could have crushed the foe completely, and a fast-moving detachment might easily have captured the Congress with the gavel still in its hand. Clinton could then have been dispatched to the aid of Burgoyne, and Gates would have been in the trap instead of Gentleman Johnny. Without an American victory at Saratoga, France would never have come in, and the colonies might still have been one of the strands of the Lion's tail — perhaps the Dominion of America.

Had the British commander-in-chief gone home a winner, he would, no doubt, be known today as *Howe* instead of *Sir William* Howe. But, alas for the success of the British arms, the bugles did not blow at Brandywine for a pursuit, and Sir William, when he went home, went not to celebrate but to explain.

APPENDIX

THE

NARRATIVE

OF

LIEUT. GEN. SIR WILLIAM HOWE, &c.

I F THE peculiarities of my situation be considered, I shall
not be thought presumptuous in desiring the indulgence
of the committee during the trespass I must this day commit upon their patience. The repugnance of his Majesty's
ministers (in this house at least) to declare any opinion
concerning the transactions of the American war during my command, although possessed of all the necessary, and only, documents, upon which a judgement could have been formed, impelled me to move, that my correspondence with the Secretary of
State for the American department, might be laid before you.
The most material parts of my conduct, the reasons upon which
I acted, the plans which I suggested and executed, appear in that
correspondence; and therefore to those who may have connected
the whole in a regular series of dates and events, the detail into
which I propose to enter may seem unnecessary. But I cannot
flatter myself that the papers have been considered with such
minute attention, nor can I presume to suppose, that all the circumstances of the American war have been invested with the
partial view of clearing the conduct of the man who commanded
the army. And, Sir, it is with that partial view I now rise —
for I mean not to call in question the justice, nor the policy of
that war. I mean not to call in question the expediency of
measures which have been framed, relaxed, or persevered in, by

the councils at home. My object, at present, is confined to the explanation of my own conduct.

Many are the censures that have been passed upon me. The misrepresentations and false arguments of my enemies have made a deep impression upon minds too prompt to decide; whilst an ignorance of the true state of facts has left the unprejudiced in doubt. Those who alone could do me justice, have been silent: and therefore to the judgement of this committee, and to the impartiality of my country at large, I at last resort, flattering myself with the hope of an ample justification.

In the course of the great variety of business which fell to my lot, during such a wide and extensive command, faults must undoubtedly be perceived, but none I hope which can be suspected to have arisen from want of zeal, or from inactivity. In all military transactions, but more particularly in those of America, where the nature of the war, in all its points, is without example, the happiest commander will he be who escapes with the fewest blots.

The facts to which I principally wish to turn the attention of the committee, and which the papers upon your table bear witness to, are

1st. That I did not neglect to furnish the minister of the American department with every information, as well as with my ideas, relative to the conduct of the war from time to time.

2d. That I did not fail to give my opinions respecting what appeared practicable to be done, with the succours required, or expected from Europe, and with the force at different times on the spot.

3d. That my plans were carried into execution with as little deviation, as, from the nature of military operations, could have been expected.

4th. That I never flattered the minister with improper hopes of seeing the war terminated in any one campaign, with the force at any one time under my command.

I shall now beg leave to trouble the committee with a narrative of those material operations of the war, which may lead to an impartial judgement upon my general conduct, which may obviate misconceived opinions concerning particular events, and which, with some few remarks upon the several passages of the correspondence as they arise, may elucidate the truth of the facts premised.

The evacuation of Boston was the first material occurrence, after my appointment to the command of his Majesty's forces in North America.

On the 9th of November, 1775, I received the Secretary of

State's order, dated the 5th of September, to abandon that town before winter, and to move the army to New-York, or to some other place to the southward; my own reasons, indeed, against opening the campaign from Boston, had been in the mean time generally set forth in a letter to his lordship of the 9th of October. The late arrival of the order, and the deficiency of transport tonnage, rendered the removal of the troops impracticable till the 17th of March following, when I embarked with about 6000 rank and file, fit for duty, and about 900 sick.

It has not been insinuated that any disgrace was brought upon his Majesty's arms by the manner in which that town was evacuated. (*a*)

My letter of the 21st of March, 1776, accounts for my carrying the army, with the incumbrances then belonging to it, to Hallifax, in preference to any other port. Concluding that the reasons there given are satisfactory, I do not trouble the committee with any farther explanation, except that I think the army by going thither, received great benefit, not only from necessary refreshments, but from the opportunity of being exercised in line, a very material part of discipline, in which we were defective until that time. I might also add, that the troops performed very essential service at Hallifax, by constructing redoubts, and other strong works, for the defence of the town and dock, which could not have been executed by the garrison.

My letters go on to show how the army was disposed of previous to the landing upon Long-Island, while waiting for the arrival of the troops from Europe, and from the expedition against South Carolina. That intermediate time, as I do not recollect, amongst the multiplicity of anonymous publications against me, any fault has been imputed, I pass over, remarking only, that from the violent heat of the weather, little active service could have been done, and that such service would probably have been attended with much sickness to the troops.

I beg leave here to say, that although, to save the time of the committee, I may omit to mention many transactions of the war, I shall be willing to solve all doubts which the members of this

(*a*) In the examination of General Robertson (one of the witnesses called by Lord George Germain) an attempt was made to prove that considerable quantities of linen and woollen merchandizes, which might be of great use to the rebels, were left at Boston, upon the evacuation of that town, although it was in my power, to have carried the whole away. But though the General was of opinion that those goods might have been removed with the army, it was merely in the idea, conceived from report, that they might have been carried away, if the holds of the transports had been well stowed; for he acknowledged that we were in great want of shipping, and that we took with us all the vessels that were fit to go to sea.

committee may entertain, with respect to circumstances not touched upon, or not sufficiently explained.

I hasten to the action at Bedford on Long-Island, the 27th of August, 1776, where a paragraph in my public letter of the 3d of September has been quoted against me as a violent charge. The paragraph is as follows. "Had the troops been permitted "to go on, it is my opinion they would have carried the redoubts, "but it was apparent the lines must have been ours at a cheap "rate, by regular approaches, I would not risk the loss that might "have been sustained in the assault, and ordered them back to a "hollow way in the front of the works, out of reach of mus- "quetry."

This paragraph, I am free to own, I added to give here the same impression that I felt of the ardour of the troops upon that occasion. But I am at a loss to know from whence it has been supposed, that carrying the lines would have been followed by the defeat of the rebel army. The facts are these: — The rebels had a body of men posted in front of the lines, to guard against an attack from Flat-Bush, and from the lower road upon their right. These troops were defeated with considerable loss. The remainder of the corps was posted behind the lines, the main army being then on York-Island; so that admitting the works to have been forced on the day of action, the only advantage we should have gained would have been the destruction of a few more men, for the retreat of the greatest part would have been secured by the works constructed upon the heights of Brooklyn, opposite to New-York, and their embarkation covered by a number of floating batteries.

On the other hand, the most essential duty I had to observe was, not wantonly to commit his majesty's troops, where the object was inadequate. I knew well that any considerable loss sustained by the army could not speedily, nor easily, be repaired. I also knew that one great point towards gaining the confidence of an army (and a general without it is upon the most dangerous ground) is never to expose the troops, where, as I said before, the object is inadequate. In this instance, from the certainty of being in possession of the lines in a very few days, by breaking ground, to have permitted the attack in question, would have been inconsiderate, and even criminal. The loss of 1000, or perhaps 1500 British troops, in carrying those lines, would have been but ill repaid by double that number of the enemy, could it have been supposed they would have suffered in that proportion.

The necessary preparations, and erecting batteries, to facilitate the landing upon the island of New-York and battering the enemy's works at Horens-Hook, occupied us till the 15th of September, when the possession of New-York was effected, as appears in my letter of the 21st of September, 1776.

From that time to the 12th of October we were employed in fortifying the heights from Macgowan's-Pass to North River, about two miles from the enemy's most advanced intrenchments, and in getting possession of Paulus-Hook. Some time was also necessarily employed in enquiries respecting the face of the country to be possessed, upon a supposition that the enemy should remove from King's-Bridge. There was a necessity of entrenching upon the height I have mentioned, in order to cover New-York in the absence of the main army. My publick letters of the 23d, 24th, and 25th of September point out all these particulars.

With regard to the knowledge of the country, so necessary to be obtained previous to the movement from New-York, I beg leave to mention the difficulties we laboured under in that respect throughout the war. The country is so covered with wood, swamps, and creeks, that it is not open in the least degree to be known, but from post to post, or from accounts to be collected from the inhabitants entirely ignorant of military description. These circumstances were therefore the cause of some unavoidable delay in our movements.

I must here add, that I found the Americans not so well disposed to join us, and to serve us as I have been taught to expect; that I thought our farther progress for the present, precarious, and that I saw no prospect of finishing the war that campaign. These sentiments I communicated to the Secretary of State in the letters last mentioned.

From the 12th of October, the day the army landed on Frog's-Neck, to the 21st of the same month, we were employed in getting up stores and provisions, in bringing over the dragoons, the second division of Hessians, the carriages and horses for transporting provisions, artillery, ammunition, and baggage. Four or five days had been unavoidably taken up in landing at Frog's-Neck, instead of going at once to Pell's Point, which would have been an imprudent measure, as it could not have been executed without much unnecessary risk.

On the 28th of October the engagement at the White-Plains took place. But it has been asserted, that, by my not attacking the lines on the day of action, I lost an opportunity of destroying the rebel army; and it has been also said, that I might have cut off the enemy's retreat by the Croton-Bridge, Sir, and assault upon the enemy's right, which was opposed to the Hessian troops was intended. The committee must give me credit when

I assure them, that I have political reasons, and no other, for declining to explain why that assault was not made. Upon a minute enquiry those reasons might, if necessary, be brought out in evidence at the bar. If, however, the assault had been made, and the lines carried, the enemy would have got off without much loss, and no way had we, that I could ever learn, of cutting off their retreat by the Croton Bridge. I cannot conceive the foundation of such an idea. By forcing the lines we should undoubtedly have gained a more brilliant advantage, some baggage, and some provisions; but we had no reason to suppose that the rebel army could have been destroyed. The ground in their rear was such as they could wish, for securing their retreat, which indeed seemed to be their principal object. And, Sir, I do not hesitate to confess, that if I could by any manœuvre remove an enemy from a very advantageous position, without hazarding the consequences of an attack, where the point to be carried was not adequate to the loss of men to be expected from the enterprise, I should certainly adopt that cautionary conduct, in the hopes of meeting my adversary upon more equal terms.

But to proceed in my narrative. — My publick letter of the 30th of November relates the further proceedings of the army, until Lord Cornwallis arrived at Brunswick in the Jerseys, in which is included the taking of Fort Washington, afterwards called Fort Knyphausen. I need not trouble the committee with other particulars in that period: But I must say I should have been highly blameable, had I ordered the noble lord to have followed the enemy beyond Brunswick, when the whole of his corps had not joined him.

I refer to my publick letter of the 20th of December for an account of the progress of that corps until the 14th of that month, when they went into cantonments, which I was hopeful they might have maintained. My first intentions were to have made Brunswick the left, and Elisabeth-Town, or Newark, the right of those cantonments; and my reason for extending to Trenton was, that a considerable number of the inhabitants came in with their arms, in obedience to the proclamation of the commissioners on the 30th of November. I took upon me to risk that post under the command of a brave officer, with the support of Colonel Donop at Bordentown, five miles distant, with a very strong corps. The two posts were occupied by nine battalions, the Hessian cavalry, and a party of the 16th regiment of light dragoons, amounting in the whole to upwards of 3000 men, with sixteen field pieces. The light infantry of the army, a brigade of infantry, and some dragoons, were posted at Prince-town, in the chain of cantonments, twelve miles from Trenton.

But it has been objected to me that I ought not to have in-trusted the important post of Trenton to the Hessian troops. My answer to this, if clearly understood, will I think be satis-factory, Military men will certainly understand it. The left, Sir, was the post of the Hessians in the line, and had I changed it upon this occasion it must have been considered as a dis-grace, since the same situation held in the cantonments as in the camp. And it probably would have created jealousies between the Hessian and British troops, which it was my duty carefully to prevent.

Colonel Donop, who commanded the two posts, was perfectly satisfied with his situation, and so was Colonel Rhall. They both had timely information of the intended attack: The num-bers of the enemy, I was credibly informed, did not exceed 3000, and if Colonel Rhall had obeyed the orders I sent to him for the erecting of redoubts, I am confident his post would not have been taken.

I would ask those who object to this part of the distribution, where could the Hessian troops have been better employed than in the defence of a post? In the last war they were esteemed not unequal to any troops in Prince Ferdinand's army, and I should do them much injustice were I not to say they were in very high order in America. Two of these very battalions had served in Germany with great credit, and the whole brigade un-der Colonel Rhall's command had given a recent proof of their bravery at the attack of Fort Knyphausen.

The possession of Trenton was extremely desireable; could we have preserved it we should have covered the greatest part of the country to the eastward of Prince-town, including the whole county of Monmouth, where I had reason to think there were many loyal inhabitants. We should also have been so near Philadelphia that we might possibly have taken possession of it in the course of the winter; though I confess I had several rea-sons for doubting the expediency of that measure at that time.

My principal object in so great an extension of the canton-ments was to afford protection to the inhabitants, that they might experience the difference between his majesty's govern-ment, and that to which they were subject from the rebel leaders. For, Sir, although some persons condemn me for having endeav-oured to conciliate his majesty's rebellious subjects, by taking every means to prevent the destruction of the country, instead of irritating them by a contrary mode of proceeding, yet am I, from many reasons, satisfied in my own mind that I acted in that particular for the benefit of the king's service. Ministers themselves, I am persuaded, did at one time entertain a similar doctrine, and from a circumstance not now necessary to dwell upon, it is certain that I should have had little reason to hope for support from them, if I had been disposed to acts of great severity. Had it been afterwards judged good policy to turn the plan of the war into an indiscriminate devastation of that country, and had I been thought the proper instrument for executing such a plan, ministers, I presume, would have openly stood forth, and sent clear, explicit orders. Ambiguous messages, hints, whispers across the Atlantick, to be avowed, or disavowed at pleasure, would have been paltry safeguards for the honour and conduct of a commander in chief.

I now return to my narrative. — Previous to the loss of Trenton I had detached General Clinton with 6000 men to take possession of Rhode-Island, the success of which expedition is mentioned in my publick letter of the 20th of December 1776. This was one material point in the general plan of operations. And here I must beg leave to call the attention of the committee to my separate letter of the 30th of November, 1776, wherein is set forth my first plan for the next campaign, with the force requisite, in order, if possible, to finish the war in one year. My propositions were, that we should have 10,000 men to act on the side of Rhode-Island, and penetrate eastward into the country towards Boston, leaving 2000 for the defence of Rhode-Island, 10,000 in the province of New-York, to move up the North River to Albany, 5000 for the defence of York-Island and its Dependencies, 8000 to cover Jersey, and to keep General Washington's army in check, by giving a jealousy to Philadelphia, which as well as Virginia I proposed to attack in autumn, provided the success of other operations should have admitted of sending thither an adequate force. South Carolina and Georgia I proposed as objects for winter. But to carry this plan into execution I informed his Lordship, that ten ships of the line, and a reinforcement of 15,000 rank and file would be absolutely necessary, besides an additional battalion of artillery. According to this calculation the army under my command would probably have consisted of 35,000 effective men, to oppose 50,000 voted by the congress for the next campaign, exclusive of the large bodies of militia, who were to be collected on the shortest notice. I mentioned at the same time the spirit infused into the people by their leaders from the strongest assurances of procuring the assistance of foreign powers, and that it was said Dr. Franklin was gone to France to solicit the aid of that court.

This letter of the 30th of November was received by the Secretary of State on the 30th of December. On the 9th of March, 1777, I received his lordship's answer, dated the 14th of January. This answer it is to be observed was by no means decisive. The determination upon my plan was postponed until the arrival of my next letter, when Major Balfour (one of my aides du camp, and then in England) was to be immediately despatched. My requisition, as has been just stated, was for 15,000 rank and file in order to complete the army to 35,000 effective men. The noble lord, in the letter I am now quoting, hopes that he shall be able to augment the army under my command to near 35,000, although he proposes sending me only 7,800. This misconceived calculation can no otherwise be accounted for, as I apprehend, than by his lordship's computing the sick, and the prisoners with the rebels, as a part of the real effective strength of the army; and yet I cannot see how such a mistake could have arisen, as my requisition was specifick, for 15,000 men, rank and file. His lordship further declares, that it is beyond his power to furnish me with the additional battalion of artillery. If any thing could be an alleviation of my disappointment in these respects, it was the assurance which accompanied it, that — "whatever degree of support the rebels had been taught to "expect from for-"eign powers, his lordship had great reason to believe that Dr. "Franklin would not be able to procure them any open assist-"ance."

During the doubts I entertained, whether the large re-inforcement I had requsted would arrive in time for the execution of the extensive plan mentioned in my letter of the 30th of November, 1776, I had information, which I thought might be depended on, that the reduction of Pennsylvania was practicable, even upon the supposition that the whole of my strength, fit for duty at the opening of the campaign, might not exceed 19,000 men. I therefore suggested, in my separate letter of the 20th of December, 1776, a second plan, which was for acting next campaign in Pennsylvania, and which, when I was told I must expect a re-inforcement of only 7,800 men, little more than half my requisition, I concluded was to be adopted.

I remarked that by this plan the march towards Boston, which I had before proposed, must be deferred until the required re-inforcements should arrive from Europe; but as these operations, perhaps of the last importance to the nation, might depend upon the exigences of the moment, I sollicited his lordship to point out any general plans that might be thought most adviseable, as well with respect to the present strength of the army, as in the event of re-inforcements, remarking to me the periods of time in which I might expect the arrival of troops. This letter having been received in England on the 23d of February, 1777, which was long before General Burgoyne's departure, the minister had full opportunity of communicating the contents to that general, and of making such changes as he might judge expedient to co-incide with the northern operations.

Presuming that it was my duty to omit no opportunity of communicating, though it might be deemed repeating, my ideas to the Secretary of State, my private letter of the 20th of January, 1777, was also full and explicit. I there assure him, that there must be another campaign, for I found that upon the good news from Quebec, in 1776, he had hoped, that a prospect was open for ending the war in one campaign. I pressed for more troops — I told him that a re-inforcement of 20,000 men was requisite, but that 15,000 would give us a superiority, pointing out Philadelphia, for the reasons before mentioned, as the principal object; I observed, that an augmentation of 20,000 men would admit of my detaching a corps thither by sea, whilst the main body might penetrate by the way of Jersey. On the other hand I observed, that if the re-inforcements were small the operations would be of course curtailed. This letter also arrived in England prior to General Burgoyne's departure. Both letters are answered the 3d of March, 1777, and brought by Major Balfour, who arrived at New-York on the 8th of May.

I had now the Secretary of State's entire approbation of my second plan, the expedition to Pennsylvania; my reasons for deviating from my former plan being, as his lordship is pleased to express himself, solid and decisive. He laments, however, that instead of augmenting the army to 35,000, which I had requested, and which I had some reason to hope for, instead of even re-inforcing me with 7,800 he could only allow me to expect 2,900 that is to say not a fifth part of the number I had required. It is to be observed, that his lordship at the same time, notwithstanding so great a reduction of the re-inforcements requisite for the operations determined upon and approved of, recommends a warm diversion to be made on the coasts of Massachuset's-Bay and New Hampshire, as far as the main plan will permit. The admiral and I however, agreeably to his Lordship's commands, consulted upon the expediency of the diversion, and in my letter of the third of June, 1777, I informed the Secretary of State, that we found it not to be practicable without interfering materially with those more important operations of the campaign which had been approved of by himself, and which were already too much curtailed from a want of a land force. — The army fit for actual duty at this time, exclusive of about 2000 provincials, was 14,000 short of the number I had expected.

But to resume the chain of my correspondence. Finding by the Secretary of State's, letter of the 14th of Jan. 1777, received on the 9th of March following, that the re-inforcements were not to be expected, I totally relinquished, in my secret letter of the 2d of April, the idea of any offensive operation, except that to the Southward, and a diversion occasionally upon Hudson's-River. I informed the Secretary of State that the principal part of the plan formerly proposed could no longer be thought of; that the Jerseys must be abandoned, and Pennsylvania be invaded only by sea; that in the former campaign my force was equal to the operations, but that in the ensuing one, from the several posts necessary to be preserved, the offensive army would be too weak for rapid success; and that restricted as I was from entering upon more extensive operations, by the want of force, my hopes of terminating the war that year were vanished; that notwithstanding the whole rebel army, 50,000 men, voted in autumn, might not be raised, the enemy would have a numerous militia in the field, in addition to their standing force, and a good train of artillery. I at the same time transmitted my distribution of the army for the campaign, by which it is to be observed, that my real effective force exclusive of 3000 provincials amounted only to 18,100 *(b)*.

The noble Lord's answer to this letter, dated the 18th of May, 1777, contains a repeated approbation of the expedition to Pennsylvania; but it is remarkable in other respects — He states his inability to furnish me with the supplies requested, and is concerned to find that I do not imagine my force to be as suitable to the operations of the ensuing campaign as I had confessed it was to those of the last. These expressions, Sir, require observation — They seem eager to catch me in the confession that my force was suitable to the operations of the last campaign, and would from thence imply, that my force was equally suitable to the operations of any other campaign. Now, Sir, even if I had not explained my idea upon the point (which however I clearly did) I think it might have been obvious to any man less acquainted than his lordship with military reasoning, that the force which had been sufficient to take possession of New-York, and other strong holds of the enemy, could not, after the necessary divisions for preserving the variety of posts we had gained, be equally suitable to the making of new conquests. For is it

(b) In stating numbers present, rank and file fit for duty is always meant.

not self-evident, that the power of an army must diminish in proportion to the decrease of their numbers ?   And must not their
numbers for the field necessarily decrease, in proportion to the
towns, posts, or forts, which we take, and are obliged to preserve ?
But his Lordship proceeds to say, that his concern (on account
of this imagination of mine) is in a great degree alleviated by the
intelligence which he daily receives, of the rebels finding the
utmost difficulty in raising an army to face his majesty's troops
— From the supposed weakness of the enemy, and the good inclination of the inhabitants, he has every reason to expect that
my success in Pennsylvania will enable me to raise amongst them
such a force, as may be sufficient for the interior defence of the
province — He declines a particular consideration of the advantages which may be expected from a successful execution of my
present plan, but is pleased to inform me (in contradiction to
my repeated representations and assertions) that he is inspired
with no small degree of hope, that this campaign will put an
end to the unhappy contest.   Thus, Sir, all my positive assurances, arising from a declared want of force, and from a plain
state of facts, are here answered with a single argument of his
own delusive hopes, built upon a supposition of the enemy's
weakness.   To what a dilemma is a commander reduced, when,
after having repeatedly complained of his deficiency of strength,
the minister, from information collected here at home, or from
hopes suggested by fears, opposes his own conjecture (I cannot
call it judgement) and tells him, that decisive success is still expected from him ?   If the powers of this country, or the extent
of his Lordship's influence, could not have raised the force required, that answer would have been satisfactory to me and no
reflection upon himself.   That answer would have relieved my
mind from an apprehension I began to entertain, that my opinions were no longer of weight; and that of course the confidence
so necessary to the support, satisfaction, and indeed, security, of
every man in a responsible situation, was withdrawn.   If the
noble Lord had thought that my requisition for more troops
was unnecessary, and that the force he had already furnished was
adequate, why did he not take the manly part of appointing
some other person to fulfil those sanguine expectations, which
from duty and conviction I had laboured to discountenance !

   In order to preserve, as well as I can, the historical chronology,
amidst such numerous events and quotations, I must in this
place remind the committee, that in my letter to the Secretary of
State of the 2d of April 1777, I enclosed a copy of a confidential
letter which I wrote on the 5th of the same month spontaneously
to Sir Guy Carleton; I say spontaneously, because I had not at

that time received any official information, concerning the plan of the northern expedition which I conceived was to take place that year. It may be recollected, that the substance of this letter was, that I should probably be in Pennsylvania at the time when the northern army would be ready to enter the province of New-York; that little assistance was to be expected from me to facilitate their approach, as a want of sufficient strength in my own army would probably not admit of my detaching a corps to act up Hudson's River in the beginning of the campaign.

On the 5th of June I received a copy of the Secretary of State's letter to Sir Guy Carleton, dated the 26th of March 1777, wherein he communicates to him the plan of the northern expedition, and adds, "that he will write to Sir William Howe by "the first packet."

I must observe, that this copy of a letter to Sir Guy Carleton, though transmitted to me, was not accompanied with any instructions whatsoever; and that the letter intended to have been written to me by the first packet, and which was probably to have contained some instructions, was never sent.

I now come to the summer of 1777, passing over the expeditions in March and April to Peeks-Kill and Danbury.

The progress of our army in Jersey being also fully mentioned in my letters upon the table, I likewise pass over the various occurrences there, previous to the embarkation at Staten-Island. But as I have been blamed for not marching, before I left Jersey, to attack General Washington, posted at Middlebrook, I must beg leave to trouble the committee with a few words upon that point.

To have attacked General Washington in that strong post I must necessarily have made a considerable circuit of the country; and having no prospect of forcing him, I did not think it adviseable to lose so much time as must have been employed upon that march, during the intense heat of the season.

Exclusive of this consideration, our return must have been through a very difficult and exhausted country, where there was no possibility of keeping up the communication with Brunswick, from whence alone we could draw our provisions; and the force with me at that time amounting only to about 11000 men, it would not admit of sufficient detachments to preserve the communication. The movement which I did make in two columns was with a view of drawing on an action, if the enemy should have descended from his post, and been tempted towards the Delaware, in order to defend the passage of the river, on a supposition that I intended to cross it. But as the position of my first column at Hillsborough must have induced that idea, and yet had not the desired effect, I determined to return to Brunswick, and to follow the plan which had been approved by the minister. These reasons, together with those assigned in my letter of the 5th of July, 1777, will I hope sufficiently account for my not attacking General Washington upon that occasion. I must also observe, that even so long before as in my letter of the 2d of April, I declared it was not my intention to undertake any offensive operation in the Jerseys, unless some very advantageous opportunity should offer.

But it has been asked, why I did not cross the Delaware, and proceed by land to Philadelphia ? To this I answer, that, from a want of sufficient means to pass so large a river, I judged the difficulties and the risk too great, more especially as the enemy had a corps ready for the defence of it, exclusive of their main army in my rear.

I have already shown, that finding the promised re-inforcements were not to be expected, I informed the Secretary of State that the plan first proposed could no longer be thought of; that the Jerseys must be abandoned, and Pennsylvania be invaded only by sea. The communication for provisions through such an extent of country could not possibly be maintained with the force then at my command. This, Sir, is surely a satisfactory answer to the charge of my not having proceeded to Philadelphia at that time by land.

In my next letter of the 7th of July, 1777, I observed "that "the war was now upon a far different scale with respect to the "increased powers and strength of the enemy, than it was last "campaign, their officers being much better, with an addition of "several from the French service, and a respectable train of field "artillery: That 50 pieces of brass cannon had been landed at "Boston, and that the rebel army in Jersey had already with it "a field train of 40 pieces — That unless the British regiments "were completed with drafts and good recruits, we should soon "lose our consequence by the current casualties of a campaign, "even without a general action: That a corps of 10,000 Russians, "effective fighting men, might insure the success of the war to "Great-Britain in another campaign: But that if they were not to "be had, and if we should succeed this campaign in the possession "of Pennsylvania, the Jerseys, and the province of New York "(which I had before said must in a great measure depend upon "the success of the northern army) the drafts of troops in that "case for the preservation of them in the next campaign, would "be great, at the same time that a considerable force would be "requisite for the reduction of the northern provinces, wherein "three armies should be employed to make it effectual: And that

"even in our present state, twenty regular battalions were em-
"ployed for the security of York-Island with its Dependencies,
"and Rhode-Island."

It may be observed, that I made various alterations from time
to time in the plans of operations, but I flatter myself they will
be found solid, so far as they relate to the distribution of the
troops to Rhode-Island, New-York, and the main army.

With regard to the main army, the question is, "Whether it
"could have been disposed to better advantage than upon the
"expedition which took place to Pennsylvania ?" — an expedition
said by some gentlemen to have been the cause of the subsequent misfortunes: Those gentlemen will, I presume, endeavour
to support this strong assertion by evidence of the officers, the
General officers, upon whose opinions they profess to have
founded their judgement. If there are any in this Committee
who have formed a similar conclusion from their own reasoning,
I trust they will this day favour me with their ground for such
opinion, unless they should be satisfied with what I am going
to state in my justification. And in making this request I know
I address myself to men of honour, who cannot mean a wanton
accusation, but who may wish to be satisfied in points not sufficiently explained.

And here, Sir, although I might shelter myself from this violent charge, by referring to the complete approbation, as well as
the acquiescence of the Secretary of State; and might answer
every objection by the short observation, that the reasons for
adopting this expedition are adjudged by his Lordship to be
solid and decisive; yet am I content to wave that justification,
and to stand entirely upon the merits and policy of the measure
itself.

Persons of some authority, I am told, have said, "that the army
"ought to have gone into New-England, others that it ought to
"have gone up Hudson's River." Permit me to examine the
propriety of both these opinions, by considering what would
have been the consequences, if either of them had been adopted.

Suppose, in the first place, it had gone to New-England, would
that measure have led to a conclusion of the war ? I think not.
For, Sir, wherever, the main body of our army had gone, there
most assuredly would General Washington have gone also, but
that he would have avoided a general action, I am authorised
to say, not only from his constant uniform conduct in that respect (and in which, no doubt, he acted judiciously) but also
from this very obvious reason: He knew we could not have kept
any part of Connecticut in the winter, except one or two places
upon the coast of the Sound; situations which could not have

forwarded the recovery of that province. — In Connecticut, therefore, there was no object for which he could have been tempted to risk a general action.

Besides, the provinces of New England are not only the most populous, but their militia, when brought to action, the most persevering of any in all North America; and it is not to be doubted that General Washington, with his main army, would have followed me into a country where the strength of the Continent, encouraged by his presence, would have been most speedily collected.

In Pennsylvania the prospect was very different. The increase of force which that country could afford to Washington was small in comparison to the other, and the defence of Philadelphia was an object, which I justly concluded would engage the whole of his attention. It was incumbent upon him to risk a battle, to preserve that Capital. And as my opinion has always been, that the defeat of the rebel regular army is the surest road to peace, I invariably pursued the most probable means of forcing its Commander to action, under circumstances the least hazardous to the royal army; for even a victory, attended by a heavy loss of men on our part, would have given a fatal check to the progress of the war, and might have proved irreparable.

These, Sir, were my inducements at the time, for carrying his Majesty's arms into the province of Pennsylvania in preference to those of New-England. *(a)*

Had the re-inforcements I required been granted, New England would have had a share in the general operations of the campaign while the main body acted to the southward. But with an army upon the smaller scale, that plan was impracticable, and I have already given my reasons why I could not carry the main army into those provinces, unless I had been really desirous of protracting the war for my private advantage, a motive which has been basely imputed to me by those who wish to perpetrate the ruin both of my professional and my private character.

The second suggestion is, that I ought to have gone up Hudson's-River, in order to facilitate the approach of the northern army to Albany. What would have been the consequences of such an expedition? Before the object of it could have been attained, the forts in the Highlands must have been carried, which would probably have cost a considerable number of men, defended, as they would have been, by General Washington's whole force. But these forts being carried, how would the en-

(a) I have omitted a computation of the strength of the New-England provinces, because it is impossible to speak of it with a sufficient degree of accuracy.

emy have acted? In one of these two ways: He would either have put himself between me and New-York, or between me and the northern army. In either case I am of opinion, that the success of our efforts upon Hudson's-River, could not from the many difficulties in penetrating through to very strong a country, have been accomplished in time to have taken possession of Philadelphia that campaign. But admitting I had at length reached Albany, what should I have gained, after having expended the campaign upon that object alone, that I had not a right to expect by drawing off George Washington, with the principal American army, from any operations on that side?

When it is considered how invidious and how minute a scrutiny has been made into my conduct, and into the motives of my conduct, I shall not be thought to speak absurdly if I say, that had I adopted the plan of going up Hudson's-River, it would have been alledged, that I had wasted the campaign with a considerable army under my command, merely to ensure the progress of the northern army, which could have taken care of itself, provided I had made a diversion in its favour, by drawing off to the southward the main army under General Washington. Would not my enemies have gone farther, and insinuated, that, alarmed at the rapid success which the honourable General had a right to expect when Ticonderoga fell, I had enviously grasped a share of that merit which would otherwise have been all his own? and let me add, would not Ministers have told you, as they truly might, that I had acted without any orders or instructions from them; that General Burgoyne was directed to force his own way to Albany, and that they had put under his command troops sufficient to effect the march? Would they not have referred you to the original and settled plan of that expedition (which is amongst the papers on your table) to prove that no assistance from me was suggested? and would they not readily have impressed this house with the conclusion, that if any doubt could have arisen in their minds of the success of such a well digested plan, they should, from the beginning, have made me a party in it, and have given me explicit instructions to act accordingly?

And now, Sir, having sufficiently, and I hope satisfactorily spoken to the two plans, which some persons have judged ought to have taken place; I return to the only one which, in my opinion, could with propriety have been adopted. — After the most mature deliberation, and frequent consultation with the Admiral, Lord Cornwallis, and other General officers; after weighing all the circumstances of every possible operation; after the most probable conclusion, founded upon the best intelligence, that General Washington would follow me, I determined on pursuing that plan which would make the most effectual diversion in favour of the northern army, which promised in its consequences the most important success, and which the Secretary of State at home, and my own judgement upon the spot, had deliberately approved.

It was not one province, but three, that I conceived we had reason to take possession of at the end of the year 1777. The first object was Philadelphia, a city from whence, by means of the River Delaware, the rebels drew the greatest part of their supplies — the capital of Pennsylvania — the capital, as it were, and residence of the Congress in North-America, situated in one of the most fertile provinces of that Continent, and in which I include the three lower counties on Delaware. Added to Pennsylvania, I concluded that the arrival of the northern army at Albany, would have given us the province of New-York and the Jerseys; all which events I was confident would lead to a prosperous conclusion of the war.

Early in July, 1777, I began the embarkation — I wished however to remain until the arrival of Sir Henry Clinton from Europe, who was to command at New-York in my absence; and until I should learn something of the progress of the northern army. On the 5th of July Sir Henry Clinton arrived, and on the 15th I received an express from General Burgoyne, informing me of his success at Ticonderoga, "that his army was in good "health, and that Ticonderoga would be garrisoned from Can-"ada, which would leave his force complete for further operations." In my answer I said, that I expected General Washington would follow me to Pennsylvania, but that if, contrary to my expectation, he should go northward, I should soon be after him. It may also be proper in this place to advert to the instructions I left with Sir Henry Clinton, and to several of my subsequent letters to that General. As I omitted to send copies of them to the Secretary of State, they are not upon the table; but I have them in my hand, and with leave of the Committee will read a short extract of them.

Extract of Instructions from Sir William Howe *to* Sir Henry Clinton, *dated 9th July,* 1777.

"UPON my departure from hence with the army, you will "be pleased to take the command of the troops mentioned in the "enclosed return, and of all other troops now here, or that may "arrive in my absence. You will make such changes in the po-"sition of them as you may judge most conducive to his Majesty's

"service for the defence of this important post, and its depend-
"encies, whereby I would be understood to include King's-
"Bridge, Long-Island, Staten-Island, Paulus-Hook, and Sandy-
"Hook; at the same time it is by no means my intention to
"prevent your acting offensively, in case an opportunity should
"offer, consistent with the security of this place, as above-
"mentioned, which is always to be regarded as a primary object."

Extract of a Letter from Sir William Howe *to* Sir Henry
Clinton, *dated 15th July,* 1777.

"I have directed the 7th and 26th regiments of foot, and
"Colonel D'Eib's regiment of Anspach to remain here under
"your orders, in addition to the troops of which you have re-
"ceived a return, and am hopeful, if you see occasion to act of-
"fensively, those corps may prove of essential use.
"Upon the arrival of Major-General Sir Thomas Wilson, you
"will be pleased to order him to join me, unless from any of-
"fensive operations you may have in view at the time, you shall
"find his presence necessary for that service, in which case you
"will keep him under your command."

Extract of a Letter from Sir William Howe *to* Sir Henry
Clinton, *dated off Delaware, 30th of July,* 1777.

"IT is not possible for me to say at this time when I shall be
"able to send re-inforcements to you, but I beg you may be as-
"sured I shall not fail to do it, as soon as expedient: In the mean
"while, if you can make any diversion in favour of General
"Burgoyne's approaching Albany, with security to King's-Bridge,
"I need not point out the utility of such a measure."

From these extracts it is to be observed, that I gave full power
to Sir Henry Clinton to act offensively, if opportunity should
offer, consistent with the defence of New-York and its Dependencies, and that the facilitating the approach of the northern
army, by a diversion in its favour, if practicable, was not out of
my thoughts, although I had received no instructions whatsoever
upon that head.
The Committee will now permit me to state the distribution
of the whole army under my command, at the time of my departure to the southward. For the defence of Rhode-Island
there were about 3000 men; at New-York about 8500, exclusive
of the sick and convalescents of those corps, and of the southern
army, and a small body of militia upon Long-Island. These
two corps I judged to be not more than sufficient for their situa-

tions at that time, especially in the view of Sir Henry Clinton's acting upon occasion, to a certain degree offensively, in favour of the northern army — My own corps, to be opposed to the enemy's principal army, was nearly 14,000, and knowing General Washington to have about 15,000, exclusive of almost any number he pleased of militia, I could not think it adviseable to weaken any of those corps, by detaching from them for an expedition to the northward by sea.

The embarkation being finished, we sailed from New-York the 23d of July, and arrived off the Delaware on the 30th. Several days must have been employed to surmount the difficulties of getting up the river, and I inferred from thence, that I should not be able to land the troops before General Washington would be in force at Wilmington, where there was also a corps: There was besides no prospect of landing above the confluence of the Delaware and Christiana-Creek, at least the preparations the enemy had made for the defence of the river, by gallies, floating batteries, fireships, and fire rafts, would have made such an attempt extremely hazardous. I had also to consider that the country below, where the troops must have landed, and where only the transports could have laid in security (I mean about Reedy-Island) was very marshy, and the roads upon narrow causeways intersected by creeks: I therefore agreed with the Admiral to go up Chesapeak-Bay, a plan which had been preconcerted, in the event of a landing in the Delaware proving, upon our arrival there, ineligible. It is to be observed, that if we could not have landed above Wilmington we should have been under the necessity of going the same route we took from the head of Elk, by way of Aikens's Tavern, otherwise called Pencadder.

Our going up Chesapeak-Bay alarmed the provinces of Virginia and Maryland, and diverted a body of their troops, which did not join General Washington until after the battle of Brandywine. Another circumstance much in our favour attended this change: Our troops by being on board ship in the hot month of July and part of August, escaped an almost certain fatality by sickness, in which the enemy suffered much at that time. But, for this I do not take credit, as I was anxious to get forward, and no delay arose from that consideration. I will, however, declare it as my opinion, that in those two months the troops should be exposed as little as possible in the field in America.

On the 16th of August we entered Chesapeak-Bay, and there I received the Minister's letter of the 18th of May, 1777, wherein I am again told, that my last plan is approved, and in the same

period, that he trusts "whatever I may meditate, it "will be ex-
"ecuted in time for me to co-operate with the northern army."
Were I to be permitted to account for this expectation, I would
say, it must have been founded upon an idea, that the possession of that most important object, Philadelphia, was to be obtained without any great efforts of the enemy for its defence —
At least I must conclude the noble Lord apprehended none.
The fact however is, that Mr. Washington opposed our progress
with his whole force. It is also to be remarked, that, although
the idea of going up Hudson's River had not entered into any of
the reduced plans which I sent home, and which met with approbation, yet, in this letter it is suggested at a time when there
could be no possibility of carrying it into execution, consistently
with the approved expedition I was then upon — I was now
under the necessity of proceeding *(a)*.

I pass over the time between the landing of the army near the
head of Elk, and the battle of Brandywine. But understanding
some fault has been attributed to me for making a division of
my force to bring on that action, I flatter myself it will not be
thought impertinent to say a few words on that subject.

To bring the enemy to an action was my object, and being
confident that General Washington was studious to avoid it, unless under most favourable circumstances, some art and some
hazard was necessary to accomplish my purpose.

The movements made on this occasion, which may be found
in my letter of the 10th of October, 1777, were not repugnant
to sound principles, and it is no small consolation to me to know
independent of the event, that I have the opinions of the most

(a) Lord George Germain, in his answer to this part of my speech, complained
of my neglect of duty in point of correspondence, by declaring that after I had
embarked for Pennsylvania, two months elapsed without his hearing from
me. I took the earliest opportunity of replying to this charge; the fact stands
thus: — On the 16*th of July* I wrote to his lordship, informing him, that I
proposed going up the Delaware, in order to be nearer New-York than if I
went up the Chesapeak, *as I once intended,* and which route I preferred to that
of the Delaware, provided the enemy discovered a disposition to defend Pennsylvania. This letter was received by the noble lord on the 22d of August.
My next letter was dated the 30*th of August,* from the head of Elk; but it
happened that the Swallow-packet, carrying that letter, had a very uncommon
length of voyage, and did not reach England till the 28*th of October,* which
accounts for his lordship's having been two months without hearing from me,
my letter of the 16th of July having reached England on the 22d of August.
The noble Lord, when he was so unusually long without receiving a letter
from me, might have conjectured the possibility of a packet's having a tedious
voyage; of its having been lost; or of its having been taken by the enemy. Indeed he might also have conjectured from the words I have quoted in my
letter of the 16th of July, that I was gone up the Chesapeak, which would
necessarily lengthen my voyage from New-York; and finally he ought to have
compared the dates of the letters themselves, and not the dates of their arrival.

judicious officers in the army on the spot, to support a measure which some gentlemen, from what authority I know not, have been pleased to censure. But at the same time that I am reflected upon on one hand, for hazarding too much, I am blamed on the other, for not making the action more decisive, and for not following up the victory more closely.

To demonstrate the impracticability of a vigorous pursuit in a hostile country (but more particularly in America than in any other country I have seen) or the inutility of attempting it farther than was done, in the peculiar state of the army at that time, would be trespassing too much upon the indulgence of the Committee. I flatter myself it will suffice to say, that from a due regard to the wounded, the importance of possessing the post at Wilmington for their accommodation, and for the security of the prisoners, no movement could have been made sooner, or more effectual, under such circumstances, than the advance of the two corps with Major-General Grant and Lord Cornwallis towards Chester; and I must be allowed to insist there was no avoidable delay in the approach to Philadelphia by Valley Forge, the Schuylkill, by the nearer route through Derby, being inpassable: nor any opportunity lost of bringing the enemy to farther action between Dilworth and German-Town. This I nearly effected on the 17th of September when he was upon his march on the Lancaster road, but the extreme violence of the weather rendered every effort to get forward impracticable. They had therefore an opportunity of evading the approach of the King's army, by a forced march into a very rough mountainous country, where it was certain they could not be followed. But my endeavours to get at the enemy, whatver was thought by those actually engaged in them, have been treated here as ill-judged, feebly prosecuted, and void of enterprise, which last censure has been even extended to the general conduct during my command.

I shall not descend to minute refutations, but I beg leave to say, and I assert it with firmness, that almost very movement of the war in North-America was an act of enterprise, clogged with innumerable difficulties. A knowledge of the country, intersected, as it every where is, by woods, mountains, waters, or morasses, cannot be obtained with any degree of precision necessary to foresee, and guard against, the obstructions that may occur. In a word, Sir, whatever may be the aim or wish of my enemies in propagating these aspersions, it is from my conscience I affirm to this Committee, and to my country at large, that I never neglected an opportunity of bringing the enemy to action, where it could have been done upon a comparative view of all circumstances at the time, and consistent with the caution indispensably requisite in a situation always so critical, that a material check to his Majesty's arms might have been productive of fatal consequences to the interests of this country in America.

The next point is the attack made upon the King's army at German-Town on the 4th of October, which has been maliciously represented as a surprise, thereby throwing a stigma upon the vigilance of the troops, but more particularly upon that of the General.

The circumstances which encouraged the enemy to make this attack are set forth in my letter of the 10th of October, 1777, as well as the reasons for making the detachments which caused that encouragement. In addition to the account there given, I beg leave to inform the Committee, that my first position at German-Town was taken to cover Philadelphia, during the operations carrying on against Mud-Island, and was therefore more extended than it otherwise would have been. It is true, however, that I did not expect the enemy would have dared to approach after so recent a defeat as that at Brandywine.

In this Idea I did not direct any redoubts to be raised for the security of the camp or out-posts, nor did I ever encourage the construction of them at the head of the line when in force, because works of that kind are apt to induce an opinion of inferiority, and my wish was, to support by every means the acknowledged superiority of the King's troops over the enemy, which I considered more peculiarly essential, where strength was not to be estimated by numbers, since the enemy in that respect, by calling in the force of the country upon any emergence, must have been superior.

I confess also it was for the above reasons I did not change my position, after making the detachments beforementioned, choosing rather to trust to the well-tried vigilance of the troops, and the activity of the patroles (though I had intimation that an attack might be made) than to give the army unnecessary fatigue, by making more cautionary preparations.

In my confidence in troops I was not disappointed; the enemy's approach was discovered by our patroles, and I had early notice of it. The line was presently under arms, and although it must be admitted that the out-posts and light-infantry in one quarter, were driven back, it must be equally admitted, that they were soon effectually supported, and the enemy repulsed from the only place where the smallest impression was made.

I cannot mention this transaction without paying a due acknowledgement to an excellent officer, Lieutenant-Colonel Musgrave, whose gallant and judicious conduct, upon this occasion, will, I hope, some day meet with its reward.

I have stated these facts, in addition to the account in my letter upon the table, principally to shew, that how much soever I may be supposed to have erred in my own conjecture, the imputation of the army being unguarded or surprised is not founded in truth.

On the 19th of October I found it adviseable to remove to Philadelphia, to expedite the reduction of Mud-Island, which proved to be more difficult than was at first supposed. To this end the possession of Red-Bank on the East side of the Delaware engaged my attention. The event of that enterprise is contained in my letter of the 25th of October, 1777, but as I understand that a pointed reference was made to it in this House, last year, by the noble Lord in the American department, I shall briefly state, to the best of my recollection, the circumstances under which Colonel Donop, a brave and gallant officer, was detached on this service. He earnestly intreated Lord Cornwallis, in whose corps he served, to express his wishes for an opportunity to signalize himself, and the Hessian troops under his command. My design on Red-Bank affording the earliest opportunity, I desired Lord Cornwallis to explain the nature of the service, and if it should meet with his approbation, to offer him the command, which he very readily accepted. On the evening of his departure Colonel Donop desired to know from Lord Cornwallis, if it was expected he should make the attack at all hazards, when Lord Cornwallis assured him from me, that he was to be guided by his own judgement on the spot, but that the attack was to be made, unless he saw good reason to the contrary. If I may conclude from the manner in which I parted with Colonel Donop, or from the approbation the directions given to him received from his immediate and most valuable commander, General Knyphausen, I have every reason to believe he went upon the service perfectly satisfied.

The committee will do me the justice to believe I have no other motive for this explanation than to make known what really passed with respect to the orders given to Colonel Donop upon this enterprise. The intrepidity and vigour with which it was attempted, reflect the highest honour on the commander and his troops, and the loss sustained upon the occasion cannot be too much regretted.

It has been asserted, than an early possession of Red-Bank must have been immediately followed by the reduction of Mud-Island, to which I in some measure agree, that is to say, after the enemy had put it in a state of defence: Before that time such corps as could have been spared from the army, must have been established and supplied with stores and provisions, with great difficulty, while exposed to the annoyance of the armed gallies and floating batteries; and before the army was drawn nearer to Philadelphia the support of a post, so detached, would have been very precarious.

I must nevertheless acknowledge my great disappointment in the time that proved necessary for the reduction of Mud-Island; but if the violent rains, by filling the trenches, and sapping the foundations of the batteries, had not caused a considerable delay in the destruction of the enemy's defences, which prevented an earlier co-operation of the ships of war, I probably should have been much less deceived in my expectations.

My dispatch of the 13th of December, 1777, respecting the movement to White-Marsh, and my conduct on that occasion, is so explicit as to make farther observations unnecessary. — The motives from which I acted at that time were, I think, just, and if they appear inconclusive to any here, I can only esteem myself unfortunate in the want of their concurrence.

The activity of the army during the winter is undeniably proved by my subsequent letters: But as many of the transactions were in their effects less important to the grand object than to the credit of the troops, the most material only were specified in my dispatches.

The entrenched situation of the enemy at Valley-Forge, twenty-two miles from Philadelphia, did not occasion any difficulties so pressing as to justify an attack upon that strong post during the severe weather, and though every thing was prepared with that intention, I judged it imprudent, until the season should afford a prospect of reaping the advantages, that ought to have resulted from success in that measure; but having good information in the spring that the enemy had strengthened the camp by additional works, and being certain of moving him from thence when the campaign should open, I dropped all thoughts of an attack. My letter of the 19th of April, 1778, gives further reasons for this part of my conduct.

From the remainder of my correspondence, gentlemen must have seen, that I continued my remonstrance for more troops. Perhaps it was impossible for the minister to send more. — Such an acknowledgement would have been no reflection upon himself, and would have relieved my mind from the uneasiness it laboured under, in conceiving, that my opinions of the necessity of re-inforcements were deemed nugatory: and that, of course, I had lost the confidence of those, who were in the first instance to judge of my conduct. It cannot be surprising, that finding myself in this situation, I desired his Majesty's permission to withdraw from the command. — I gave the true reason for that request — the loss of confidence. — The reason was tacitly acknowledged to be well founded, for it was acquiesced in; and his Majesty was pleased to appoint a successor to the command of the army.

With regard to the complaint I made of the loss of confidence, the noble Lord in the American department must have done great injustice to my sensibility, when he expressed an opinion, upon a former occasion, that I alluded merely to the slight put upon my recommendations; not but that I confess I was mortified to find, that brave officers, whose eminent services I had strongly and faithfully represented, were not rewarded at home with the distinction expected for them by the army in general, as well as by me. It were a matter of small moment if the evil went no farther than to my personal mortification: but if it be true that the spirit of military men is raised or depressed by the conferring or with-holding of their sovereign's substantial approbation, such slights may prove of very dangerous tendency.

The noble Lord, on a former day, thought proper to treat my recommendation of Captain Emmerrick with a certain air of contempt and ridicule. He had forgot, it should seem, that he himself sent Captain Emmerrick to America, and, in the very extraordinary terms contained in his Lordship's letter of the 25th of April, 1776, originally recommended him to my attention. His Lordship best knows the purpose for which he sent him out, and whether he was a proper person to raise a body of men, or to be trusted with money for such a service.

When I received my orders to return home, as soon as Sir Henry Clinton should arrive at Philadelphia, I confess I became cautious of hazarding exploits which might have reduced the army of my successor, though a fair opportunity happening to present itself, I did make one attempt, which, had it succeeded, would have proved a severe stroke upon the enemy. Upon the whole, I flatter myself it will be found, that I made no disadvantageous use of the army under my command, and that I never made deceitful representations of the situation of affairs, but freely communicated my sentiments upon the force necessary to suppress the rebellion: and I am to this hour confident that if sufficient re-inforcements had been sent from hence, and the plan of operations which I took upon me to propose, had been adopted in its proper extent, the war in North America would now have wore a very different aspect.

I have heard it has been said, that my civil commission was

inconsistent with my military command — and that my mind was more intent upon bringing about a peace by negociation, than by force of arms. Sir, thinking it my first duty, I certainly should have preferred the former mode of conciliation, and my brother and I for that purpose did go to the utmost verge of our very limited commission and instructions. But our proceeding in the character of Commissioners never for one moment suspended our military operations. We soon saw that the leaders of the rebellion were determined, from interest, if not from principle, to prevent a reconciliation with Great-Britain, and therefore our joint endeavours were invariably exerted in the prosecution of the war, to as great an extent as the force in our hands would permit.

The reflection, that the civil and the military commission were incompatible, has, I know, been applied particularly to my conduct. I boldly assert it to be ill-founded, as I am certain I never delayed to seize an opportunity of attacking the enemy, consistently with my duty of weighing the risk of ruining the cause I was engaged in by a considerable loss of troops: and indeed those who are acquainted with my commission and instructions, as a Commissioner of peace, must know, that from the restrictions they contained, it was next to an impossibility, that my military could materially interfere with my civil duty.

I have trespassed, I fear, too long upon the patience of the Committee — The great importance of the subject, and the detail of facts, I have been necessarily led into, will, I hope, plead my apology. I shall trouble you with but a word more; in support of the measure of proceeding to Philadelphia. Before I came from thence, I had every reason to be perfectly satisfied of the advantages that would have ensued from that operation, if the councils at home had thought the Post proper to be preserved. The inhabitants in general of the province of Pennsylvania, those of the lower counties on Delaware, and those of the lower part of Jersey, were forward to return to their allegiance, and even to assist offensively in compelling his Majesty's revolted subjects to their duty. This favourable disposition, however did not appear immediately — An equivocal neutrality was all I at first experienced; our successes and apparent ability to retain our advantages, induced the inhabitants at last to be less reserved. Secret intelligence, which, until that period, had been extremely difficult to procure, was then so good, and so readily obtained, that I could not but attribute it to the possession of Philadelphia, which convinced the country of the superiority, and persuaded them of the established power, of his Majesty's arms. The difficulties of the Congress, in raising supplies, and in recruiting Mr. Washington's army, then indeed became real, and had the appearance of being unsurmountable. But the French treaty, and our orders to evacuate Philadelphia, by which measure the protection of his Majesty's forces was to be withdrawn from the province, made a sudden and melancholy change in our affairs. The rebels were inspired with fresh hopes; the friends of government were dismayed. — But it is not my intention to animadvert upon orders sent from hence after my recall, nor upon the future prospects of the war. — My view is merely to justify my own conduct during the time I was honoured with the command *(a)*.

This Narrative has, I fear, been too prolix; but the subject was so complicated with matter, and the circumstances necessary to be brought into a clear point of view, were so numerous, that brevity would not have been consistent with perspicuity. Had I laboured to make my Narrative short, it would have been obscure. Sensible as I am of the great attention and indulgence with which the Committee has honoured me, I now hasten to the conclusion.

The Secretary of State, as appears in his letters, has signified in the most flattering expressions, his Majesty's approbation of every material part of my conduct, during the whole of my command. His Lordship's own personal applause is also very warmly conveyed throughout his correspondence; all his letters however, may with propriety be said to have been private letters, until they were laid before this House. The knowledge of the approbation they contained was confined within his Lordship's breast and mine. When calumny first became busy with my reputation, I could have wished his Lordship's sentiments more generally known: — though it would not perhaps have become me to have obtruded upon the world those official declarations in my own favour. But I must ever think it would have been an ingenuous, an honourable, and a liberal part in the noble Lord to have avowed, openly in parliament, the approbation, which it is to be presumed he was convinced I deserved, because he had advised the King to bestow it. Such a

(a) Mr. Joseph Galloway, in his evidence to the Committee of the House of Commons, positively asserts, that I advised him, and the other magistrates, to go over to Washington and make their peace. The truth is, as soon as it was known that orders were arrived for the evacuation of Philadelphia, Mr. Galloway came to me on behalf of himself and the other magistrates, and requested my advice and assistance concerning the measures to be adopted for their welfare. I assured him, that if they chose to go with the King's army, they should be taken all possible care of; but if they rather chose to stay behind with their property and families, I could have no objections to their enquiring previously whether Washington and the Congress would grant them protection and security.

conduct would have stopped the current of ill-founded accusation against me. Such a conduct would have secured to himself the confidence, and to his country the chearful services, of future Generals.

And now, Sir, having endeavoured to bring before you, by the most impartial quotations, all the evidence that I thought necessary to collect from the papers on your table, I shall only remind you, that the House has ordered the attendance of several of the most respectable officers who served in America during my command. Their testimony may confirm the truth of the facts I have advanced, and will undoubtedly explain and prove any other material circumstances, which you may think necessary for your investigation.

And, Sir, if the House of Commons, or any other individual member, shall have any charge or accusation to make against me, I declare myself ready and willing to meet it. The Committee is open for the reception of any other papers, and for the examination of any other witnesses. My only wish is, that every possible light may be thrown upon every part of my conduct.

I move that Earl Cornwallis be called in.

—

BOOKS CONSULTED AND QUOTED

Adams, Charles Francis, *Studies Military and Diplomatic*, 1911.
Adams, John, *Works, With Life of the Author*, 10 Vol., 1850–56.
Adams, John, *Familiar Letters to Wife*, 1876.
Adams, John, *Warren-Adams Letters*, 1925.
Adams, Randolph G., *Headquarters Papers of British Army*, 1926.
Adams, Randolph G., *Papers of Lord George Germain*, 1928.
Almon, John, *Remembrancer*, 1775–80.
André, John, *Major André's Story of the Meschianza*, 1894.
André, John, *Journal*, 1903.
Arnold, Isaac N., *Life of Benedict Arnold*, 1880.

Bancroft, George, *History of United States*, 10 Vol., 1848.
Barrow, Sir John, *Life of Richard Earl Howe*, 1838.
Barrow, Sir John, *Naval History of Great Britain*, 1776.
Beard, Charles & Mary, *Rise of American Civilization*, 1927.
Belcher, Henry, *First American Civil War*, 2 Vol., 1911.

Carrington, Henry B., *Battles of American Revolution*, 1877.
Channing, Edward, *History of United States*, 6 Vol., 1909.
Clark, Jane, *Responsibility for Failure Burgoyne Campaign*, 1930.
Clinton, Sir Henry, *Historical Detail Seven Years Campaigns in North America*, unpublished MS. in W. L. Clements Library.
Clinton, Sir Henry, *Narrative Relative to Conduct of War*, 1783.
Clinton, Sir Henry, *Observations on Answer of Cornwallis*, 1783.
Clinton, Sir Henry, *Observations on Stedman's History*, 1794.
Cobbett's *Parliamentary History of England*, 36 Vol., 1806–20.
Coffin, C., *History of Battle of Breed's Hill*, 1835.
Cornwallis, Charles Earl, *Answer to Clinton's Narrative*, 1866.
Cresswell, Nicholas, *Journal*, 1924.

Dexter, Franklin B., *Literary Diary of Ezra Stiles,* 3 Vol., 1901.
Dictionary of American Biography, 2 Vol., 1928–9.
Donkin, R., *Military Collections and Remarks,* 1777.

Ellis, G. E., *Siege of Boston,* 1876.
Ellis, G. E., *History of Battle of Bunkers's (Breed's) Hill,* 1895.

Field, Thomas W., *The Battle of Long Island,* 1869.
Fisher, Sydney G., *Struggle for American Independence,* 2 Vol., 1908.
Fiske, John, *American Revolution,* 2 Vol., 1896.
Fitzpatrick, John C., *Diaries of Washington,* 4 Vol., 1925.
Force, Peter, *American Archives,* 1837–53.
Ford, Paul Leicester, *Orderly Books of Revolution,* 1891.
Ford, Worthington, *Writings of George Washington,* 14 Vol., 1889–93.
Fortesque, J. W., *History of British Army,* 11 Vol., 1915.
Franklin, Benjamin, *Complete Works,* 10 Vol., 1887–8.
Frothingham, Richard, *Battle of Bunker Hill,* 1900.
Frothingham, Richard, *Siege of Boston,* 1849.

Galloway, Joseph, *Letters to a Nobleman,* 1779.
Galloway, Joseph, *Reply to Observations of Sir William Howe,* 1780.
Galloway, Joseph, *Letters From Cicero to Cataline Second,* 1781.
Galloway, Joseph, *Letter to the People of America,* 1778.
Gentleman's Magazine, 1778.
Germain, Lord George, *Hints for Management of an Extended Inquiry,* unpublished MS. in W. L. Clements Library, Ann Arbor, Mich.
Gordon, William, *History of Rise etc. of Independence,* 3 Vol., 1794.
Graydon, Alexander, *Memoirs of a Life,* etc., 1811.
Greene, Francis Vinton, *General Greene,* 1897.
Greene, Geo. W., *Life of Nathaniel Greene,* 3 Vol., 1878.

Hamilton, Alexander, *Works* (Edited by Henry Cabot Lodge), 12 Vol., 1904.
Hastings, Geo. E., *Life and Works of Francis Hopkinson,* 1926.
Heath, William, *Memoirs of General Heath,* 1798.
Howe, Sir William, *Narrative Before Parliament,* 1780.
Howe, Sir William, *Observations upon a Pamphlet,* 1780.
Howe, Sir William, *Orderly Books, Charlestown,* 1890, New York, etc.

Howe, Sir William, *View of Evidence Relative to Conduct of War*, 1779.

Howe, Sir William, *Schedule of Correspondence*, 1779.

Hudleston, F. J., *Gentleman Johnny Burgoyne*, 1927.

Hughes, Rupert, *George Washington*, 3 Vol., 1926, et seq.

Irving, Washington, *Life of George Washington*, 5 Vol., 1856.

Johnston, Henry P., *Campaign of 1776*, 1878.

Jones, Thomas, *History of New York During Revolutionary War*, 1879.

Lear, Tobias, *Letters and Recollections*, 1906.

Lecky, W. E. H., *The American Revolution*, 1926.

Lee Papers, 4 Vol., Coll. N. Y. Hist. Soc., 1872–5.

Little, Shelby, *George Washington*, 1929.

Lodge, Henry Cabot, *Life of Washington*, 2 Vol., 1920.

Lossing, Benson J., *Field Book of Revolution*, 2 Vol., 1851–2.

Lossing, Benson J., *Two Spies: Nathan Hale and John André*, 1886.

Marshall, John, *Life of Washington*, 5 Vol., 1926.

Mc Coy, Samuel, *This Man Adams*, 1928.

Montresor *Journals*, (Edited by G. D. Scull), 1882.

Moore, Frank, *Diary of American Revolution*, 2 Vol., 1860.

Moore, Frank, *Songs and Ballads of American Rev.*, 1865.

Moore, Geo. H., *The Treason of Charles Lee*, 1860.

Nevins, Allen, *American States During and After Revolution*, 1924.

New York Historical Society Collections, 1869.

Nickerson, Hoffman, *The Turning Point of the Revolution*, 1928.

Northumberland, Hugh Percy, *Letters From Boston* etc., 1902.

Orderly Books, Charlestown, 1890, New York and Penn. in MS. only.

Pennant, Thomas, *Amer. Annals, or Hints & Queries*, 1810.

Pickering, Timothy, *Adams-Cunningham Letters*, 1824.

Reed, William B., *Life etc. of Joseph Reed*, 2 Vol., 1847.

Robertson, Archibald, *Diaries*, 1930.

Scull, G. D., *The Evelyns in America,* 1881.
Sheldon, W. H., *The Jumel Mansion,* 1916.
Shewkirk, Pastor, *Journal* (reprinted in full in *The Campaign of 1776,* by Henry P. Johnston, 1878).
Sparks, Jared, *Writings of Washington,* 1834.
Stedman, C., *History of the American War,* 1794.
Stiles, Ezra, *Literary Diary of,* 3 Vol., 1901.
Stryker, Wm. S., *Battles of Trenton and Princeton,* 1898.

Trevelyan, Sir George Otto, *The American Revolution,* 3 Vol. 1908.
Trevelyan, Sir George Otto, *George III and Chas. Fox,* 2 Vol., 1921.

Van Tyne, Claude H., *Loyalists in American Revolution,* 1902.
Van Tyne, Claude H., *The American Revolution,* 1905.
Van Tyne, Claude H., *The War of Independence,* 1929.

Walpole, Horace, *Memoirs etc. of George II,* 1847.
Walpole, Horace, *Letters,* 2 Vol., 1890.
Walton, Joseph S., *Washington in Chester County,* 1898.
Watson, John F., *Annals and Occurrences of N. Y. City,* 1846.
Watson, John F., *Annals of Philadelphia,* 1857.
Weems, Mason L., *Life of George Washington,* 1837.
Whitlock, Brand, *La Fayette,* 2 Vol., 1929.
Wilkin, Walter H., *British Soldiers in America,* 1914.

GAZETTES AND NEWSPAPERS

Boston *Gazette.*
London *Gazette.*
National *Gazette* (P. Freneau, Editor).
Pennsylvania *Gazette.*
Rivington's *Gazette.*
Gazette of the United States (John Fenno, Editor).
New York *Gazette* & *Mercury* (Hugh Gaines, Editor).
American *Minerva* (Noah Webster, Editor).
Porcupine's *Gazette* (William Cobbett, Editor).

INDEX